D0926567

RICHTHOFEN

A TRUE HISTORY OF THE RED BARON

WILLIAM E. BURROWS *1937-*

HARCOURT, BRACE & WORLD, INC. · NEW YORK

To

HELEN BURROWS

with love, respect, and appreciation

CONTENTS

ILLUSTRATIONS

PREFACE

This book grew out of an article I wrote in 1968 for the New York *Times Magazine* to commemorate the fiftieth anniversary of the Red Baron's death. That article went as far as 2,500 words can go, I think, in sketching Manfred von Richthofen. But no article can do justice to his remarkable life and important afterlife. That is why this second effort was undertaken.

A novelist would be hard-pressed to dream up a character to match Richthofen. He was, on the surface, an average young man of his class, who sought glory with a compulsion that drove him out of World War I's grim trenches and into the new fighting environment of the air. Through a combination of luck and skill, Richthofen became Germany's premier air ace and the greatest Wagnerian hero it has ever had. The Prussian aristocrat achieved the fame he wanted and, in due course, became more valuable as a propaganda tool than as an air fighter, a fact he gradually came to realize and loathe. Prussian tradition, the military and propagandistic needs of his country, and his own peculiar personality combined to make him the war's highest-scoring ace, forced him to defend his title in a way similar to the tragic tradition of the bull ring, and finally killed him. But Richthofen achieved martyrdom in death, and was to become at least as valuable in a future war as he had been in the one that consumed him. Was the Red Baron—around whom a mystique gathered that eventually spread to the movies and comic strips—a hero or a villain, a sadistic killer or a knightly patriot—or all of them? What part did his family, and particularly his mother, play in shaping his character, and what about his renowned passion for shooting and hunting, and his indifference to women?

Richthofen was killed when he was twenty-five years old, and, unfortunately, most of those who have been interested in him cared only about the last two of those years—his "productive" years, if that word applies to a man who works at war. Writing the biography of such a man, especially of one who, by his own admission, was not scholastically inclined, raises problems. He wrote practically nothing except short letters to his parents, even shorter combat reports in which he drily claimed recognition for kills, and an extensively edited and censored book for his country's propaganda effort. Most who knew him are dead. Others have memories which a half-century and another war have faded.

Books and articles about Richthofen have tended to concentrate almost entirely on the air fighter, rather than on the man as a personality and as a hero. They have devoted disproportionate space, for example, to raking over candidates' claims for killing him, the honor for which is relatively unimportant, and have hardly bothered to ask why he became a hero in the first place and how he felt about it. The artilleryman who pulled a howitzer lanyard often killed as many of the enemy in thirty seconds as Richthofen did in eighteen months. Why was the artilleryman not a hero? What, then, constitutes a hero and what purpose does he have in war? The answer, I think, serves a more useful historical purpose than does a determination of who actually squeezed the trigger of the gun that killed him or a simple recounting of each of his eighty official victories, which can be done on a chart.

Friends who knew I was writing this book asked many questions while it was in preparation, but there was one question asked by everyone: "Do you *like* Richthofen?" I cannot imagine that question being unanimously asked of Henri Troyat while he was writing his biography of Tolstoy. It further underlines the nature of Richthofen's mystique that people—even those who only know the Red Baron as a comic-strip character—feel one must either be for or against him, that there can be no dispassion for a soldier. Such attitudes are so simple-minded they contribute nothing to their subject. There is no question but that Richthofen enjoyed his work. So, however, did countless others who fought beside and against him, on the ground and in the air. Some adapted easily to killing, while most learned to kill so that they could live. The line between the two is far from clear, and I submit that neither group would have gotten the chance had the world not been ripe for the war and turned them loose in the first place. If there has to be a condemnation, it should be placed on higher heads than those of junior officers.

I have started each chapter with a quotation or two that seemed to me to sum up its meaning. One comes to mind here: "Biography," wrote Philip Guedalla in *Supers and Supermen*, "like big game hunting, is one of the recognized forms of sport, and it is as unfair as only sport can be."

New York   WILLIAM E. BURROWS
New Year's Day, 1969

ACKNOWLEDGMENTS

Authors like to call what they write *their* books. That is rarely the case with nonfiction, and certainly not with this book. Instead, many persons have poured information into my funnel, leaving me only to sift it critically and try to write about it clearly. Some have contributed unknowingly through *their* own books, and since they are too numerous to list here, the bibliography should be taken as an extension of my sincere appreciation. This book combines facts and opinions. The facts come from those acknowledged. The opinions are my own.

Major Werner S. Lottermoser, Assistant Air Attaché, Embassy of the Federal Republic of Germany in Washington, D.C., helped prepare the way for much of my visit to his country. I am grateful to Colonel Horst D. Kallerhoff, the commander of West Germany's *Jagdgeschwader* 71 "Richthofen," and to his officers and men for extending every possible hospitality and service during my stay with them, and particularly to Lieutenants Georg Schaub and Arnold Bormann, for being "faithful native guides" and research assistants. Research in Bonn was made possible by Lieutenant Colonel Helmut Wollin, of the Defense Ministry's Military History Department, who tracked down material from his government's archives. Major Botho Teichmann, a former operations officer in the second Richthofen Wing, trudged around Berlin gathering information and new sources on World War II, and brought them to me. Mr. Hans Georg von der Osten of Cologne, one of the last of the "Gray Eagles," patiently recalled anecdotes about his friend, the subject of this book, and shared them with great pride. I am also grateful to the late Mrs. von der Osten, who shared tea and cookies with a stranger.

Research in London was as fruitful as in Germany, largely because of Mr. F. S. White, Ministry of Defence Library (Air), and the staff of the Imperial War Museum. I would particularly like to thank Miss Rose Coombs, a master of British military history, and Mr. J. F. Golding and Mr. Edward Hine, of the Photographic Section, for supplying hundreds of pictures that yielded considerable information. My appreciation also goes to Mr. William Conway of Gruppe 66, the International Society of German Aviation Historians, who rallied his London membership on my behalf, and to Mr. Jack Beaumont, who allowed me to spend two profitable afternoons in his musty basement.

Mr. Charles Donald, an American who has devoted most of his life to studying Manfred von Richthofen, is in a category by himself. I am especially grateful to him for supplying material by the pound, including rare photographs and fascinating conversation.

The literary effort was aided by Mr. Richard Severo, a reporter of the New York *Times* and a friend and teacher, who read successive stages of the manuscript and gave needed editorial criticism, and Mrs. Walter Zarek and Dr. Peter Fenner, who helped in translating source material.

Finally, my deepest appreciation to Joelle, my wife, for reading the manuscript more times than anyone else could have stood, for making helpful suggestions throughout, and for cheerfully putting up with all the discomforts that came with "the writer." Now she knows why authors acknowledge their wives, and why acknowledgments do not suffice.

PART I  THE HUNTER

ONE · A BRITISH HAWK—FALLING

"Hawking is a sport of great antiquity, and the hawker watches keenly the flight of his bird as it dives upon its prey. Though he hunts by proxy, as it were, his nerves are taut with the excitement of the chase, imagining himself in the place of the hawk. This hunting instinct passes down through many generations."

—TYRREL M. HAWKER,
Hawker, V.C.

The wind always had to be reckoned with. It blew down from the Channel and over the fishing villages that hugged the coast between Cherbourg and Boulogne. Then, almost capriciously, it turned eastward and passed over the Gothic spires of Amiens, over the red clay roofs of Corbie and, still farther on, over the long trenches filled with men who, in two years, had turned the rolling wheat fields along the Somme into a wasteland. The wind followed the Somme right to the German lines.

It was bringing a particularly cold and wet November to northern France. The infantry had the worst of it, of course, because they had to live in the muddy trenches and were always shoveling out collapsed walls, buttressing those near collapse, and bailing out deep pools of cold brown water which their boots absorbed and held. Worse, there were heavy frosts at night, bringing everything from common colds to compound pneumonia and flu to the soldiers who lived in the mud. A battalion of British Tommies near Bertangles, just north of Amiens, had about a hundred men a day reporting for sick call. Comfort came to the British soldiers only with the thought that the Germans on the other side of the barbed wire were every bit as sick and miserable as they were.

The German armies that had marched across Belgium and into the northern French provinces in August, 1914, were pointed, at least on Prussian General Staff maps, toward Paris. The arrows drawn on those maps in smoky Berlin war rooms represented huge columns of men that were expected to capture Paris, turn south, and then move back toward the east to trap and crush the French army against its own heavy fortifications and the Swiss border—all in a matter of weeks. It had seemed perfectly logical to the generals of cavalry, infantry, and artillery the month before as they looked down at their sprawling maps and mumbled confidently to each other about salients, feints, pincers, and envelopments.

But the plan had not worked. Some of the field commanders, who owed their ranks more to the Kaiser's patronage than to ability, were not mentally or emotionally capable of following other people's plans. Others not only followed the plan, but also, in an effort to build instant reputations as great generals, moved their men far ahead of it. They moved so quickly, in fact, that supplies, food, and reinforcements could not keep up with them. As a result, the German drive stalled east of Paris and curled into a sweating knot around the Marne before August was over. That gave the French a chance to gather their wits, their guns, and the British, and start hammering back. From then on, every time the Germans tried to regain their momentum with a push to the west, the Allies extended their battle lines northward to block them, until the lines stretched through Amiens, across the Belgian frontier, over the Flanders plain, and to the North Sea.

The sides soon balanced one another. Then they began feverishly to dig defensive positions, so the enemy could be held back until enough reinforcements came for one great decisive attack. But enough reinforcements never came. No matter how many battalions of fresh infantry were brought up, how many squadrons of cavalry were assembled, or how many batteries of howitzers were used, the enemy was always too strong to be overrun. So the war became one of attrition. Hundreds of thousands of young men were told to slaughter each other until someone thought of a better plan. At the end of August, 1916, General von Falkenhayn, who had replaced General von Moltke after the Marne fiasco, was himself dismissed by the Kaiser, for losing 525,000 men in the battles of Verdun and the Somme. The losses themselves were acceptable, Falkenhayn was led to understand, but he had absolutely nothing to show for them, and that was unpardonable. Falkenhayn had at least done no worse than the enemy. British casualties at the Somme amounted to 57,470 men during the first twenty-four hours alone.* Then autumn came, bringing torrents of rain, early snow, and a persistent mist, which combined to grind the Battle of the Somme to a halt on November 18. The troops on both sides dug their trenches deeper, settled into them, and began to concern themselves with listening for incoming artillery, occasionally probing each other's defenses, separating maggots from their rations, trying hard to remember what it had once been like to be clean, and looking upward at the airplanes that flew several thousand feet above them and worlds away.

The aviators of No. 24 Squadron, Royal Flying Corps, lived in warm sheds at their airdrome just outside Bertangles. They slept on beds with clean sheets or on canvas cots, and were therefore much more comfortable than the infantry, although few of them thought so. They liked the mud no more than the infantry did, because it was slippery, and taking off and landing on it was dangerous. They bragged to each other that crashing because of the mud could be even worse than the infantry's compound pneumonia and flu.

---

* Final German casualties at the Somme came to 650,000. The British had 419,650, and the French, 194,450.

But the infantry felt no sympathy for the aviators. They knew all about the hot food and fresh coffee the aviators got three times a day, and about their servants and long, drunken, womanizing leaves in Amiens and Paris, and about their warm sheds, clean beds, bathtubs, soap, reading lamps, and free whisky. No wet trenches, no lice, and no barbed wire for the aviators. No artillery shells that suddenly landed in the middle of maybe twenty men and blew most of them to pieces. No hearing the survivors moan and cry all night, and no stench from the ones who did not survive but who were buried too deep in the mud to find. How could there be sympathy for men who flew high over the trenches and just looked down at the war, who only fought *when they wanted to?* What could it be like to hide in a big white cloud or drop down, land, and casually walk away when the war got to be too much? The ones who were shot down in flames died horribly enough, to be sure, but that was their fault. They were not as good as the next man. At least they were not just anonymous parts of a helpless, frightened mob caught in an eruption of earth and steel or in the impersonal spray from a machine gun they could not even see. No. The aviators had a fair chance. They looked down at the real war but did not live in it, and they were luckier than they knew.

Major Lanoe G. Hawker, the leader of No. 24 Squadron, did not feel lucky as he walked slowly to his airplane early in the afternoon on the last day of his life. He was concerned about the wind, the mud, and the frail, inadequate biplane he was about to fly into combat. Hawker was a slender man who sported a neatly clipped brown mustache and the Victoria Cross, and he did not worry easily. He was the product of an unbroken line of army and navy officers that went back to the reign of Elizabeth I, and, like the others of his caste, carried himself with a dignity and firm gentility that did credit to his home and schooling.

When Lanoe was ten years old, he watched his father leave

for the Boer War, and then he and his younger brother said good-by to their mother and tutor and went off to boarding school in Geneva. Life in Switzerland became an endless series of fist fights between the brothers and those classmates who had been told by their parents that England had no place in South Africa. Lanoe and his brother banged Swiss heads together at least once "to show that England could not be insulted with impunity," even though the odds had been twelve to two that England *could* be insulted with impunity. The boy's ordinarily happy disposition began to wear thin. One day, the sister-in-law of the woman who ran the second school attended by the Hawker boys, became angry with Lanoe and grabbed him by his ear. He quickly twisted away and, shaking from rage, shouted, "You have no right to touch me. I am in Miss Stable's charge, not yours, and anyhow, my mother says no one is to pull my ears; they're too big already." And they were. Lanoe was on his way to becoming a frail young man with a disproportionately large, angular head set between outsized ears. But there were also large, limpid eyes, too serious for a boy his age, and a firmly set, straight mouth.

Lanoe returned to England after two years and was sent to a school that prepared boys to be officers in the navy. He could not play strenuous games, like rugby, because of a deviated bone in his nose, which caused breathing problems. He went out instead for fencing, and developed good co-ordination and an aggressive attack. Three years later, he went to the Britannia Naval College, at Dartmouth. An unreported case of jaundice strained his heart and forced him to leave after a year. He never returned.

Recuperation started at home with a stamp album, but when Lanoe was strong enough to get outdoors, he changed to kites, then to model gliders, and finally to rubber-band-powered airplanes. He read everything he could find about flight, and took some of the books about flying with him to the military academy at Woolwich, which he entered in February, 1910. Lanoe graduated from there a year and a half later, at the age of twenty, and was commissioned in the Royal Engineers.

During his stay at Woolwich, Lanoe and his brother became founding members of the Royal Aero Club and spent every free weekend at the Hendon airdrome trying to learn all they could about real wood-and-wire flying machines. The airplanes at Hendon looked, on the one hand, like imposing vehicles, but, on the other, uncomfortably like larger versions of the wood-and-paper models Lanoe had designed and built as a child.

It was on one of those weekends at Hendon that Lanoe begged his first ride in—or, rather, on—an airplane. Perched on a small flat seat beside the pilot, with feet firmly pressed to a rail, cap eagerly turned backward, and white knuckles grasping anything for dear life, Lanoe Hawker lurched and bounced over the grass and finally bounded awkwardly into the air. Actually flying through the air. The sensation was fantastic. It was so deliciously exhilarating that it made his flesh tingle. As the small, sputtering engine pushed Lanoe in wide, graceful circles around Hendon, he peered straight down through tears brought by the wind and, for the first time, saw the earth the way the birds did.

Hawker joined the Royal Engineers and spent the next three years on dull peacetime garrison duty. Then a request for pilot training was finally approved, and, on the eve of war, he was sent to the Central Flying School. Three months later, Hawker was posted to France with a scout squadron. Within a year, he had become the first Royal Flying Corps combat pilot to win the Victoria Cross. He was given his country's highest military medal for routing three German airplanes on one patrol. One of them had to make an emergency landing behind its lines, and another crashed in flames. He had, in fact, shot down nine airplanes, which, by the standards of 1916, made him a man on the way up among the new and daring breed of British combat pilots. He had also combined practical experience from his time in the Royal Engineers with imagination and mathematical ability to invent a rocking platform for realistic aerial-gunnery practice on the ground, warm boots for cold-weather flying, a new gunsight, and other items useful to military pilots. Hawker had, in short, what they call on fitness reports "leadership potential." The twenty-five-year-old officer was therefore encouraged by being given command of England's first fully equipped scout squadron. When he woke on the morning of November 23, 1916, ten months later, Major Lanoe G. Hawker, V.C., D.S.O., looked like a good prospect for general.

He stood in front of his airplane and felt the Channel wind blowing gently against his face. It would not be so gentle up there. In a few minutes it would again carry him, the way it always did, far over the German lines, and probably to China, if he let it. It carried British aviators over the Germans so that they could drop their small black bombs or lean far out of their cockpits to point and click clumsy cameras at gun emplacements and new trenches. Then, their missions over, they had to swing their light airplanes into the stiff head wind to get home. The wind was no friend. Flying into it not only quickly drained the gas that fed their engines, but, worse, slowed them so much that intercepting German scouts had enough time to plunge into and maul their lumbering formations. The Germans had to fight the same wind on their way to British targets, of course, but relatively few of them did that. They preferred to wait for the British to come to them, and since General Trenchard thought there would be no victory without a continuous air offensive, the British always did.

It was one o'clock. The rain had stopped several hours before, but the sun was only just breaking through dark, towering clouds that slid eastward on a fast wind. Although the last of the Somme battles had ended five days earlier, small, probing attacks against the Germans at Bapaume, thirty miles northeast of Bertangles, were still being planned by the infantry. It was therefore necessary, the infantry explained, to photograph German defensive positions from the air thoroughly. Two-seater observation airplanes had been doing that, unmolested, since well before noon, under the watchful eyes of scout pilots from No. 24 Squadron's C Flight. But when C had finished its patrol and returned to Bertangles less than half an hour before, Long, its leader, anxiously reported to Hawker that large formations of Hun scouts had suddenly begun prowling over Bapaume. Hawker knew that the Germans were after easy meat, and, when properly attacked, few things were easier than the underarmed, plodding observers. If the Germans were in their new Albatroses, it would be all the worse, even for his D.H. 2 scouts. He therefore decided to fly with the one o'clock patrol, not as squadron leader—the commander of all three flights in the squadron—but as an ordinary member of A Flight, led by Andrews. He told Long and Pashley to get their airplanes ready to join A Flight over Bapaume in an hour. Then Hawker climbed into the airplane that squatted obstinately in front of him.

The first D.H. 2 was completed early in the summer of 1915. But a year and a half later, the new, sleek German Albatros scouts had made it a dangerous antique. Its pilots nicknamed it the "Spinning Incinerator." It was, basically, a ten-foot-long coffin-shaped box rounded on top and made of wood and canvas. The box supported two fabric-covered wings whose delicate, evenly spaced ribs could be clearly seen when the sun was behind them. When a D.H. 2, its engine full open, passed overhead at ninety-three miles an hour, it was pretty and graceful looking. Its tail, which looked like an afterthought, was held on by metal tubing that started midway out on the wings and tapered back, like two large stepladders, until it met to form a V, at the apex of which the tail was attached. Everything—wings, tail, tubes, box—was held precariously together with what looked like thick piano wire. It was painted beige underneath and a shade of brown on top and sides that exactly matched the mud at Bertangles. There were large concentric red-white-and-blue circles hand painted at the ends of the wings. These identified the D.H. 2 for the Germans who wanted to shoot it to pieces, an admitted drawback, but they also made it easier for other British pilots and for Allied antiaircraft gunners on the ground to identify. The latter occasionally shot at anything that flew by, regardless of nationality, in what British pilots scornfully called "fits of boyish exuberance." The D.H. 2 was slightly more than twenty-five feet long, weighed 943 pounds before its fuel, Lewis machine gun, extra ammunition drums, and pilot were stuffed in, and could be set completely ablaze in less than five minutes with one match applied anywhere except to the tubing and hard rubber tires. Since its designers were unable to figure out how to make a machine gun fire through a spinning propeller without shooting off its blades, they decided to mount its engine on the back of the box, where it would push the D.H. 2, rather than pull it, and seat the pilot in an open cockpit at the very front.

This was where, behind his machine gun, Hawker now huddled in woolen underwear, uniform, fur-lined flying coat, and thigh boots. He flipped a switch that sent electricity to the engine behind him. When the current and the gas in the engine's cylinders touched, there was a loud sneeze, which sent a shudder through the wooden box, along the intricate network of crisscrossing cables, and out over the large, cloth-covered wings. The little engine caught and settled into a more or less even roar. Blue smoke came out of the cylinders in thin streams and was drawn back into the propeller, where it was chewed up and sent tumbling into the mud and wet grass behind the airplane. The noise was loud and irritated even the few men at Bertangles who liked D.H. 2's. Hawker pulled his goggles over his eyes and adjusted them until they felt comfortable. Then he kicked the rudder-pedal bar back and forth and moved his joy stick around to see whether the ailerons, elevator, and rudder were working. They were. Andrews had already started his engine, and the other two regular members of the flight, Saundby and Crutch, were about to start theirs. It was all right to take off.

The valve that controlled the flow of gas to the engine had

only two positions—"stop" and "full speed"—so when Hawker released the brake, his D.H. 2 jumped forward and started to roll through the mud as fast as it could. The longer it rolled, the faster it went, and if the pilot pulled back on the stick when it was rolling fast enough, it lifted into the air. It was as simple as that. After a short roll into the wind, Hawker's plane rose from the Bertangles airdrome and climbed steeply, but gracefully, toward the last of the dark clouds. Then it turned northeastward and was soon joined by the three other scouts. They formed a squat diamond, with Andrews in front, Hawker a little to his left, Saundby a little to his right, and Crutch behind.

They could see beneath them and far off to the right St. Peter of Corbie, a thick, dark-gray cathedral similar, from 11,000 feet, to Notre-Dame, which stood in the center of the town and seemed to rise obliviously above it. Small tan homes and shops crowded against the church and looked as though they were clinging to it for protection against the bedlam that surrounded and snapped at them. Isolated, pock-marked farmhouses and barns scattered along the roads leading to the town were stragglers, and they had paid for it. Many had large holes in their stucco sides, exposing jagged rows of gray tree branches, like the ribs in a cadaver. There were high columns of black smoke at several points on the eastern horizon, and, below, toy autos and lorries inched along narrow brown roads and over bumpy fields toward toy soldiers who worked or rested near tents, sheds, and lonely, battered houses or in the sandbagged trenches that went up and down the rolling hills. The D.H. 2 offered a fine view.

Less than ten minutes after taking off, Crutch signaled that his engine was running rough, and then swung away from the formation to land at No. 9 Squadron's airdrome for repairs. The others continued to drone on through the biting air over Albert, more than halfway to Bapaume, with a quarter of their strength already gone. Crutch had been right to drop out, because a cripple in combat would be a dangerous liability—especially if they ran into the Albatroses—but all the same, it was a bad omen. And there was still the cold. The thin layer of grease that covered Hawker's face only partially blunted the air that struck it. Rear-mounted engines allowed for a fine view, all right, but they deprived the pilot of the warm air that flowed back from front-mounted engines. On the other hand, a rear-mounted engine, though it limited visibility in that direction, protected his back against bullets coming from behind.

A Flight crossed the front lines at 1:30 P.M. Hawker routinely fired five rounds from the machine gun that was mounted on a swivel in front of him to make sure it was not jammed. At about that moment, all three pilots noticed a battle taking place near Grandcourt, a few miles to their left, between Nieuports and enemy scouts. But when they turned to join in, perhaps forgetting their mission, the Germans broke off and flew eastward, so the D.H. 2's were again pointed toward Bapaume and the camera-carrying two-seaters they were supposed to meet there.

Twenty minutes later, a couple of two-seaters were seen flying low and slightly to the northeast of Bapaume. Friendlies? Three pairs of eyes squinted at the dots for a long time, to be absolutely certain. No. The black Maltese crosses on their wings made them Huns. Easy meat. Andrews pushed his stick forward, bringing his D.H. 2 into a shallow dive in the direction the Germans were heading. He would lead the attack. Hawker and Saundby would fly on his sides to catch the Germans when they tried to get out of Andrews's way. But the Germans saw the attacking Englishmen in plenty of time, and when A Flight was only halfway through its dive, the two-seaters casually banked eastward and began pulling away. At the height of his frustration, Andrews took a quick look around, and that was when he saw the other dots far above him.

Bait. The two-seaters were bait for a trap. No thought now of easy meat. Get out of there. As Andrews kicked on his rudder bar and simultaneously moved his stick to one side, bringing his scout into a wide right turn, the dots began dropping on the three English pushers at more than one hundred miles an hour. Hands and feet were suddenly soaked with perspiration, while mouths went dry. Saundby, who had imitated his flight leader's every move, was now a little ahead of Andrews as both prepared for a dash to the safety of their lines. But Hawker, either because he thought Andrews had turned back on account of engine trouble or because he was too intent on catching the disappearing two-seaters, continued to fly eastward without looking up. The dots were now unmistakably Hun scouts and they were headed right for Hawker.

Andrews, seeing that his squadron leader was probably seconds away from being shot to pieces, continued his circle, with Saundby still off his right wing. When the circle was completed, both D.H. 2's went after Hawker in an effort to head off the first of the Germans, who at that moment was looking down at the unaware Englishman from between the black barrels of two Spandau machine guns. Andrews never took his eyes off that German. He held the stick with his left hand and grabbed the handle of the Lewis gun with his right as he and the German converged on a point a couple of hundred feet above and behind Hawker. It was not really close enough for Andrews to fire effectively, but in another moment it would be too late. He squeezed the trigger until twenty-five bullets had arced out toward the German. With gunpowder fumes in his nostrils, Andrews watched the startled German turn his scout on its side and roll over into a steep dive. There was no telling whether the Hun had been hit, but at least the clatter from Andrews's gun had gotten him off Hawker's tail. It had also awakened Hawker to the fact that a free-for-all was developing between A Flight and ten fast German scouts.

Hawker looked up in time to see another German coming at him. The Englishman, too, banked sharply away and rolled into an upside-down fall, which made the earth spin deliriously as it turned quickly over, like an enormous brown pancake, until it became the sky.

Andrews had no sooner lost sight of the German he had shot at than his own airplane was violently shaken by bullets coming from behind that tore into its engine and gas tank. The engine stopped. In spite of the airplanes swarming around him and the sound of their machine guns, the first thing he noticed was how quiet it had become. The familiar rasping sound of his own engine was suddenly gone, and it made him fully realize that he was flying a crippled airplane through a battle. No, he was not really flying it, so much as he was trying to keep it out of a spin that would end fatally. The D.H. 2 liked to spin. As he crouched deep in his cockpit, waiting for the Hun's second burst to hit him in the back, he turned his scout around until it pointed west, into the wind. Then he gently pushed forward on the stick until the silent airplane started into a long, ever faster glide toward the British lines. He could hear the wind whistling through cables and around the red-and-white, candy-striped struts that held the upper and lower wings together. He took a last look back and saw Hawker down at about 3,000 feet in a circling fight with a German scout.

Saundby had twisted himself out of the way of several Germans when the attack began. Then he went after the one who had turned his flight leader's airplane into a glider and who, after smashing Andrews's cylinders, gas tank, and cam box, and ripping large holes in his wings, was carefully closing in for that last burst that had to send the Englishman—the "Lord," as Germans contemptuously called British pilots—to his death. But Saundby had in the meantime pulled to within twenty yards of the thoroughly absorbed German and emptied most of a forty-seven-round drum into his airplane at almost point-blank range. He watched, almost hypnotized, as his bullets punched a line of splintering holes into the plywood between the tail and the Hun's head. The German began to sway from side to side, and finally dropped away and disappeared without giving Saundby the satisfaction of seeing flames. When he saw that Andrews was nursing his D.H. 2 back to the lines, however, he, too, disappeared in search of another German. The observers that should have been protected were forgotten. Andrews now had to concentrate on fighting the wind. Major Hawker could take care of himself, he thought.

The pilot of the bullet-nosed Albatros that now followed Hawker around a tight circle at 3,000 feet near Bapaume, two miles inside German lines, did not know who his opponent was, but he knew the Lord's airplane intimately. He had been one of several German pilots who test flew the first D.H. 2 to arrive in France after it crashed almost intact behind German lines a year and a half later. He had tested its maneuverability and absolute speed limits at all altitudes in climbs, dives, and turns, the reliability, range, and accuracy of its machine gun, and the number of minutes its thirsty engine allowed it to stay in the air. Then, while another German pilot flew it and took defensive action, he made simulated attacks against it to find its most vulnerable side.

The German therefore knew that his opponent could not defend himself from the rear. There was no chance of being shot at if he stayed behind and slightly above the Englishman. That was requisite number one, and, having achieved it, he could think about the kill. He knew that his Albatros was about twenty miles an hour faster than the D.H. 2 at their present altitude, that it could climb more quickly, and that it carried two machine guns to the Englishman's one. It could not, however, turn tighter circles than the D.H. 2, which might make staying on its tail difficult. But the German knew that if he could stay in the circle with his opponent, they would slowly lose altitude while the wind blew them farther and farther behind German lines, until the Englishman ran out of gas. If that happened, the Lord would have to either land and be taken prisoner or be shot out of the sky. No pilot would get into such a predicament. He would therefore try to escape. So the German knew that all he had to do was wait for the Englishman to break the circle and run for home. Then he would have him. Then he would kill him.

Hawker realized immediately that he was not up against what his pilots called a "nervous type." The Hun was doing all the right things. He had not yet let his hunger for a victory force him into a mistake. Not yet. But there was still time. Ten minutes before, Hawker had turned off his engine to prevent it from choking, and started a long dive at 11,000 feet to catch the pair of two-seaters that had been speeding eastward. He had no sooner turned off the engine than he heard machine-gun fire coming from above, and, at almost the same instant, bullets passed close by. To hell with those two-seaters. He put his scout into a roll and then into a leaflike spiral. At the same time, he pushed his fuel valve to "full speed" to get the engine going and pulled out of the spiral with a little less than full power at 10,000 feet. That was when he had run into this smart Hun, who had been below all the time, probably waiting for him. Hawker got off a few ineffective shots at the German while each tried to get into firing position, but neither would allow such an advantage, so they settled on opposite sides of a 300-foot-wide circle. They went around about twenty times to the left. Then Hawker made a figure eight, leading the German into about thirty more circles to the right and, by that time, dropping to 6,000 feet. They continued that way, round and round, like two dogs snapping at one another's tails, as the minutes passed and they neared 3,000 feet.

The German was now slightly higher on his side of the circle, and had a clear view of the Englishman hunched in his cockpit. He looked down and closely observed the man he was waiting to kill. He noted every movement of the Englishman's head and tried hard to penetrate through the goggles that masked the eyes looking up at his. But because of the goggles and the tan leather cap, he could not see the expression on Hawker's face and he regretted it. An arm came out of the Englishman's cockpit and coolly waved up at him. The German smiled, but did not wave back. "No beginner," he thought.

When Hawker's altimeter showed 1,500 feet, he began to get desperate. Half an hour had passed, the gas was critically low, and he figured he had drifted well over two miles behind the lines. He would be in the arms of the German infantry in ten minutes if he stayed in this mad circle. Where was Saundby? Where, for that matter, were Long and Pashley? He could now see trees, houses, and roads spinning by where, an eternity before, there had been limitless, free sky. He continued to look up at the German, but the dark blur he caught in the corner of his eye—the earth—now seemed like a giant mouth that wanted to swallow him. The circle *had* to be broken. With his eyes still on the German, Hawker jerked back on the stick, putting his D.H. 2 into a couple of high, twisting loops. When he came out of the last of them, he rolled to one side, then to the other, and, with his altimeter showing 300 feet, began the dash for home.

"Now." The German snapped his Albatros into a tight bank and went straight for the Englishman's tail. Both airplanes sped 150 feet above flat, pock-marked fields. They skimmed over groups of gray-uniformed German soldiers who held flattened hands over their eyes to block out the sun as they watched the terrier go after the rat. Most of them had seen it before, but it was always interesting, so they stopped piling sandbags and opening crates and watched the airplanes for as long as they could. It was a good excuse for a cigarette. Some of the soldiers wanted to fire their rifles or machine guns at the Englishman, but he was too close in front of their man, so they just watched.

Hawker, trying to throw off the German's aim, kicked his rudder bar back and forth, putting his scout into a series of zigzags. Two blue-gray eyes followed him, first to one side, then back across the black Spandaus to the other. Then back again. The eyes sent the picture to the brain for analysis. It was a trade-off, thought the German. The Englishman was zigzagging to present a more difficult target. But he lost speed every time he did it.

Whether he succeeded in dodging bullets long enough depended on how close they were to the lines. The German was certain the Englishman would not make it. Every time the swerving airplane passed in front of his Spandaus, the German squeezed their triggers and watched a short line of bullets go out toward the growing target. He liked the sound of the guns, the sudden smell of gunpowder, and, most of all, the feeling that his bullets were ripping into canvas, smashing wooden braces, cutting control cables, and perhaps imbedding themselves into flesh. But the Englishman still would not fall, and the front lines were now 1,000 yards ahead.

The German was now within sixty feet of the Englishman and firing almost continuously. If the D.H. 2 made it to the British lines, its pilot would immediately drop to a safe landing, and the German would be robbed of his hard-earned prize. With 900 of his 1,000 rounds gone, and the first row of British trenches in sight, the German's guns jammed. He cursed and frantically tried to clear them. They were clear again. He carefully lined up the small gunsight between his Spandaus with the Englishman's engine. The gloved hand wrapped around the Albatros's stick, and the boots resting delicately on its rudder pedals moved fractions of an inch in exact duplication of the hand and boots in the airplane ahead. The German again squeezed his trigger. More bullets came out of the twin Spandaus. Another quick taste of powder.

Then the German saw the English scout suddenly straighten, hang limply in the air for a second, and fall. It smashed nose-first into the ground, burying its machine gun in the mud, splitting and crunching wood, and tearing fabric. It stayed in that position for a moment, tail pointed upward, and then came crashing down in a tangle of cables and a thin cloud of dust. The wreckage bounced once and came to rest in a waterlogged shell hole 500 yards inside the German forward lines. Its pilot lay somewhere in the debris with a bullet in his head.

The young German put his Albatros into a tight, climbing

turn until it pointed east. He looked around for other airplanes, and seeing none, let himself look down at his victim. He tried hard to be calm as he studied what he had done. But his heart pounded from excitement. There was no other feeling like it. He felt potency surging through his body and waiting in his fingers to be used again. Two of them had fought for the sky. One was the victor. *He* was the victor, and therefore he owned the sky for as far as he could see and as far as his guns could reach.

He pulled gently back on the stick and aimed his Albatros toward a higher altitude, where it would catch the wonderful wind that always carried him home. He thought the wind could carry him to heaven. It was the eleventh time Baron Manfred von Richthofen had felt that way.

TWO · "LEARN TO OBEY THAT YOU
MAY LEARN TO COMMAND"

*"Na, so you have managed to become a reserve lieutenant—that is
the chief thing—that is the thing you must be these days—socially,
professionally, in every connection! The doctorate is the visiting card,
but the reserve commission is the open door—that's the essential thing
these days!"*

—KARL ZUCKMAYER,
The Captain from Köpenick

"Idiotenhaus!" The word was used by Prussian officers in 1916,
not to describe the war rooms of the Allied generals with whom
they were locked in a murderous stalemate, but to describe their
own Foreign Office. The milksop diplomats and dangerous liberals in the Reichstag, they warned Kaiser Wilhelm, were losing
the war for the Fatherland. So far as the diplomats and liberal
parliamentarians were concerned, the feeling was mutual, and it
formed the basis for a vicious power struggle that swept through
Berlin's private clubs, its most fashionable tea salons, and into
the Kaiser's drawing rooms. Only the city's most informed citizens
knew about the accusations that went back and forth between
the General Staff, the Foreign Office, and the Reichstag. They
went to the Tiergarten on Sundays to debate it along tree-lined
gravel paths and over tables spread with beer, sausages, and
newspapers that promised great offensives which would break
the stalemate once and for all. There was always information
about the next offensive, and about the nation's war heroes, but
rarely statistics on German casualties.

The other citizens—the great majority—did not go to private clubs and fashionable tea salons, so they knew little or nothing about the war within the war. They did know, however, that the one in France and Russia was supposed to have been over by Christmas, 1914, but it was still going on. The ordinary people of Berlin, who stood ten-deep along the Unter den Linden and watched, hats in hands, as their sons marched west under the Brandenburg Gate and disappeared to the sounds of steel hoofs, caisson wheels, and boots, were becoming restive. The parades were still impressive. Girls still threw flowers and kisses to the endless gray lines. Cavalry officers still looked dashing as they guided panting stallions past the crowds. Gun carriages still looked menacing as they rumbled over the cobblestones. Fifes, drums, and snapping flags still stirred something. But not many of the sons were coming home. Even the oldest in the crowds that lined the Unter den Linden could not remember when so many men had marched out of Berlin and so few had returned.

The Prussian army had fallen on evil times. It had been born during the Thirty Years' War, which ended with the Peace of Westphalia in 1648. During the next two and a half centuries, it was fed with the sons of conservative *Junker* landowners, and it grew to adolescence, maturity, old age, and senility by digesting them. It had reached maturity by beating Napoleon in 1813–14, and the prestige from that victory made it arrogant. It then took on the liberals and constitutional reformers in its own country, with results that proved more significant than the wars won with gun and sword outside its borders. In a long series of vicious battles, it fought off all attempts by civilians to control it, and by the time Germany was unified in 1871, the Prussian officer corps was seriously trying to control the civilians. It was to prove to be supremely ironic that the old-line officers' collective senility would cause the collapse in 1918 of the very monarchy they had defended against mounting liberal opposition for more than a century. And the man who was eventually to accomplish what the liberals never could—the total, if degrading, subordination of the Prussian generals to civilian control—would win their obedience by promising resurrection after the humiliating defeat of 1918. His name was Adolf Hitler.

The old-liners would blame 1918 on the *bourgeoisie* and the Communists, who, they said, stabbed them in the back at home while they faced their country's enemies. They especially scorned the *bourgeoisie* within their own ranks. Since there had not been enough *Junkers* to supply officers for the army after Germany was unified, the Prussian officer corps had had to dip into the middle class for them, and it did so with loathing. Military journals read by the officers who led the young men to France and Russia in 1914 warned, as they had for decades, that the forces of turmoil were becoming stronger and that "whole masses had declared war on God and the King." The army was "the only fixed point in the whirlpool, the rock in the sea of revolution that threatens on all sides," the journals warned, and they insisted that officers be totally bound by their personal oaths to the Kaiser.

Most of the young officers who came to the rock in the whirlpool were from the wealthier sections of the middle class. They were sent to the army in the 1880's and 1890's partly because the growing threat of socialism had made their fathers conservative and partly because fathers and sons wanted to be accepted by a feudal *Junker* aristocracy whose approaching end they could not yet see. Possession of a commission became an important sign of social acceptability, and was eagerly sought. Most of the new bourgeois officers adapted themselves well to the colors—in many cases, too well. They embraced and exaggerated the thoughts, manners, and what they imagined were the full-time vices of their noble comrades in arms. While many made brilliant theoretical and practical contributions to their corps, others plunged into heavy drinking, brawling, gambling, and dueling with swords (which left wounds that often became infected), in what they imagined was the proper pastime of aristocrats on garrison duty. The authentic *Junker* officers became disgusted by the bourgeois invasion that brought vulgarity to their austere, but dignified lives, and reacted with arrogance. That, too, was copied. The officer corps began to abound with arrogant junior officers who easily lent themselves to magazine satire, ridicule in books, such as *The Captain from Köpenick,* and alienation from most of society. The average, relatively modest and usually correct, Prussian officer—or, at least, the officer who was taken to be Prussian —had become an almost unbearable lout.

But lout or not, he belonged to a still-elite fraternity which, on the eve of the war, had behind it an impressive string of victories against the Danes, the Austrians, the French, and the Reichstag. While it held power, the force to be dealt with was the Prussian officer corps. It developed its own traditions of command, obedience, and honor, and it fed off those traditions. The legends of the Teutonic knights, who rode valiantly into lone combat with lances, squires, and their honor, were dusted off and passed from one generation of young officers to the next. Battle techniques had been developed by the time of Napoleon, and depended, first, on the clear and comprehensive formulation of an objective, and then on flexible maneuvering in a constant effort to find and destroy the enemy. Individual initiative was stressed, as was duty to God and King, and to underlings, who were to be used and protected, but never abused. The officer-candidate, standing in front of his examining board, was likely to be asked: "What is the first duty of an officer?" The answer was expected to be: "The first duty of an officer is to his men."

From the generations of Prussian officers who lived by that code came the generals whose names the new lieutenants—even the bourgeois lieutenants—knew as well as their own: von Scharnhorst, von Gneisenau, von Boyen, von Blücher, von Kleist, von Rauch, and von Yorck. No one knew von Richthofen when Germany went to war.

Major Albrecht Baron von Richthofen was one of the first in his family to become a professional soldier. A cousin of his father had been a general somewhere, but aside from him and a scat-

tering of distant relatives with reserve commissions, the Richthofens had for the most part worked at farming, raising merino
sheep, and milking their dairy herds along the Oder River in
Silesia. They were gentlemen farmers much like their English
counterparts, so when they were not supervising the work in
their fields and scrupulously balancing ledgers, they were hunting and horseback riding.

The line went back at least as far as Sebastian Schmidt, a native
of Coblenz, who lived in Bernau between 1543 and 1555, and
who had been a pupil of Martin Luther. Sebastian married the
daughter of a Berlin town councilor and had a son named Samuel.
Sebastian also happened to be a friend of Paulas Schultze, a
devoted courtier of Emperor Ferdinand I, who was rewarded for
his services to the Crown with a coat of arms and a Latinized
name—Praetorius. Since Schultze had no heirs, he adopted his
friend's son, Samuel. After Schultze's death, Samuel took his coat
of arms and new fortune to Frankfurt, where he became a judge
and then mayor. His son, Tobias, married into the nobility and
more money, and became one of the first Germans to buy land in
Silesia, then populated mostly by Slavs. Tobias's son, Johann, was
awarded the surname von Richthofen by Emperor Leopold I.
Because the family remained loyal to the German-Austrian
Empire during the War of the Austrian Succession, in which
Spain was thrown out of Silesia, they were given knighthood and
a barony by Frederick the Great. From then on, every Richthofen was called *Freiherr*, or Baron, and, with eight exceptions,
they settled near Liegnitz and Schweidnitz and worked to maintain their lands and name.

The exceptions included four Richthofens—Karl, Hartmann,
Ernst, and Praetorius—who became conservative members of the
Reichstag and a fifth, Oswald, who became a state secretary of
foreign affairs under Kaiser Wilhelm II. The sixth, another Karl,
became a law professor at the University of Berlin. The two most
interesting of the eight were Walter and Ferdinand. Walter came
to New York with his English bride in the mid-1870's, and then

moved to Denver, where he dabbled in real estate, gold mining, and cattle and horse breeding. Although he became an American citizen, he had a castle built of gray stones, with the Richthofen coat of arms set on its north tower. It still stands in Denver, along with a few other buildings he erected, and a Richthofen Place was named in his honor. Since cattle breeding was Walter's greatest pleasure, he wrote a book, *Cattle-Raising on the Plains of North America,* which was published in 1885, and which has been credited with helping to start the cattle boom in that part of the country. Ferdinand von Richthofen (1833–1905), became the only member of the family to be mentioned in the Encyclopaedia Britannica. He explored China seven times, taught geology and geography at the universities of Bonn, Leipzig, and Berlin, and wrote several books on his specialties. One of them, *Natural System of Volcanic Rocks,* was written and published while he lived in California in 1867–68.

Albrecht, who was born in 1859, decided as a child that he wanted to be a soldier. After going through cadet school and a military academy, he joined the cavalry. It made sense. In Germany, as elsewhere, riding was practiced by the landed gentry almost from birth. That made entrance into the cavalry relatively painless, and the cavalry was favored by soldiers of the aristocracy. After all, riding to war was better than walking. Albrecht took his profession seriously, which was why, though sweating from exertion one day during winter maneuvers, he dove into the icy Oder to rescue three of his ordinary soldiers whose horses had lost their footing. The Rittmeister, or Cavalry Captain, came out of the water with a severe chill, which he ignored and covered with more perspiration. The chill caused complications that settled in his ears and finally made him deaf. A medical board decided that he was unfit for active service, so he was promoted to major and retired with a pension wholly inadequate for a man with servants, serfs, and property. Major Albrecht Freiherr von Richthofen became convinced that glory had eluded him. But two things made his fate palatable. First, he was married to the former Kunigunde von Schickfuss und Neudorff, an auburn-haired beauty from an old family with enough wealth so that, combined with his relatively small inheritance, the lands could be kept. Second, although their first child had been a girl, born on August 8, 1890, which Albrecht considered nice, but unimportant, their next two had been boys, which was most important. They were born in Breslau, while he was stationed there. The first came on May 2, 1892, and was named Manfred Albrecht, after an uncle in the Imperial Guards. The second, Lothar, was born on September 27, 1894. Albrecht had decided even before he was married that his first son, according to the custom in many Prussian military families, would follow his father into the army. His determination on that score doubled when he lost his hearing.

Manfred was not a cherubic child, but he had his mother's soft, straight handsomeness and, as he grew, a relatively strong physical disposition. Long blond curls hung to his shoulders until after his second birthday, when they were cut off, revealing a pair of well-shaped, almost forgotten ears. His dresses went about when his curls did, and, freed of both, little Manfred began accommodating his life to that of his sister, Ilse, and to a world of goat-cart rides, doting servants, dogs, horses, and the grapes and berries that could be picked and eaten while he explored his father's woods and fields. He also accommodated himself, with interest and increasing arrogance, to the Slavs who worked on his father's land and who, his parents and relatives said, were Orientals and therefore inferior to Prussians, and even to Germans.

The Richthofens moved to their estate at Schweidnitz, about forty miles southwest of Breslau, after Albrecht's retirement. There, Manfred, who was almost nine, discovered guns. His father told him hunting stories that captured his imagination and prepared him for his uncle Alexander, a frequent guest in the Richthofens' three-story white stone house. Alexander von Schickfuss, his mother's brother, was a dedicated hunter. When he tired of hunting deer and boar in the Silesian hills, he visited a friend's game preserve in Hungary and shot bear, wolves, and lynx. When that bored him, he took his rifles to Norway and then, he told the wide-eyed Richthofen boys, to Africa and India for lions, tigers, elephants, and other huge and dangerous beasts. They were enthralled by Uncle Alexander's stories, and became even more so when they visited his home and saw more than 400 mounted heads, dozens of skins, and racks of pistols, rifles, and shotguns, all polished to a shine and stacked in large glass cabinets. Manfred decided that he, too, would be a great hunter and kill mighty animals. He asked his father for an air rifle, was given one, and started his hunting career around Schweidnitz by going after all the squirrel-sized animals he could find. During a vacation at his grandmother's, Manfred used his rifle to kill three of her tame ducks, and pulled a white feather out of each for trophies. He brought them into the house for exhibition. When his mother began to scold him, his grandmother stopped her, because, she explained, Manfred had been quite right to confess his misdeed. But he had not been confessing; he had been bragging.

Manfred was sent to Wahlstatt, a cadet school in Berlin, when he was eleven. He took an immediate disliking to the cold gray former monastery, and to its tiny, Spartanly furnished rooms, long hours of study, unappetizing food, and its motto: "Learn to obey that you may learn to command." He also disliked the harsh penalties that came when the motto was disobeyed. Mostly, the little boy disliked being so far from home, far from his parents, far from his own room, and far from his rifle, horses, and dogs. He decided to study exactly as much as he had to in order to keep from being expelled, but to use his energy where it would best relieve his frustrations—in athletics and gymnastics. He put apple-tree climbing at Schweidnitz to good use on wooden horses and parallel bars and began to surprise teachers who at first had thought his slender build and delicate appearance would not stand the rigors of military life. Manfred was always stronger than he looked. He actually won prizes for gymnastics in his first year at Wahlstatt, which made his instructors take a more lenient view of his scholastic shortcomings. Nevertheless, he was not considered bright, and was soon lost in the majority of average boys at the school. His spirits only picked up toward the end of the academic year, because he knew he would soon leave Wahlstatt for a summer of swimming, riding, shooting, and eating real food, rather than mush. Furthermore, his mother had just given birth to a new brother, Karl Bolko, whom he had never seen.

Before Manfred went to Wahlstatt that first year, he had heard a story that the house at Schweidnitz was haunted by the ghost of a man who had hanged himself from a rafter in the attic. The twelve-year-old, returned home for vacation, determined to find the ghost and bash its supernatural brains in. He talked Lothar into joining the hunt and got permission from his mother for both of them to spend a night in the attic. Then he asked the caretaker to show him the supposed spot at which the body had dangled. Under it, the children pushed their bed and began a vigil. They were soon asleep. The next thing Lothar knew, he was sitting up in the black musty room listening to something roll loudly and erratically across the floor. There it was again, this time close by. Terrified, he pushed and pulled Manfred out of his sleep, and both listened as the bumping sound again came over the floor boards. Manfred picked up a stick next to the bed, climbed down, and advanced slowly toward where the sound was coming from. He was poised to deliver the hardest blow he could, when the light went on, and he saw his mother and Ilse grinning at him. Each held a fistful of chestnuts. Baroness von Richthofen recalled later that she and her daughter came close to being severely clubbed that night by a boy who did not show the fear he must have felt.

Years later, Manfred told of the time he made his first "ascent" —to the top of the highest church steeple in Wahlstatt. He described a tingling climb with a friend over the eaves to the uppermost of the steeple's lightning rods. There, he said, he looked down at the town from his tiny perch and was thrilled beyond anything that came later, even the view from 20,000 feet. He tied a handkerchief to the rod, and claimed to have seen it, still tied in place, ten years later. Breaking the monotony of school at Wahlstatt apparently drove him to desperation.

Richthofen would later sum up his six years there this way: "I found it difficult to bear the strict discipline and to keep order. I did not care very much for the instruction I received. I was never good at learning. I did just enough work to pass. In my opinion, it would have been wrong to do more than was just enough, so I worked as little as possible. Consequently, my teachers did not think a great deal of me. On the other hand, I liked sports, and particularly gymnastics, football, and so forth. I could do all tricks on the horizontal bar. So I received some prizes from the Commandant."

He could not, apparently, do *all* the tricks on the horizontal bar. A fall during one leap loosened cartilage in his leg, which made him limp until an operation repaired the damage. All in all, he could reflect in the spring of 1909, when he turned his back on studies at Wahlstatt for the last time, that it had been a miserable ordeal. He never complained to his parents about the school, and hardly mentioned it to Lothar, especially after it was behind him. But he later warned Karl Bolko about the evils of the place and urged the youngest Richthofen to avoid military education if at all possible. Manfred was not a blindly obedient youth. Obedience when you enjoyed your work was one thing, he explained, but being obedient for six years of misery was something else. Bolko idolized Manfred too much to follow that advice, so he eventually went to the cadet school to learn for himself.

But Wahlstatt was now finished. Manfred, at seventeen, looked forward to another summer out of doors, and particularly to hunting, before autumn came, and with it, the senior school at Lichterfelde. He spent as much time as possible roaming over the wooded hills around Schweidnitz in search of game birds, foxes, otters, deer, and marten. They required careful stalking. He was good at that. He practiced walking silently through brush and timber and put other hours into training himself to send a bullet exactly where he wanted it to go. Walking deep into the dark forest, through dense foliage and silently over leaves and brittle twigs that could give him away, excited him, as did pitting his senses against those of his prey. The thought that somewhere ahead a flushed animal, perhaps looking fearfully back at him, was running for its life thrilled him. Having successfully stalked it, which was to conquer another living thing in its own environment, he would put a bullet into it to seal his victory. The bullet would be placed cleanly. That was important to Manfred, because he knew that the bullet gave him so great an advantage that if it was not aimed perfectly, the sport would somehow be unfair. He wanted it to be fair. Anything less than that would be haphazard shooting, which, to Manfred, amounted to butchery. But there had to be a kill, because when he trudged home without one, he felt he had not measured up to his father, and that was important to him. So he worked hard at becoming a good shot, and by seventeen he was. The carcass was, as he had been taught by his father and uncle, the most dramatic testimony to his prowess. Trophies were important to him, as they were to every hunter he knew, because they were undeniable proof of his victories and they confirmed, in the most tangible and unmistakable way, that he had competed and was better than his victim. He strained for victories in all outdoor activities, and, as he grew older, developed a deep hatred for being denied the plaudits that were supposed to come with them.

Lichterfelde was better than Wahlstatt. The school was on the southern edge of Berlin and only five miles from Potsdam, an important military garrison behind the New Palace erected by Frederick the Great. Based on past experience, Richthofen was nonetheless filled with misgivings throughout the train trip to Berlin. He was still not sure about a lifetime of soldiering, especially if it was all like Wahlstatt, which still brought bitter, depressing memories. "My father wished it," he said later about his career, "so my wishes were not consulted." Before he finished his first week at Lichterfelde, however, he began to reap the benefits of being a young adult in a senior school, and he liked them. No more drill books, field regulations, standing orders, and the constant spit-and-polish cadet life. No one punished him for a crooked tie, leftover food, or a speck of dust under his bed. No more nonsense. All that was set aside for the real business of soldiering. Studies began to interest Richthofen. He had classes in military history and went on field exercises with real soldiers stationed at the Potsdam garrison. And, delightfully, there was Clausewitz, the patron saint of the General Staff. One at a time, he took the famous ten-volume work out of the library and pored over it in his room. The first three books, *On War*, were called masterpieces by his teachers, and dealt with the philosophy of war and the creation of sweeping new strategies. The next seven books were slower going, and were concerned with the Italian campaign of 1796–97, the campaign of 1799 in Switzerland and Italy, the wars of 1812–14, Waterloo, and papers on the campaigns of Gustavus Adolphus, Turenne, Luxembourg, Munnich, Frederick the Great, and others. He did not know it at the time, and probably would not have cared much if he had, but his counterparts in the École Militaire, in Paris, and at Sandhurst, in England, were also reading Clausewitz in the winter of 1909.

Richthofen had genuinely free time at Lichterfelde. He "did not feel so isolated from the world, and began to live a little more like a human being," he said. The young Baron made friends with Prince Frederick Karl, and together they roamed Berlin in their off-hours looking for occasional quiet beers and decent restaurants. They also competed against one another in gymnastics and on the playing field. Richthofen admitted that his friend usually beat him, but deserved to do so, because he trained harder. The admission was a good indication of their friendship, since Richthofen took more than average pride in his body's ability to win prizes. At eighteen, he was five feet eight inches, which was as tall as he was going to get. He was slim and still looked a little fragile, but he had remained strong for his build and could withstand great physical punishment and pain, which he was proud of.

He left Lichterfelde at the end of 1910 and entered the Berlin War Academy for a year of final polishing. Richthofen did not like the stuffiness of the War Academy and compared it with Wahlstatt. But the end of his formal education was now in sight, so he could not think of dropping out, and decided to bear up under the final lectures. He was given up-to-the-minute instruction on the state of the German army and the armies around it. There were briefings on the political situation in Germany, and, though politics in neighboring countries were mentioned, his teachers laid particular emphasis on the troubles at home, which, they said, were caused by liberal encroachments against the army and the Crown. Richthofen found such intellectuality boring. When he looked back on the "not overly agreeable" War Academy, he could find only one incident that amused and interested him:

"One of our instructors bought a very nice, fat mare. Her only fault was that she was rather old. She was supposed to be 15 years old; she had very stout legs, but she jumped wonderfully. I rode her often, and her name was Biffy.

"About a year later, when I joined the Regiment, my Captain, von Tr————, who was very fond of sports, told me that he had bought a funny little mare, a fat animal, who jumped very nicely. We were all very interested in meeting the fat jumping horse that bore the strange name of Biffy. I had forgotten the old mare of my instructor at the War Academy. One fine morning, the animal arrived, and I was astonished to find that the ancient Biffy was now standing as an eight-year-old in the Captain's stable. Meanwhile, she had changed her master repeatedly, and had greatly risen in value." The Captain, Richthofen added, had paid more than twice as much for Biffy as had his teacher at the War Academy. "She won no more prizes for jumping, but she changed her master once more, and fell in the beginning of the war," he recalled.

Richthofen ended his formal education, and immediately after passing the final examination enlisted in the 1st Regiment of Uhlans, which was stationed near Schweidnitz. Uhlans were cavalry lancers who specialized in reconnaissance and light combat, and were thought to be the most dashing of soldiers, which suited the Baron well. Life was getting much better.

He was awarded his epaulettes in the autumn of 1912. "It was a glorious feeling, the finest I have ever experienced, when people called me lieutenant," he said. Then he settled into the pleasant life of peacetime garrison duty so close to home that he could ride there on weekends. His father gave him a mare named Santuzza when he received his commission, and he spent the rest of that idyllic autumn training the horse to jump.

The state of the rest of the sprawling Richthofen family that autumn was less than idyllic. The former Emma Maria Frieda von Richthofen, a distant cousin of Manfred, had, the previous May, deserted her husband and three children to run away with a relatively unknown writer named D. H. Lawrence. Frieda, a tall, green-eyed blonde, had become bored as the wife of a professor in England, and within a month of meeting Lawrence crossed the Channel with him and went to Metz to celebrate her father's fiftieth anniversary in the army. They separated there, but by the end of the month were reunited in Munich and began living together. The family was scandalized. Frieda, then thirty-two, had had everything her wealthy and influential family could provide, including a good school in the Black Forest and the social whirl of Berlin, before she married. She went to Berlin at the age of seventeen, after her schooling, and stayed for a year with her uncle Oswald, then Undersecretary of State, in his residence in the Tiergarten, was introduced to the Kaiser at a ball, and sampled all of the city's glittering culture. Since Frieda had always been considered an emancipated woman, no one was shocked when, before she was twenty, she married an English teacher fifteen years her senior. She settled in Nottingham and spent the next twelve years having three children and, as she put it, sleepwalking through the days. Being the wife of a foreign teacher had been one thing, but taking up with a writer was something else, and her liaison with Lawrence in Munich, followed by a *walk* through Bavaria and Switzerland to Italy, was too much for her mortified parents. Her mother expressed the hope that none of their friends would read Lawrence's works, and her father, reflecting on the fact that her lover was six years younger than she and the son of a coal miner, told her she was a "*Kellnerin.*" Waitresses in German beer halls were considered somewhat less than chaste by the Richthofens. Manfred's parents undoubtedly knew about the calamity, and although their reactions have not been recorded, they are easily imagined. Their oldest son's emotional involvement had to do chiefly with horses, which could be physically dangerous but was at least morally safe.

It was not Manfred's year for horsemanship. The day before he was to load Santuzza on a train for steeplechase competition in Breslau, he decided to ride her once more around the course at his base. The mare struck a fence on her last jump and came down heavily on her shoulder. Richthofen hit the ground hard enough to break his collarbone. Several months later, he entered another horse in a steeplechase at Breslau, with this result:

"My horse did extremely well on a run over about half the course, and I had hopes of winning. I approached the last obstacle. From far away, I saw that the obstacle ahead was bound to be something extraordinary, because a large crowd was watching it. I said to myself, 'Keep up your courage. You are sure to get into trouble.' I approached the obstacle at full speed. The people waved to me and shouted that I was going too fast, but I neither heard nor saw. My horse jumped over, and on the other side, there was a steep slope and the river Weistritz. Before I could say knife, the horse, having jumped, fell with a gigantic leap into the river, and horse and rider disappeared. Of course, I was thrown over the head of the horse. Felix left the river on one side, and I, on the other. When I came back, the weighing people were surprised that I had put on ten pounds, instead of losing two, as usual. Happily, no one noticed that I was wet through and through."

But he did not stop there. Still later, he entered a horse in the long-distance Kaiser Prize race, a cross-country event open only to the German army. Early in the race, his horse stepped in a rabbit hole, and Richthofen was again thrown hard to the ground. In spite of a throbbing shoulder, he remounted and rode another forty miles, to win the race. After dismounting, the winner was told that he had again broken his collarbone. He was taken to a military hospital in a state of delight. By the beginning of the summer of 1914, Richthofen had bought another horse, named Antithesis, which he planned to race later in the year.

Newspapers in Germany had been warning through most of the winter and spring that war was almost upon Europe, but Richthofen and his fellow officers, now stationed six miles from the Russian-occupied Polish border, did not believe it possible. They were too happy to go to war. The battle plan against France and Russia had been drawn up nine years earlier by Field Marshal Alfred von Schlieffen, but the contented junior officers had not been told about it. Had they known of the plan in the 1st Uhlans on August 1, 1914, Richthofen and his messmates probably would have toasted its postponement for another nine years, and then gone back to training horses and playing cards. The mother of a young officer friend of Richthofen's visited them that afternoon and asked apprehensively about the newspaper headlines. They assured her that the journalists were wrong. Who, they asked her, was in a better position to know than the cavalry, the very eyes of the army? There had been several alerts in the past few weeks, but there had been so many, in fact, that they were now just shrugged off or laughed at. Relieved, the woman invited her son and his friends to a celebration dinner.

Halfway through the meal, with oyster shells and champagne bottles littering the table, Count Kospoth, the district resident officer in Silesia, walked into the room. He watched, horrified, and then explained to the laughing young men that he was on a hastily ordered inspection tour of the frontier. All bridges in the area were being placed under heavy guard that night, and fortifications were being built that very minute at strategic positions in the vicinity. The news stopped the festivities for a moment, but only for a moment, as the mother again searched the faces around her. Another false alarm. The drinking and laughing started again, and Count Kospoth, visibly frustrated and angry, tried one last time to explain the gravity of the situation to the gay young cavalry officers. They ignored his pleading and offered him a glass of champagne. The next morning there was war.

THREE · OBEYING

The great questions of the day "are not decided by speeches and majority votes, but by blood and iron."

—BISMARCK,
to the Prussian House
of Delegates

Late on the night of August 2, Richthofen took a patrol of Uhlans out of the garrison at Ostrowo and along a narrow road leading to the frontier, six miles to the east. A map stuffed in his pocket showed the way, but it was unnecessary. He had memorized it during identical maneuvers over the past year. The soldiers reached the Prosna River, which formed the frontier, at about midnight. They clattered over a wooden bridge, and a moment later Richthofen rode into enemy territory for the first time.

The silent horsemen, with their lieutenant leading, continued to gallop through the darkness toward their objective. The only sounds were made by hoofs pounding hard soil and by the clinking of swords and spurs. They were enough. The noise traveled down the road ahead of the cavalrymen and echoed from bushes and trees that seemed to press in on them from either side. Yet no one fired at them or, apparently, even saw them.

Richthofen had expected resistance at the bridge and wondered why there had been none. He was exhilarated at finally leading men into war, but thought it a strange war, and did not know whether he was relieved or disappointed at not being shot at. This was not the way war was supposed to be. The Russians should have guarded the bridge, but they had stupidly not done so, and now he was well past it and nearing the objective as the horizon ahead began to lighten. He had been so certain that there would be terrible shooting that before leaving Ostrowo he had scribbled his family a last will and testament, thanking them "for everything" and adding that he had saved a few hundred marks, which he was carrying. Saving that much from a junior officer's pay was not easy, even in a remote garrison, so he was proud of himself.

Then he saw the church on the outskirts of Kielce. His orders were to observe the village and report enemy troop movements. The church would make the best observation post. He had often studied its spire through field glasses from the German side of the river, and until now it always seemed close but untouchable. Now it stood in front of him. Richthofen raised his arm to signal a halt. After looking around, he slowly led his men to the village priest's house, where they stopped again. He dismounted, straightened his tunic and cap, and rapped smartly on the door with his riding crop.

The priest, a tall man in black robes, opened the door, smiled soothingly, and said good morning to the twenty-two-year-old lieutenant standing stiffly in front of him. Richthofen tried to look as serious as possible. He did not return the older man's affability, although he was inclined to do so. Instead, he concentrated on his own words and tried hard to believe them. He announced his name and regiment. Then he told the priest that it was his painful duty to inform him that war had been declared, that the village was occupied by German soldiers, and that at the first sign of hostility by its inhabitants, he, the priest, would be shot. The cleric probably did not believe the uncomfortable-looking young man, but he had to humor him, so he accompanied the soldiers to his church and was then asked to climb to its belfry.

Richthofen had the ladder removed. He reasoned that the ties between the Catholic and Russian Orthodox churches made the priest a security risk, but he was wrong. The Poles disliked the Russians who occupied their country at least as much as they did the Germans who were trying to. Richthofen wrote a detailed report on events of the past twelve hours. When it was completed, it was given to a dispatch rider to be taken back to Ostrowo.

Some of the citizens of Kielce ignored the Germans who occupied their church. Others spoke politely to them. Still others sold them fruit and vegetables. Four days passed. Every day another Uhlan was handed a dispatch that said there was nothing to say, and rode west with it. What a colossal joke it would be if they had captured an observation post in enemy territory without there being an enemy. Richthofen decided that he could only follow orders, and if the war *had* been called off, someone would eventually get word to him. The priest was released with token apologies.

Just after midnight on the fifth day, Richthofen was shaken out of sleep by a sentry who whispered excitedly that there were Cossacks in the street in front of the church. He climbed out of his blankets and, after taking the stairs two at a time, ran out of the building. It was dark, and a misty rain was falling. He and the sentry entered the churchyard, where they joined the third and final member of the patrol, who was waiting with the horses. The mounts were led through a hole made in the rear wall of the yard a few days earlier for such an emergency. Richthofen told the man with the horses to lead them to a nearby field. Then he and the other, each carrying a carbine, went back through the hole and across the yard to where they had started from. They carefully looked over a section of wall nearest the end of the main street. Cossacks, about thirty of them, standing in small groups, were talking to townspeople. Some carried lanterns, which lighted them from the waists up in misty balls of flickering yellow and sent long shadows jumping over their faces. Black and brown beards, ammunition belts crossed over a rainbow of shirts, large fur hats and green caps, and thick hands holding rifles or resting easily on sword handles. A few were in deep conversation with the priest. The Germans quickly retraced their steps across the yard, joined the Uhlan with the horses, and walked to a wood several hundred yards away. They spent the rest of the night under dripping bushes. At dawn, Richthofen returned to the wall in time to see the last of the Russians ride away. He decided against returning to the church, however, for fear of a trap. None of his dispatch riders had come back, so he was left with two men in an unsafe position. The danger did not bother him. It excited him. But he had been sent to Kielce to observe Cossacks and had done that. Staying too long meant risking his life and those of his men for nothing, and he thought that would be stupid. It was time to leave. The next day, three mud-spattered and unshaven cavalrymen climbed wearily on their horses and rode out of Kielce, having had their first brush with the enemy.

They were received at Ostrowo as though they were ghosts. The garrison had gotten word that Richthofen and what was left of his patrol had been slaughtered by Cossacks in a bitter, if not epic, fight. The story did not make the newspapers, but it reached Schweidnitz soon after the letter with the last will and testament. While their son was dismounting to the cheers of his fellow officers and taking in their excited explanations of what they thought had happened to him, Baron and Baroness von Richthofen were accepting condolences in a parlor that looked like a botanical garden. When Manfred heard about his battle with the Russians, he slowly walked to his barracks, showing even more exhaustion than he felt. He dictated a cable to his parents, wrote another report, took a bath, and then fell into a sound sleep. The mud on his crumpled uniform might as well have been his Fatherland's highest decoration.

Within twenty-four hours, he and three other lieutenants were crowded into a second-class compartment on a commandeered train that was moving westward with the men, horses, and equipment of the 1st Uhlans. The lieutenants did not know where they were going. No one told them that Germany was leaving only three corps, backed by three reserve divisions, on the Russian front. Everything else was being poured into France in an effort to conquer it before the Russians had time to mobilize fully. When France had been crushed, within six weeks, the General Staff plan stipulated, German armies would turn around, move back across their country, and wipe out Russia by Christmas.

Richthofen found his compartment too confining for "four war-like youths," and the whisky bottle being passed around did not make him feel better. He gathered his belongings and went to the luggage car, where he spread a tent cloth on straw and began enjoying more light and a steady stream of fresh air. He noted the train's first stops and correctly guessed where it was going. There were always large crowds waiting. Cheering people handed flowers and candy up to the open hands that belonged to the smiling, confident faces nudging each other out of the way in every window. The 1st Uhlans, in particular, were given loud ovations, Richthofen later recalled, because word had spread ahead that they actually had fought the Russians and had been mentioned in the first communiqués. The cavalrymen felt like heroes and tried hard to act the part. Lieutenant Wedel, whose mother had been reassured the day before the war, and who had fled Kielce with Richthofen, pulled a Cossack sword out of his bag and showed it to girls at every stop. The dark spots on its blade, he told them, were dried blood. That was the signal for his friends to start inventing short hair-raising stories of vicious hand-to-hand combat. In truth, Wedel had taken the sword away from a frightened Polish policeman.

Near Busendorf, the train stopped in a tunnel, which seemed to someone like a good place to fire his rifle. Hundreds of soldiers, who knew they were nearing the front, took the loud shot as an attack. In a moment, almost everyone had his rifle poking out a window. Gun flashes, deafening reports, and shouting suddenly turned the dark tunnel into a scene of chaos, as bullets ricocheted off sooty stones and railroad cars, and officers ran into each other while screaming at their men to stop. No one on the dented train that came out of the tunnel was hurt, and an immediate investigation to find the man who fired that first shot produced no one. The line of cars that pulled into Busendorf had thousands of nicks and a number of pockmarks and cracked windows that made them look as though they had been under attack. The soldiers who got off were reluctant to discuss the matter, which was taken by some of the citizens of Busendorf to mean that they had somehow been in a battle that was too cruel to be remembered. The civilians were proud of their soldiers, especially because the war was little more than a week old.

The next day, the 1st Uhlans climbed onto horses weakened almost to the point of collapse by the sweltering train trip, and slowly rode north toward Luxembourg and Belgium. People in the small towns on the other side of the border did not cheer as the Germans rode by. The faces that looked at the Uhlans were sullen and contemptuous, which startled many of the Saxons, Hessians, Prussians, and others who, a few days before, had been bombarded with flowers and wishes for Godspeed. Richthofen noticed a strange uniform in one town and, not taking chances, had its wearer arrested. The indignant policeman informed the second lieutenant that if he were not immediately released, he would send a formal complaint to the Kaiser. Richthofen believed him and, since he had no idea what official policy was toward Luxembourg, he let the policeman go.

The horses were so well recovered by the time the Uhlans crossed into Belgium that they went forty miles in one day, and reached Arlon. It was time for a short rest. The French were only twenty miles away, and Richthofen, becoming increasingly excited, decided to take a bicycle across the town to St. Donat's Church, climb the steeple, and get his binoculars on the enemy. When he found that the French were still too far to be seen, he left the tower and returned to the street, where he saw that the tires on his bicycle had been slashed. A glance at the young men who surrounded and glared at him left little doubt as to who used the knife, or why. He said later that the incident amused him, and he would have been perfectly happy to have fought with the crowd, because "I felt absolutely sure of myself with a pistol in my hand." He was less than amused, however, at having to walk for half an hour to get back to his regiment.

On his return, he was told that a cousin, another Richthofen, had been killed close by. News of the death, together with an increasing awareness that, contrary to what he had been told, the Germans were not liked by their neighbors, put him in a somber mood. If it was toughness the Belgians wanted, then it was toughness they should have. "Later on, I heard that the inhabitants had behaved very treacherously several days before toward our cavalry, and later, toward our ambulances. It had therefore been found necessary to place quite a number of these gentlemen against the wall." Richthofen had not been the one to order the executions, but under the circumstances he thought that shooting civilians was entirely justified.

On August 21, the Uhlans were moved up to Virton, from where they could hear the artillery and see smoke for the first time. And also for the first time, the advancing cavalrymen passed dead and wounded going the other way. They saw hundreds of men in red-stained bandages limping or being carried from where the smoke was. They passed wagons piled with bodies whose booted legs hung over the backs and bounced in lifeless cadence over every bump. There were many more bodies behind the French lines. The French Third Army had marched into the side of the German Fifth Army. The Germans turned on them and poured so many bullets into the Frenchmen that their machine guns became too hot to touch. The French, dressed in their peacetime sky-blue blouses and scarlet trousers, made ideal targets as they marched in parade-like lines toward the German guns. They were cut down with the wheat that grew around them. Then they retreated, and while German infantrymen smoked and waited for their guns to cool, the Uhlans were brought up to find the French and see whether they could fight some more.

Richthofen was ordered to take fifteen men on a scouting patrol into a heavily wooded part of the Argonne near the village of Meix-devant-Virton. He scanned the trees through field glasses from the top of a low hill, and seeing nothing suspicious led his men down into the thick forest. He stood his horse to one side at the edge of the tall trees as his men filed past. It was the worst possible place for horsemen, he thought, visualizing a sniper behind every tree and under every bush. Front and rear guards were posted when the patrol entered the wood, but they slowly bunched up during twenty uneventful minutes. Someone noticed fresh hoof prints in the damp soil, and Richthofen, the hunter, again looked carefully around. He could not see past the nearest trees. Thirty more minutes of silence, except for the lulling sounds of their horses' hoofs and the clanking of equipment. Then the riders in front rounded a turn and reigned to a halt. In a moment, all of the men were looking at freshly felled trees that formed a barrier across the path. There was a small stream to their left, with a fifty-yard open field and a barbed-wire fence beyond. A steep, rocky ridge hemmed them in on the right. Richthofen rode forward and looked at the trees lying in front of him. Again he tried to penetrate the foliage with binoculars. Sunlight came down in long, widening beams, which filtered through an umbrella of branches that blocked out the sky. All eyes moved slowly around, focusing on separate leaves, and still saw nothing to justify a fear that grew worse by the second.

The rifle fire started an instant after a bush rustled to one side of Richthofen. The first sensation was of terrific noise, as sharp cracks rebounded from thick timber, and multiplied. There were small puffs that could not be individually distinguished, but which seemed to form a hazy circle around the men caught in the center. Two horses bolted near Richthofen's, threw their riders, and leaped over the barricade. Another fell behind him.

Richthofen raised his arm and gave the signal for "close up and follow order" as he turned his horse tightly around for a retreat. Those behind mistook it for "come forward." They charged ahead and bunched in front of him, while bullets dug into the tangled mass of men and horses. Some of those who fell lay still. Others tried to crawl into the bushes for protection. Richthofen's orderly's horse was hit and went down in front of Richthofen, forcing the patrol leader to jump over both of them, and so run into other Uhlans, who could not get out of his way. The orderly was pinned under his horse, but was not hurt, and eventually walked back to the German lines. The clearing began to fill with smoke, which floated through shafts of sunlight and further obscured the French cavalrymen, who were firing their carbines as fast as they could reload them. The Germans finally stumbled, as much as retreated, out of the clearing and then became organized enough to gallop as fast as possible away from the ambush. Bullets were still going past them when they rounded the bend and made for their lines.

Richthofen returned to his camp stunned, but unhurt, and minus ten men. He estimated that there were a hundred Frenchmen behind the trees, which was probably more than twice as many as there really were, but an ambush will do that to victims who cannot see their attackers. He had thought that morning that he might end the day by winning the Iron Cross. When the sun went down, he was shaking from nerves and exhaustion and preferred to do anything except write a report of the day's action. Manfred von Richthofen's war had begun.

He wrote to his mother, complaining about being attached to the infantry for reconnaissance and probing, and added, with some annoyance, that he was sure "Lothar has already been in big cavalry charges such as we will probably never ride in here." He understood that his younger brother was in one of the dragoon regiments that were rushing to capture Paris. Their attack was blunted, of course, and while Manfred begrudged the glory he thought was going to Lothar, the latter was meeting the same stiff resistance and experiencing the same frustration as his Uhlan brother. Karl Bolko, true to his word, had gone to Wahlstatt, so he, too, was miserable, although he did not find the school quite as disagreeable as Manfred had.

Richthofen's mind was taken off his and the war's shortcomings when an order came for a second patrol. This time, he and another officer were to take a small group of Uhlans in another direction, and again find the French. They spent the next day following the enemy, and that night decided to stay in a large monastery. Richthofen and the other officer, whom he identified only as Loen, wrote "a very decent report" before going to bed. They also determined that their hosts, the monks, "were extremely amiable. They gave us as much to eat and drink as we cared to have, and we had a very good time."

In the middle of the night, a sentry came into the officers' room shouting that the French were there. Richthofen was apparently too tipsy and sleepy to reply. Loen, however, stumbled out of bed in his nightshirt and asked what Richthofen considered to be an intelligent question: "How many are they?" Two Frenchmen had been shot, answered the soldier, but there was no telling how many others were around the monastery. "When you find out," said Loen, "call me again." Richthofen thought Loen handled the matter superbly, and both were snoring again within minutes. The monks gave them a large breakfast early the next morning, after which the patrol left to scout meadows and valleys in the area. They found that the French had withdrawn. They also found that their own army had withdrawn, so they withdrew after it, with little else to add to their report. Three days later, someone decided that the monks were helping the French; several of them were hanged from lantern hooks.

It became apparent to Richthofen by the middle of September that the cavalry was finished. The French forts at Verdun, which guarded the approach to Paris, could not be taken. The Germans therefore began to dig their trenches and string barbed wire in preparation for a siege. The British Expeditionary Force, which had retreated from Mons, re-formed and was pumped full of fresh troops. It then counterattacked, fighting the Germans to a standstill. A 300-mile-long line of parallel trenches was dug by both sides, which Richthofen began to brood about, as he wrote one report after another that reported nothing. Horses could not charge into barbed wire, and were large enough for machine gunners in trenches to hit while blindfolded.

As if to confirm his belief that the cavalry was doomed, Richthofen was transferred to the Signal Corps, where he first crawled to the trenches with dispatches, and later laid telephone wires between the trenches and the command posts behind them—fine work for a cavalryman. The men in the trenches openly despised him for being a "base hog," which in army slang meant someone who lived in the relative comfort of a rear area. Richthofen determined not only to kill enemy soldiers, but also to become one of the boys. He borrowed rifles from the trench soldiers and got off occasional shots at the enemy. He also threw a few grenades at them. The French responded by throwing a few grenades back, which further angered the German infantrymen, who explained with every adjective they could think of that they had to live with the French and he did not. They tried hard to persuade him not to become one of the boys, and were always relieved when the "base hog" scampered out of their trenches and went back to his base.

The autumn frosts came, and Richthofen, now bored to the point of depression, decided to go hunting. He had noticed on patrols through La Chaussée Forest that there were many wild pigs left in its denser areas. He went there on days off and, with an orderly, built a sheltered seat on a tree branch, where he sat every free night, waiting under full, clear moons and in snow for a pig to cross under him. He admitted that he had usually "become an icicle" by morning. One night, he saw a fat sow swim across a nearby lake to get into a potato field. She repeated the

trip, taking the same route, on several following nights. Richthofen, deciding to kill her, sat in the bushes between the lake and
the potato field one night, and, while the sow was swimming,
shot and wounded her. He waded into the cold water, pulled out
the squealing animal, and finished her with his knife. Another
time, he saw several pigs cross a path in front of him while he
was riding through the woods. He dismounted in time to see a
large boar bringing up the rear of the procession, and put a bullet into him at twenty yards. The boar's head was stuffed,
mounted, and sent to Schweidnitz, where it was hung. It was not
the Iron Cross, but it seemed like the only trophy he could get.

Then the Iron Cross (Third Class) came. It was in recognition
of his cavalry exploits and trips to the trenches with messages
and telephone wire. Since the medal was given to more than five
and a half million men between 1813 and 1918, it was far from
the most prized award bestowed by the Kaiser. But it *was* something Richthofen could hang on his tunic to prove that he had,
after all, at least gone to war. He wrote to his mother to tell her
the "glad tidings," and assumed that she would inform his father.

Richthofen passed that winter and the early spring of 1915
sitting in cold dugouts and watching the war go on without him.
Sometimes he looked up and saw lone airplanes fly by on observation missions—missions that six months before had been the
job of the cavalry. Now, the Imperial Air Service was the eyes of
the army. The Uhlans, he reflected, were its dirty hands. He had
no idea which side painted black crosses on its airplanes' wings
and which painted red-white-and-blue circles, because airplanes were so new to war that national insignia were mostly
unknown to men on the ground. All airplanes looked alike to
most soldiers on both sides and, accordingly, were shot at with
impartiality.

Richthofen began to debate becoming an aviator. Training
took months, which meant that by the time he finished, the war
would probably be over and he would have nothing to show for

the effort. Yet what did he have to show now? He would not become a pilot because, as everyone knew, they were just chauffeurs—mostly sergeants. The observers in the back seats were officers, though, and he had heard they sometimes thrashed the pilots with canes when annoyed at the way the airplane had been flown. Finally, he hated smelly, smoking, dirty engines. He hated pumps, wires, pistons, and sticky black oil. He loathed mechanical gadgets of all kinds and admitted that he not only knew nothing about them, but did not really care to learn. They could never equal the sweet scent of hay and leather, or the wonderful, clean pleasure he imagined came when jumping a stallion over enemy gun emplacements during a fast cavalry charge.

Richthofen was still mulling over the possibilities of flying when, one day in late April, word came that a large-scale attack was being planned in his area. It would be against Verdun itself. He stopped thinking about airplanes, and, instead, wondered what part he and the Uhlans would have in the assault. His question was answered when he was ordered to report to the Supply Corps.

At that, the Prussian went into a rage, and rebelled. His hand trembling, he wrote a short letter to his commanding officer, which, he said later, began, "My Dear Excellency: I have not gone to war to collect cheese and eggs, but for another purpose." He ended with a request for transfer to the Air Service.

The letter was forwarded up the chain of command and approved by the end of May. With his superiors in the Supply Corps "snarling" at him, Richthofen happily packed his bags and headed for the No. 7 Air Replacement Section at Cologne for observer training.

FOUR · THE EYES OF THE ARMY
LOOK DOWN

"Laughing through clouds, his milk-teeth
still unshed,
Cities and men he smote from overhead.
His deaths delivered, he returned to play
Childlike, with childish things now put away."

—KIPLING,
R.A.F.

At seven o'clock one morning in early June, 1915, Cavalry Lieutenant Manfred Freiherr von Richthofen, lately of the Supply Corps, climbed a ladder resting against the drumlike body of an Albatros observation plane. Then he carefully lowered himself into its front cockpit, a three-foot-wide, leather-rimmed hole, and felt his way onto the wooden seat inside.

Knowing that his instructors and the twenty-nine other pupils in his class were watching from a safe distance, Richthofen determined to look as though what was about to happen to him was the most natural thing in the world. He squirmed until he felt almost comfortable and tried to figure out what to hold. When the engine started, his look of composure washed away in a blast of air and smoke. His safety helmet, strapped loosely under his chin, blew off and pulled backward against his neck. His partly buttoned jacket filled with air until it looked like an inflated brown sausage, and his scarf unwound and disappeared. The noise was so loud that the pilot behind could not hear him, no matter how he shouted, so he scribbled a note and tried to pass it back. It, too, disappeared in the rush of air. Then the noise and vibrations became worse, and the biplane started to move.

As it bounced over the field and gained speed, the passenger in the front seat gritted his teeth, grabbed the rim of the cockpit as hard as he could, and told God that if he were allowed to return safely to earth, he would never try to leave it again. When the tail came off the ground, he felt a little sick to his stomach, and realized that the Albatros, now rolling on two wheels and going faster every second, was delicately balanced on the edge of flight. He hated the bouncing, but was beginning to move to its rhythm, the way he did on horses, when it stopped suddenly. The ground seemed as close as it had a moment before, but now he was going fast and quite smoothly, so he guessed he was flying.

Richthofen began enjoying what he was doing before the Albatros passed one hundred feet. The wind hit him harder in the face than during take-off. The noise was almost painful. But he forgot about them when he looked down. Things he had spent a lifetime looking up to, and accepted that way as a matter of natural proportion, like trees and buildings, were now very small and out of proportion. He was larger than they were, which was somehow not as it should be. It made him feel powerful. He was trespassing in God's domain and, incredibly, getting away with it. Things that were impossible to see from the ground, that his senses had spent a lifetime adjusting to not seeing—like the full expanse of a road, or most of Cologne—could easily be taken in from this three-dimensional world. This fascinated him. He saw the huge cathedral in the heart of Cologne, and when he looked out at the dark spires built to reach toward heaven, he was overcome with the feeling that he was privy to some secret forbidden to mortals. The long spires were reaching up toward *him!* He was delighted, and looked eagerly around for other views to make himself feel as powerful as a bird of prey, as potent as God. He was, he later recalled, master of the air. Then the almost giddy lieutenant remembered that, to test his sense of direction and navigational ability, he was supposed to direct the pilot to a point several miles away. Richthofen looked out again and realized that he was lost.

When he landed, an instructor made a point of telling him that had he looked straight down, instead of admiring distant scenery, he would have noticed the airdrome and might have taken bearings from it. Richthofen made himself look embarrassed. The only thing he was really sorry about was being on the ground. He began counting the hours to his next flight.

Some of his classmates in observer school were also cavalrymen who had become disillusioned with war on the ground. Others were reserve officers who, except for the war, would have been in civilian professions. Their attitude toward military discipline was far from Prussian, so, for the first time, Richthofen mingled with soldiers who had no military tradition in the Prussian sense. They had volunteered for flight training, and the majority were more concerned with airplanes than with the code of military behavior. They worried much more about navigation and other practical knowledge needed to accomplish their jobs than with polished buttons and the protocol of saluting. They were, in other words, individuals before they were soldiers. Somewhere deep within Richthofen, the streak of individuality that had made him despise Wahlstatt made him take to his new way of life and to the men in it. The pilots seemed to care about only their airplanes, and since an observer's life depended on that, Richthofen came to sympathize with them. It was unfortunate, he thought, that pilot training took so long. Piloting looked like fun, but in June, 1915, observers had the more important jobs of locating and reporting on enemy armies, and Richthofen thought he should be important.

If he had illusions about his place in the war, he did not

have many about the war itself, not even as early as mid-1915. He hitched rides on airplanes to get to Schweidnitz on weekends, and during one visit astounded his mother with a pessimistic prediction about the war's outcome. It was on a Friday night, just after he walked in, when his mother mentioned the victories she had been reading about in the newspapers. "I don't believe we will win this war," he told her. Manfred was usually cool and down to earth, the Baroness later recalled, "so I did not believe I heard right." He repeated it, adding, "You have no idea how strong the enemy is. Have you heard about our retreat at the Marne?" His mother said she had not. He told her about the Marne, about the hopeless immobility of the trenches, and about the resources Germany's enemies were marshaling against it. The conversation moved to the dinner table, where Manfred (who, curiously, for a hunter, did not like to eat meat) picked at his food and at the Fatherland's future. The best Germany could hope for, he continued, was a stalemate.

Richthofen worked hard at Cologne and was the first of the thirty to finish. Several did not qualify. On June 10, he was sent to the No. 6 Air Replacement Section at Grossenhain for two more weeks of training. The observation course would later be expanded to twelve weeks, but in that first year of discovery that aerial observation was an important tool for the army, observers were scarce, and were cranked out as quickly as possible. Besides flying, Richthofen had classroom instruction in map reading, camouflage recognition, troop and artillery spotting, bomb dropping, use of compass and telescope, meteorology, and photography. He had to draw maps in flight of what he saw and have them finished and ready for use before the Albatros landed. Finally, he was taught enough about the airplane's engine and control system so that in case of a forced landing he could make emergency repairs sufficient to get it into the air again.

Two weeks and about fifteen flying hours later, Richthofen

was awarded his observer's badge and told to report to a holding unit on the eastern front, from where he would be sent to whatever combat unit needed him. The area suited him well, because he would be defending his homeland in Silesia against the "Slav menace" and because what had happened in France had left bitter, frustrating memories. He reported to the holding unit during the last week of June, and the next day was sent to the 69th Squadron, which reported enemy troop movements to the Austrian Sixth Army under General von Mackensen.

Richthofen's first pilot, Lieutenant Zeumer, was one of Germany's pioneer combat fliers, and a man noted for reckless daring. Zeumer and Richthofen began flying over Russian positions on an average of twice a day. Zeumer sometimes flew so low that Richthofen could see Cossack horses bolting at the sound of their engine. Cossacks would scatter from roads and bridges when they approached on a low run, but that did not stop them from sending up vicious fusillades as the Albatros passed. Many of the Russian horsemen were from the remote regions of their country, including Turkestan and the Asian steppes, and were not used to airplanes. They also had no protection to speak of from their own tiny and often confused air force, which made them hate and fear German airplanes all the more. There were grisly stories about what the Russians did to captured German fliers. Zeumer did not seem to care. He went out of his way to take chances that other pilots shook their heads at. But the others knew what it took Richthofen a while to discover. Little Zeumer had an almost feverish light in his eyes and sallow, tight skin. He often wet his lips with his tongue and went into coughing fits in the thin air of high altitude that wracked his sunken chest. They called Zeumer "The Lunger," because he was tubercular, and the doctors said he could not be cured. He therefore flew with no fear of being killed. He welcomed it, in fact, rather than slowly waste away to the "bugs" he had in his chest. Ironically, except for Richthofen, Zeumer was to live longer than any other member of the

69th Squadron. Richthofen respected him, but soon realized that their reasons for fighting were sufficiently different to cause friction. Flying with a man who wanted to die violently began to affect Richthofen's nerves. There were arguments and denunciations, and blistering definitions of bravery and suicide.

Then Richthofen heard that Count Holck was coming. The Count was one of Germany's pre-eminent racing-car enthusiasts and a noted sportsman. Richthofen had been wondering about his next pilot, and when he heard Holck's name mentioned, he knew immediately that the Count was his man. He anxiously awaited his appearance, expecting him to show up "in a 60 h.p. Mercedes or in a first class sleeping car." Instead, the Count walked into the officers' mess one afternoon, carrying toilet articles and followed by his small dog. He explained to the officers who gathered around him that his train had stopped thirty miles away, and, after waiting for what he considered more than enough time, he got off and started walking along the tracks, thinking the train would catch up. Since it never did, he just kept walking. His luggage was on the train, being tended by his servant, Holck added, and both would doubtless be along shortly.

Richthofen liked the Count, and they got on well together, each appreciating the other's sportsmanlike or adventuresome qualities. They went on as many observation patrols as possible. This, Richthofen decided, was the way it should have been in the cavalry. "The glorious thing about the Air Service," he noted, "is that you feel you are a perfectly free man and your own master as soon as you are up in the air." Holck felt the same, so they enjoyed their work, and they took the Count's dog along on every flight to make their airplane's crew complete.

Richthofen discovered on his last flight with Holck, however, that sportsmanship could be pushed too far. They had not been ordered to fly that morning, because the squadron was moving to a new airdrome, but the Russian armies were retreating in front of Mackensen, and they wanted to see what the withdrawal looked like. What they saw as they flew over the retreating enemy thrilled them. Everything seemed to be on fire. Long lines of infantry, artillery, and Cossacks threaded through blazing towns and along roads that passed the smoking, gutted remains of houses and barns. Livestock that could not be eaten had been slaughtered in the fields and left to rot, rather than be abandoned to the Germans. Wagons that could not carry wounded or supplies had been burned. Bridges had been blown up or set on fire to slow the enemy. The Baron and the Count took in the panorama of war on all sides and the hundreds of smoke columns rising from the countryside as far as they could see.

When the direction of the retreating Russians had been noted, Holck swung the Albatros around and tried to head for the new airdrome, which was being set up to keep pace with Mackensen's advance. But he was not sure where it was. They were flying at 4,500 feet as they approached the town of Wisznice, which was burning, when they saw a thick column of smoke directly ahead. Going around it would have taken five minutes. Richthofen turned and looked at Holck, and the Count smiled, so he knew what Holck was going to do and smiled back in agreement.

A moment later, they flew into the greasy black smoke and could see nothing. It was hot. Their eyes began to itch and smart. They breathed in putrid gases, coughed, and tried to adjust their goggles tighter, which only let in more smoke. The Albatros started to reel violently. Then it fell. The hot, turbulently rising air caught the light wings and pushed them over, throwing the Albatros into a tumbling spin. Richthofen felt himself coming out of his seat, so he locked his hands on the cockpit rim and pulled against gravity for all he was worth. He barely caught a glimpse of Holck struggling to regain control of the airplane, with consternation on his face, but not fear. All Richthofen could think of, for the second time since the war started, was the stupidity of dying for nothing. He was afraid.

They were still tumbling, and he could not even guess how much altitude they had lost, when the blackness below turned into a sea of orange. It was like falling down the chimney of a giant blast furnace. He could hardly keep his eyes open, and every coughing spasm brought in hotter, fouler air. Up was black and down was orange, but they kept reversing themselves by the second. After what seemed like forever, Richthofen finally felt the Albatros straighten, stagger uncertainly for a moment, and head toward gray.

The crew of the blackened biplane, dazed and still coughing, re-entered sunlight at 1,500 feet. They were about to congratulate themselves when the engine sputtered and started to lose power. Richthofen and Holck looked down and saw Russians, who also heard the engine sputter, and who were now shooting at them. The Germans began losing altitude as the sputtering became worse. Landing in the middle of Russians was unthinkable. Richthofen imagined himself at the end of Cossack swords, and another look at Holck told him that the Count was contemplating the same thing. They had to get the dying Albatros back to their lines. It sputtered on, still losing altitude, as the gunfire increased. Carburetor trouble had been repaired before in flight, but never by Richthofen and Holck, who only vaguely knew where it was, much less how to take it apart. Bullets were now hitting struts and wing wires, which twanged irritatingly, and punctured stretched linen like hailstones going through a drum. When the Albatros was well under 1,000 feet, several bullets went into its engine, and one knocked off a piece of the propeller. Both stopped. Holck tried to keep the airplane's nose up as it skimmed silently over clusters of trees, then over bushes, and finally bounced into a long, sliding crash that left a furrow almost to another cluster of trees. The landing gear and a wing ripped off, but everything else stayed together. Richthofen and Holck climbed out, soot covering their faces except where goggles had been, and ran for the cover of the woods, followed by Holck's equally sooty and thoroughly terrified dog.

They watched from bushes as first one soldier and then several came toward them. Richthofen held their only weapon—a pistol with six cartridges. They stared at the advancing men, trying to make out whether they were wearing German spiked helmets or Russian khaki caps. The first soldier wore nothing on his head. The German aviators hardly breathed as the soldiers came nearer, and they hoped that the dog would do the same. Then they saw spiked helmets. The infantrymen who soon circled them were grenadiers of the Prussian Guard who had overrun Russian positions that morning. After a brief explanation, Richthofen and Holck were returned on horseback to their new airdrome, but without the dog, which disappeared into the woods and was never seen again by its master.

Germany had been fighting a two-front war for more than a year. Since it was winning on the eastern front, but at a stalemate in the west, the high command decided to pull out more of the men who were chasing the Russians and send them to France. Richthofen and Holck were two of them. They found orders waiting at the new airdrome telling them to report to different squadrons on the western front. Richthofen's orders were intriguing. He was to report to an airdrome at Ghistelles, a village near Ostend, Belgium, on August 21, for duty with the Mail Pigeon Detachment. Pigeons were used by the army for carrying messages in combat areas, but he was certain they were in no way connected with the Air Service, and would not require aerial observers even if they were. He guessed that "Mail Pigeon Detachment" was the code name for a secret unit, and wondered what it was all the way to Brussels. He was met at the train station by, of all people, little Zeumer, who, still coughing, and looking worse than ever, immediately began whispering about "Large Battle Planes." The Air Service, he said, was forming its first long-range bomber group for use against England. No, Zeumer said, impatiently, not against English soldiers in France—against targets *in* England.

The first bomb to fall on British soil, a pear-shaped twenty pounder, had been pitched over the side of an airplane on the morning of December 24, 1914. It had made a small crater in a garden near Dover and had been ignored. Since then, occasional German single-engine observation planes had ventured across the Channel to drop bombs on Dover Harbor. The pilots considered their missions successful if there were explosions, and the people below considered them "a bit of a nuisance," explosions or not. But the huge silver Zeppelins were something else again. They started bombing Norfolk less than a month after the first airplane raid, and worried the English far more. Kaiser Wilhelm, the oldest grandson of Queen Victoria, issued orders for Zeppelin bombings only after long soul-searching. He worried about the irreplaceable historic sites and landmarks scattered around London and about the safety of his relatives in Buckingham Palace. But his admirals, who rightly considered the Royal Navy to be Germany's deadliest enemy, applied increasing pressure on Wilhelm to grant permission to bomb shipping and port facilities as part of the counterblockade against England. The Kaiser finally approved limited Zeppelin bombing, but forbade the dropping of explosives on London's residential areas and, "above all, on royal palaces." * The docks along the Thames were consi̱ered in bounds, however, and were held to be all over the eastern third of the city. London's eastern suburbs were bombed for the first time on May 31, 1915, by an army Zeppelin, which made the navy furious. The admirals heatedly explained to Wilhelm that everything in London, including the Stock Exchange, was vital to England's war effort and should be hit. He finally agreed again, but with the proviso that the raids be launched only on weekends, when

---

* Major Raymond H. Fredette, *The Sky on Fire*, New York, 1966, p. 31.

many Londoners were out of town. The admirals countered that such restrictions would put their airships at the mercy of the weather, and continued to press for unrestricted bombing. Wilhelm at last sorrowfully agreed, and set the stage for unlimited attacks against London that autumn.

The ghostlike Zeppelins that began to appear high over London, sliding silently through the city's broken mist and dropping lines of small bombs, killed 557 people and wounded another 1,358 between 1915 and 1918.* The damage caused by the "Zeps" was negligible, but it made the English angry enough to invent the world's most advanced air-defense system, which was quickly to be resurrected in a future war when Germans again crossed the Channel to bomb their cities. For all the Zeppelins' majesty, which showed to excellent advantage in four- and six-column photos in German newspapers, after a year they became, for the amount of destruction they caused, too vulnerable for sustained operations. British scout pilots, pushing their biplane interceptors to the limit, eventually got the hang of bringing down the airships. They would fire incendiary and exploding bullets into the attackers' helium containers, and then speed away before the almost inevitable fireball erupted. The shortcomings of the Zeppelins—the largest and most inflammable target Home Defence pilots could imagine—were recognized by a handful of officers in Germany even before the raids began.

One of those officers was Major Wilhelm Siegert, a beak-nosed individualist with a salt-and-pepper crew cut and a mangled right hand, which he got when he rushed in front of a runaway airplane rolling toward a crowd at an exhibition. He was one of the new bourgeois officers who ignored Prussian tight-collar discipline and insisted that large airplanes and not saluting would win the war. He believed that the airplane's main function was to drop bombs, and if one could be built big enough to fly a long distance with many bombs, enemy war

---

* *Ibid.*, p. 262.

ministries could be destroyed as well as enemy soldiers, and thus Germany would triumph. After months of lobbying, he was given permission to form a special squadron of heavy bombers for use against England, which, appropriately, would be called the England Squadron. It was so secret at the time Richthofen arrived that it was still code-named the "Mail Pigeon Detachment—Ostend."

Siegert's next problem was getting his bombers. Since his ultimate weapons, the huge Gotha G IV and Giant bombers, were still being designed, he had to make do with smaller bombers, called "Large Battle Planes," that could not reach London. When the first Gotha was completed, its seventy-eight-foot wings were larger than those of any bomber used by the Germans over England in World War II. Its three-man crew was able to bring about 1,000 pounds of bombs to London at up to 14,000 feet, and fly even higher on the return trip, after the bombs were gone. The Gothas were sealed to float for eight hours in case of trouble over the Channel. The Giants, with 138½-foot wing spans, were even more extraordinary. They were powered by four large engines (to the Gotha's two), carried up to nine men, nearly 4,000 pounds of bombs, radios, advanced navigational equipment, and a bombsight. Neither airplane proved any more effective than the Zeppelins, because there were never enough of them to come close to bombing London into submission. Whereas the "Zeps" were flying dinosaurs, the monster bombers were a portent of things to come. They killed 836 Englishmen and wounded almost 2,000 more during 1917–18.*

Siegert was told that he would not even have Gothas until February, 1917 (they arrived a month late), so he had to use the Large Battle Planes and a variety of observation types adapted to light bombing, against "local" targets, such as Dunkirk, Calais, and Saint-Pol. The Large Battle Planes were the

* Ibid.

first of the so-called "G-type" bombers, the forerunners of the Gothas and Giants. Richthofen disliked them at first sight. He christened them "apple barges" because of their clumsiness and hated the position of his observer's seat, which was directly between the two propellers and afforded no view of the explosions caused by the bombs he released. "This always made me wild," he recalled, "because one does not like to be deprived of one's amusement. If one hears a bang down below and sees the delightful grayish-whitish cloud of the explosion in the neighborhood of the object aimed at, one is always pleased." During one flight, he became so annoyed at not seeing the results of his labor that he abruptly signaled to Zeumer, sitting behind him, to turn the bomber enough for the explosion to be seen. In using his hand to make the motion, he stuck a finger into one of the spinning propellers, and thereby gave his first drop of blood for his country. The gash grounded him for a week, which he spent on the beach at Ostend thinking about how much he hated "apple barges."

Spare time was passed bathing in the ocean or lying on warm sand or lounge chairs in front of the Palace Hotel, while orderlies brought coffee and cool drinks and talk turned on the value of bombers and the absence of women. Most Belgian women avoided the Germans. They particularly avoided them at beaches and shore fronts, because, contrary to German assurances, they were convinced that the Royal Navy planned to bombard them.

They were right. Richthofen and several other aviators were having their coffee one morning when they heard alarm bugles and were warned by an orderly that the British fleet was approaching. Some of the officers left their deck chairs and, running in brightly striped bathrobes, went to get telescopes and binoculars. Sure enough, columns of smoke on the horizon soon appeared through the low mist and turned into about eighty gray cruisers, destroyers, minesweepers, and torpedo boats. The morning haze finally burned off enough so that the vessels could

fire at German coastal guns and Ostend's harbor without fear
of hitting the town. Richthofen and his friends, still in bathrobes, ran up to the roof of the hotel with their telescopes to
watch the fun.

There was an orange flash and a puff of smoke in front of
one of the ships. Then the aviators heard a deepening whistle
as the shell arced miles over the water and came in. A geyser
went up in the surf where Richthofen had been bathing. There
was another flash and another whistle. Sand, chairs, and striped
beach umbrellas in front of the hotel were thrown into the air.
They came down in splinters and shreds of colored cloth and
were scattered around a smoking hole. The fun was over. Richthofen and the others, barefoot and holding their robes closed,
ran down several flights of stairs and into the cellar as the next
twelve-incher whistled in. There were two more explosions. Then
the British turned their guns on the harbor, rail yards, and German coastal batteries. The shore guns and the ships traded
shots for half an hour, while German bombing planes dove on
the attackers, raising fountains of white water around them. The
light cruiser H.M.S. *Attentive* was hit by bombs. When the German fire became more accurate than the British, Admiral Bacon,
who commanded the flotilla, ordered his ships to withdraw. One
naval shell struck the hotel, causing considerable damage but
no injuries. Fortunately, Richthofen said, the British destroyed
their own property, since the Palace had been built with their
capital.

Richthofen's vivid recollections of the domestic animals at
home in Schweidnitz prompted him to spend five marks for a
puppy he bought from a Belgian. The "little lap dog" was almost
entirely great Dane. Zeumer, who accompanied him on the day
of purchase, also picked one of the litter. They decided to name
their pets after a pair of trained monkeys which had performed
throughout Europe. Zeumer called his dog "Max," and Richthofen named his "Moritz." Max was killed by an automobile

soon after Zeumer bought him, but Moritz kept growing until, as Richthofen put it, "my tender little lap dog became a colossal great beast." He took the beast to bed with him and gave him "a most excellent education" in the observer's cockpit of a Large Battle Plane. "He behaved very sensibly," his master said. "He seemed much interested in everything, and looked at the world from above. Only my mechanics were dissatisfied when they had to clean the machine. Afterwards, Moritz was very merry." The mechanics, all enlisted men, could do nothing but clean up after Moritz. But when the dog began to destroy billiard balls and rip up the green felt under them, the officers' mess committee complained to Richthofen. There was probably a great deal of secret delight when Moritz, chasing a rolling airplane one day, was struck on the head by its propeller. Moritz came out of the confrontation with one ear shorter than the other, so Richthofen had the other clipped to match. There was at least some consolation in knowing that his dog's skull had broken the propeller. Moritz also liked to snarl at foreigners, which amused Richthofen, who took his "hound" with him to bases in Russia and France.

Richthofen had his first air fight during the morning of September 1. He and Zeumer had taken up an "apple barge" to see how it would handle in combat, although neither had ever seen another airplane in the air. When Richthofen did see one, his heart started beating faster. It was a Farman biplane of the Royal Flying Corps on an observation mission over German lines. Richthofen motioned to Zeumer that the Farman was coming at them, and then realized that no one had told him how to shoot down another airplane, but he picked up an automatic rifle lying at his feet, unlocked its safety catch, and prepared to fire when the enemy went by. Richthofen, the methodical stalking hunter, was not prepared for the Farman and his "apple barge" to pass one another at more than 150 miles an hour. The enemy was past before he could take careful aim, so the four shots he got off only warned the downward-looking Englishmen that they were not alone, which apparently pleased them. They turned and started to chase the "apple barge." Richthofen squirmed angrily. He could not get a clear shot at the English from his front seat for fear of hitting his own airplane's tail or Zeumer's head. But his counterpart, also sitting in his airplane's front cockpit, had no such trouble firing straight ahead, and sent several bullets into the Large Battle Plane's tail. Zeumer put the clumsy bomber into the tightest circle he could, trying to get behind the smaller Farman and give Richthofen a clear shot, but the English pilot hung on. When both airplanes had circled for five fruitless minutes, the Farman left and disappeared over the British lines. Recriminations started as soon as the Germans landed, with Richthofen blaming Zeumer for not flying well enough to get him into firing position, and Zeumer countering that the Farman would have been theirs if Richthofen had been able to shoot straight.

They took off again that afternoon for another try, and chased an observation plane without getting close enough to shoot. Neither had much to say to the other. Zeumer knew he was one of the best pilots in the Air Service, but wondered how much better he would have to become to outmaneuver the enemy. And Richthofen, silent and hardly looking at Zeumer, began to feel that although he was an expert marksman, he would never be expert enough to hit anything moving as fast as that Farman. Still, he thought, it *had* been exciting, certainly more exciting than dropping bombs.

The French began a massive bombardment and assault along the Champagne front on Thursday, September 23, capturing more than a hundred German heavy guns and 25,000 prisoners before the Germans could recoil enough to stop their advance. Along with many other men thrown in to plug the hole, including the Prussian grenadiers who had found him and Holck after the Wisznice escapade, Richthofen and Zeumer were ordered to fly an "apple barge" to an airdrome behind the Champagne front.

Richthofen was based at that airdrome for only a week, but it turned out to be an important one.

After a few days of flying G-type bombers, Richthofen went up in an Albatros observer with a lieutenant named Osteroth. Three miles over the French side of the lines, Richthofen spotted another Farman. This time he had a machine gun attached to a swivel, which could be inserted in holes on either side of his cockpit. He was also sitting behind his pilot. Osteroth pulled the Albatros beside the Farman, whose two French aviators looked back at the Germans but took no defensive action. Richthofen took careful aim along his gun barrel at the first enemy airplane he had ever seen at close range. Then he fired a short burst. His gun jammed. While he tried to clear it, the French observer began shooting back. Neither pilot turned his airplane away; instead, both droned on together, like two men-of-war firing broadsides into one another. When Richthofen's freezing fingers cleared the jam, he shot the rest of his hundred rounds into the Frenchmen. The Farman slipped and began to fall. "I thought I could not believe my eyes," Richthofen later recalled. "I suddenly noticed that my opponent was going down in curious spirals. I followed him with my eyes and tapped Osteroth's head to draw his attention." Osteroth put the Albatros into a diving bank and followed the Farman, which was then fluttering, all the way down. "Our opponent fell and fell and dropped at last into a large crater. There he was, standing on his head, tail pointing toward the sky." Richthofen was beside himself. He had hunted in the air and finally won. He had made his kill, and he wanted to report it and be rewarded. It seemed as though the Albatros would never land. When it did, Richthofen breathlessly told his squadron commander about the kill, and Osteroth supported him. He was shaken when he was informed that no credit could be given for kills that fell behind enemy lines. He insisted that he and Osteroth had seen the Farman crash and had even plotted its exact location on their map. On his honor as an officer, he said, shaking, he *had* shot down the Farman. No one doubted his honor, shrugged his superior, but rules were rules.

When Richthofen's anger subsided, he began to think hard about two-seater observation planes, about how difficult it was to shoot from them and how easy to shoot at them. The new single-seat scouts were the answer for making kills, but you had to be a pilot for that, he thought, as he slid under his covers that night.

Richthofen was still thinking about fast, agile single-seaters on October 1, when he and Zeumer boarded a train for Metz. They had been posted to Germany's second and only other large bomber group, which, Richthofen understood, had a few new Fokker monoplane scouts, in addition to its contingent of "apple barges." Halfway to Metz, Richthofen, being hungry, walked to the dining car. Seeing an empty seat, he asked the lieutenant sitting on the other side of the table whether it was free. The lieutenant looked up, smiled, and said softly that it was. Richthofen sat down, cleared his throat, and smiled back at the man sitting across from him. The face looked familiar. It was square, with neatly parted blond hair, a wide nose, thick lips, and large boyish eyes. It was a shy face. Richthofen thought he had seen it in the newspapers.

"Lieutenant von Richthofen," he said to the man opposite him.

"Lieutenant Boelcke," came the equally formal reply.

Oswald Boelcke was another of the new bourgeois officers. He was the fourth, and sickliest, of six children whose father had been a teacher and was then a professor. Boelcke had not been a particularly obedient child, and, like Richthofen, had never been a distinguished student. But he had managed to make his way through the Prussian Cadet Corps, and was commissioned in August, 1912. He was sent to a communications troop, saw airplanes for the first time there, and secretly decided to become a pilot. He mentioned the subject to his parents only in mid-1914, when he was already enrolled in flying school. He was awarded his pilot's badge two weeks after war broke out, and was posted to his older brother's observation squadron in France. Oswald flew an Albatros; his brother, Wilhelm, spotted for the artillery.

Boelcke became bored during the winter of 1914–15 with observation and photography missions, and with occasionally dropping hand grenades on the French. Receiving the Iron Cross (First Class) that February did nothing to raise his spirits, because he was not a medal seeker. While he was wondering what the alternatives were to flying observation planes, the French were answering the question for him. They had come out with a highly secret device that allowed a pilot to fire a machine gun, bolted down in front of him, through a spinning propeller. That meant that instead of a pilot having to fly the airplane in one direction and, if he was alone, shoot a gun in the other, he could simply point his airplane toward a target and squeeze the trigger. The device was a small triangular piece of steel, which was clamped onto both propeller blades at a point in front of oncoming bullets. Some rounds passed through the spinning propeller; those hitting the steel tabs ricocheted off, instead of chopping the wood to pieces. It was crude, but it usually worked, and French scouts began mysteriously to take their toll of unarmed or poorly armed German two-seaters on observation missions. Germany's answer was the placing of a movable gun in the rear cockpit of its two-seaters, which could be fired up, down, and to either side. It was not as effective as having a gun that fired through the propeller, but it was an improvement on automatic rifles. Boelcke had asked for, and received, permission to fly in a group at Douai, France, which had the new two-seaters.

July 6, 1915, had been a lovely summer Sunday. Boelcke and his observer, a dapper little officer named Lieutenant Wuehlisch, had been ordered to escort an unarmed observation plane and protect it from aerial attack. They were in the air less than fifteen minutes when Boelcke saw a French two-seater coming toward him from above. He slid out of the Frenchman's way and stayed low to hide his airplane against the patchwork of farmlands under him. It worked. The Frenchman passed over and continued toward the German lines. Then Boelcke, ignoring his assignment, turned and followed the enemy for thirty minutes, during which he climbed above them and moved slightly to one side to give Wuehlisch a chance to bring his gun to firing position. Unaware that the Albatros was closing in, the French pilot continued on over his own territory, while his observer, Count Beauvicourt, looked down intently and tried to pick out the boundaries of his estate. Wuehlisch began firing at forty yards. The French pilot went into a spiral dive to shake off the Germans. But Boelcke stayed behind and above him through a series of tight turns, steep dives, and every other maneuver the Frenchman could think of. Every time Boelcke heard the machine gun stop, he looked behind, and he saw Wuehlisch desperately trying to unjam it. So he concentrated on staying with the French airplane, which by that time was shooting back. Wuehlisch finally put seven bullets into the pilot and five into his observer. They went down in a vertical dive, spun twice, and crashed into a wooded area. Both Frenchmen were killed, Count Beauvicourt landing on his own property.

The fight was an important one because it was the first in the air that had been waged according to plan. Boelcke, in making his report, explained what he had done to force the Frenchmen into a poor position. He related how he had continuously kept his Albatros in range, so his gunner could keep firing, while looking out for other airplanes and trying to think ahead of the enemy pilot. Wuehlisch was given the Iron Cross for his gunnery. Boelcke, who already had one, was congratulated. From that day on, however, he was also watched closely by his superiors.

A few months earlier, Roland Garros, a French aviator of prewar barnstorming and record-breaking fame, had been forced down behind German lines in one of the airplanes with metal deflector tabs on its propeller. It was captured before Garros could set it on fire, and was sent to a twenty-four-year-old Dutch engineer named Anthony Fokker. Fokker had previously offered his airplane designs to the Allies, but was turned down. The English came to regret that decision to the point of trying secretly to bribe him with $10,000 to leave Germany, return to Holland, and make airplanes for them. The German secret service intercepted the message, however, and Fokker did not find out about it until after the war. Since he thought his airplanes were good enough to transcend nationalism, Fokker took his designs to Berlin, where they were accepted. Garros's airplane was sent to Fokker for examination and improvement. The Dutchman did not trust the metal tabs, because they *could* be cut by bullets and because some of the ricocheting bullets could go back toward the pilot. The problem, Fokker reflected, was like that of trying to throw stones between the turning blades of a windmill. If a gear could be attached to the propeller shaft that would regulate the timing of the bullets coming from the machine gun, they could be made to pass over the airplane's nose while the propeller was in the horizontal part of its rotation—a simple interrupter gear.

Fokker demonstrated his device to a group of generals at a military airdrome outside Berlin less than a week after he received Garros's airplane. Flying one of the designs that had come out of his factory, a swallow-like single-winger, or monoplane, Fokker peppered a target on the ground and sent the cynical generals nearby running for cover. When he landed, Fokker was told that his invention would have to be tested in combat before it could be put into service. The young designer agreed to do that, too, and was disguised as a lieutenant in the Air Service and sent with his monoplane to Boelcke's squadron at Douai. Fokker then went up to find a victim. After a few uneventful patrols, he noticed an enemy two-seater below and closed in for the kill. The Dutchman carefully maneuvered behind the observation plane and pulled up until he was within point-blank range. Then he became nauseated at the thought of killing the unsuspecting men in front of his gun. He turned away, still unnoticed, and landed at Douai without having fired a shot. Fokker told the Germans that he was finished with "combat" flying and was returning immediately to his factory. Before leaving, however, he explained the workings of his airplane and its interrupter gear to Boelcke. It was exactly what the Lieutenant had been waiting for. He took the monoplane up without permission, and so pleased his superiors with his initiative that he was allowed to continue testing it with the understanding that he would not fly close to enemy lines and chance its capture.

Boelcke was delighted with the monoplane. It easily outflew the two-seaters. He also flew captured two-seaters, and learned where their blind, or unprotectable, sides were. Boelcke thought about everything he did, and thought hard. He reasoned that diving on an enemy with the sun behind him blinded his victim. Clinging to certain types of cloud formations, or their shadows, provided excellent concealment. To prove his budding theories, Boelcke shot down a Bristol biplane on August 19, but was not credited with the kill because it fell behind French lines. No matter. In September, he was given an improved, more powerful Fokker monoplane, which he used to get his third kill. His fourth came at the end of the month, when he dove into ten French airplanes trying to bomb the railway station at Metz just before the Kaiser was to arrive for an inspection. He scattered the formation, and was mentioned in dispatches because of his day's work. He was also photographed for the newspapers and interviewed by German reporters. Boelcke was a publicity man's dream, because, in addition to his aerial exploits, he had jumped into a canal in August to save the life of a drowning French boy. Residents of Douai almost demanded that Boelcke's commanding officer recommend his lieutenant for the Lifesaving Medal. It is believed to have been the only instance during the war when Frenchmen made such a request for an enemy soldier, and the young German was as proud of that medal as he was of his Iron Cross. Now, the Air Service's premier hero was on his way to Metz, and was sitting across the table from a very ambitious second lieutenant.

"Tell me," asked Richthofen, "how do you manage it?" Boelcke knew what Richthofen meant, and laughed. But Richthofen would not be put off, and repeated the question, even though he saw that it had embarrassed Boelcke.

"Well, it's very simple," Boelcke finally answered. "I fly close to my man, aim well, and then, of course, he falls down." Richthofen shook his head. He told Boelcke that he did the same thing, but that his men did not fall down. They continued chatting over a bottle of wine, and, as the minutes passed, Richthofen became convinced that Boelcke's secret was not his innate superiority as a pilot, but, rather, his Fokker monoplane and its synchronized machine gun. Before Richthofen left the table, he resolved to do two things: cultivate Boelcke as best he could and persuade Zeumer to teach him to fly. Then he would apply to flying school with a decent chance of being accepted. Drawing maps and taking pictures from the back seat of an Albatros, or occasionally trying to hit another airplane with a pop gun, Richthofen decided, was ridiculous. A hunter should fly scouts.

Richthofen did persuade Zeumer to teach him to fly an old two-seater at the Metz airdrome. He spent every off-duty minute circling the field to get the feel of the airplane, while Zeumer sat coughing in the rear cockpit, watching his joy stick move erratically and remaining ready to grab it if Richthofen got into trouble. But the pupil did not get into trouble, and on October 10, 1915, ten days after meeting his idol, Richthofen was judged ready for his first solo flight.

"There are some moments in your life which particularly tickle the nerves, and the first solo flight is one of them," Richthofen later remembered. What happened the evening he flew alone for the first time was, indeed, tickling. "The Lunger" told

Richthofen that he was ready, walked out with him to the old biplane, and explained once more every movement the soloist was to make and the theory behind it. Richthofen listened carefully and absorbed almost nothing. He felt like telling Zeumer that he was too frightened to go through with it, and asking if they could postpone the flight to the following evening. But Prussian pride prevailed, and Richthofen strapped himself onto the seat and started his engine. When the biplane was rolling at the proper speed, he eased the stick forward, and the tail came up. A little faster, and he pulled it back. He was flying. "With contempt of death," he later noted, somewhat dramatically, "I made a large curve to the left, stopped the engine near a tree—exactly where I had been ordered to do so—and looked forward to what would happen."

What happened was that Richthofen crashed. Having cut his engine for the long glide that was supposed to end in a smooth landing, Richthofen felt his airplane move unexpectedly to one side. He overcorrected with the stick and pedals, and the biplane hit the ground hard, bounced, and nosed over. "I lost my balance," he explained to Zeumer, who pulled him out of the cockpit of the crumpled airplane. Richthofen tried again two days later, with the laughter and sarcasm of his companions still ringing in his ears, and made a series of successful, if not perfect, landings. The Air Service had strict rules for the certification of its pilots. Diplomas were awarded only after completion of a proscribed training program and a series of rigid tests. But Richthofen looked so eager that his commanding officer allowed him to take the first test two weeks later. He flew a series of figure eights and landed with his engine turned off. He was told that he had failed. He repeated the test several more times, finally satisfied his examiner, and was then enrolled at the large pilot-training school at Döberitz, just west of Berlin. Elated, Richthofen again packed his bags, and on November 15 hitchhiked to Döberitz on a Large Battle Plane.

Döberitz was going to be difficult. Richthofen was informed

soon after he arrived that, having passed his first examination, he would have to get through a second, and if that was successful, a third. No one knew better than Richthofen that he was not a born student. But he also knew that he now desperately wanted to be a pilot. If he could take Wahlstatt, he thought, he could take Döberitz. He probably did not realize it at the time, but that had been the purpose of Wahlstatt, and the purpose behind all Prussian military education. The end, he told himself, was worth the effort. So he applied himself with grim determination to passing the second examination, and when he had done so, to getting through the third.* That final test mostly involved cross-country flights, which he decided to practice

---

* According to the *Handbook of German Military and Naval Aviation (War), 1914–1918*, published by the British Air Ministry in October, 1918, for "Official Use Only," the second German pilot's test consisted of: (A) ten smooth landings from 1,600 feet; (B) five smooth landings from 3,250 feet with full fuel tanks and ballast equivalent to the weight of an observer; (C) landing three times under the following conditions: after the student had reached at least 1,600 feet, a rocket was fired by the instructor on the ground; the student would then turn off his engine, irrespective of his airplane's position, and land as close as possible to where the rocket had been fired from; (D) two half-hour flights at above 6,500 feet with a 160-pound ballast, and (E) a one-hour flight with full fuel tanks and a 170-pound ballast, a half hour of which was to be above 1,600 feet.

The third examination entailed: A, B, and C of the second examination repeated; (D) five landings outside the airdrome on unknown ground from 1,600 feet; (E) two cross-country flights of 30 miles with ballast in place of an observer; (F) two cross-country flights of 60 miles with an observer, who had to photograph a series of prearranged landmarks; (G) a cross-country flight of 155 miles with an observer, in which the student had to land without crashing and return to the airdrome before sunset; (H) fly to 11,700 feet with an observer and a full war load, then drop to above 9,750 feet and stay there for an hour; (I) go into several aerial combats against an instructor and his observer in another airplane; the student had to attack his instructor and be photographed by him from a distance of 80 feet, then the simulated attack was reversed so the student had to fly defensively, and (J) firing from the air at moving and stationary ground targets by the student and his observer. A recording barograph, or altimeter, was carried on all flights to make sure the airplane was at its prescribed altitudes.

while also doing some hunting. Relaxation for most of the students at Döberitz meant going into Berlin for girls and beer, both of which were abundant. Richthofen preferred to hunt pigs. He learned from more advanced students that if he made "emergency" landings on estates around Döberitz, he would be given food and drink, and probably be introduced to pretty daughters who were captivated by brave airmen. If food, drink, and daughters, thought Richthofen, why not pigs? He discovered the Buchow estate, six miles from the airdrome, and befriended its owner, who allowed him to spend whole nights stalking the wild pigs on his property. Richthofen made the flights with a sergeant, who flew the two-seater back to Döberitz after depositing him, and returned early the next morning to bring him back. The sergeant finally smashed several of the trainer's wing ribs while landing in a snow squall to retrieve Richthofen, but got him back to Döberitz in time for classes. Pig hunting was suspended while Richthofen's instructors tried to get details of the incident. Long cross-country practice flights were also made more interesting. Richthofen landed at the Fokker factory at Schwerin to entertain himself by watching them put together the monoplanes he hoped to fly in combat. He flew as far as Schweidnitz, and, after landing on an open field near his parents' home, visited, ate, and hopped back to Döberitz along a route that took him to the lawns of friends and relatives. War experiences were traded for hot food and steaming coffee that were much tastier than what he was fed in the mess.

Richthofen finally passed his third examination, without a crash, and was justifiably proud of himself.* He was notified on

---

* Only 50 per cent of the students passed, according to the Air Ministry *Handbook*. Twenty-five per cent were washed out because of crashes, 12½ per cent because of poor health or undesirable conduct, 6¼ per cent because they lacked "necessary moral qualifications" and nerve, and another 6¼ per cent because they crashed during advanced training or during night landings.

Christmas Day, 1915, that his pilot's certificate would be awarded. He was posted to the 2nd Fighting Squadron, near Verdun, in March.

Determined not to be just another "chauffeur," Richthofen bolted his own machine gun to the center of the wing above his cockpit, which gave the Albatros two guns, including his observer's. The other pilots laughed at him, but not for long. He saw a French Nieuport while on a patrol one day, but when he flew after it, the Frenchman turned and darted toward his lines. Richthofen, who was high above the Nieuport, put his Albatros into a long dive, which increased his speed enough to overtake the enemy as he neared his trenches. When Richthofen thought he was close enough, he stood up and fired short bursts into the Nieuport, and then watched as it nosed up, turned over, and fell. Thinking the Frenchman was faking, Richthofen followed him into a spiraling dive and stared, fascinated, as he crashed into trees near Fort Douaumont. His observer slapped him on the back while he turned and started for their airdrome to claim the victory. But credit was again withheld, because the Nieuport had gone down on its own territory and there were no witnesses, except Richthofen and his observer. Although not mentioned by name, Richthofen's kill was cited in the unit's dispatches of April 26, and he informed his mother accordingly.

On another patrol, four days later, Richthofen watched a Fokker scout attack three French airplanes. Because of a strong head wind, he could not reach the lone Fokker and help, so he had to watch as another French formation arrived. The German pilot, attacked from several directions at the same time, was soon forced onto the defensive and disappeared into a cloud. Richthofen was relieved, thinking the German had escaped, but learned later that the Fokker had gone straight down through the cloud and crashed. Its pilot, shot through the head, was his old friend Count Holck.

Richthofen continued to learn his trade in the following weeks. He flew through a thunderstorm, skimming a hundred feet over ground he could hardly see in the pouring rain, and landed at the airdrome soaked and swearing never to do it again unless on direct order. His commanding officer eventually permitted him to share a new Fokker monoplane with another pilot. The other man crashed it behind French lines, and burned it. They were given another, which Richthofen destroyed. Its engine stalled after take-off, forcing him into a violent crash landing, which smashed the Fokker to splinters. Richthofen walked away.

At about that time, the Germans launched another major assault against Verdun, but the French rallied once more, and beat it back. The 2nd Fighting Squadron was therefore loaded on railway cars in June and sent to the central Russian front, which the high command again hoped to conquer in lieu of the impenetrable approach to Paris. Living conditions on the eastern front were so wretched that many Germans preferred to live in the railway cars. Others, including Richthofen, pitched camp near a wood beside their airdrome. They erected a tent and "lived like gypsies," which made Richthofen happy.

The squadron's main job was bombing, and in spite of Richthofen's image of himself as a great air fighter, he enjoyed his work. The lack of opposition from Russian airplanes made most bombing missions easy, and he began to relish the havoc he created as bombs exploded in his wake. He also enjoyed strafing with a machine gun, a job that pleased him more when done to Russians than it would against Westerners. "It was particularly amusing to pepper the gentlemen down below," he said, adding that "half-savage tribes from Asia are much more startled when fired at from above than are educated Englishmen. It is particularly interesting to shoot at hostile cavalry. An aerial attack upsets them completely. Suddenly, the lot of them rush away in all directions of the compass. I would not like to be the commander of a squadron of Cossacks which has been fired at with machine guns from airplanes." When he was not bombing and strafing Russians, he was shooting at the deer, wolves, and lynx in the local forests. Life became, as he would say, very amusing.

One afternoon, Oswald Boelcke appeared. He was on his way back to Germany from a tour of air groups in Turkey. The trip had been arranged by the high command with the double purpose of giving Boelcke a rest after his nineteenth kill and showing the German and Turkish forces fighting the Arabs and the British on the Arabian Peninsula that they had not been forgotten because of the Fatherland's two other fronts. Boelcke had shot down more airplanes than any other German, and was being touted by Berlin as the world's greatest combat pilot. He told the awe-struck bomber pilots at dinner that night that he had just dropped in for a few hours to visit with his brother, Wilhelm, who happened to be the commander of Richthofen's squadron. It was not quite true. The younger Boelcke had been ordered to start an elite mobile scout squadron to grapple with increasingly better and more determined British squadrons on the western front. He was looking for talent. Richthofen was one of the pilots sitting around the dining table who smiled at Boelcke whenever their eyes met. He remained in the group that followed the Boelcke brothers to a lounge after the meal, and listened attentively while Oswald described conditions in France and some of the outstanding Allied pilots the Germans were encountering there. When it was late, the officers of the 2nd Fighting Squadron left in ones and twos, taking respectful leave, as if they sensed they were at an audition, until the brothers were finally alone in a room full of cigarette smoke and empty glasses.

Oswald explained to Wilhelm why he had come and added that, judging by what he had seen and heard that evening and previously, Richthofen wanted to become a scout pilot. He knew something of the Prussian's background, of his wealthy family, and of his renowned passion for hunting and apparent indifference to women and alcohol. What about his temperament?

Would he fit into a hunting squadron? Would he have the patience to stalk in the air the way he did on the ground, the obedience to follow instructions as quickly as was necessary in air-to-air fighting? Did he have the eyes and reflexes to be successfully aggressive?

Wilhelm told Oswald that Richthofen had had a difficult start in flying, and although he still tended to be ham-fisted, he was working hard to become better. He knew almost nothing about how airplanes worked, or about their machine guns, and showed little inclination to learn. That trait would have to be watched, Wilhelm said, because it was the sure sign of a glory-seeker who did not feel he should be bothered with details. Details won battles, Wilhelm added, which Richthofen should have learned in school. But he was eager, and being hungry for fame—even too hungry—was not a bad thing if the fundamentals could be beaten into his thick skull before he got killed. If he lived through his first patrols, the older Boelcke advised the younger, he would probably make a good scout pilot. And there was one more, named Erwin Boehme, who was an old man of thirty-seven and an exceptionally skilled and courageous pilot. Why not take him, too, asked Wilhelm, and have an old tiger among the cubs.

Early the next morning, Boelcke packed his bag and then went to Richthofen's and Boehme's quarters. He invited them to join a new group called "Jagdstaffel 2," and if they accepted, to be at Lagnicourt, France, on or about September 1. Jagd is German for "hunting." They accepted.

FIVE · THE GOSPEL ACCORDING
TO BOELCKE

*"Like the other combatant forces, they [the Air Service] were a
destructive arm in the great battle on land. This, indeed, became
their main object, and the aerial combat was only a means of attain-
ing it."*

—LUDENDORFF,
Ludendorff's Own Story

British observation planes, protected by scouts, were on the offensive. They were hurting the German army, Boelcke told the
eight pilots gathered around him at Lagnicourt on September
8, 1916. They had to be stopped. He pointed to a new Albatros
scout parked nearby. One of the eight, Sergeant Major Leopold
Reimann, had flown it to Lagnicourt when he reported, a week
before. The Albatros scout, Boelcke told his "cubs," could beat
anything the British and French had. They would use it to stop
the British, to shoot them down. "And I," Boelcke said, "will
show you how."

The cubs had been straggling into Lagnicourt when Boelcke
arrived, on August 27, with a Lieutenant Gunther and sixty-four
"other ranks" to set up an airdrome. Jagdstaffel, or Jasta, 2's first
day was recorded in its logbook: "Quarters: Officers to be bil-
leted in Bertincourt, men to live in huts. Machines; none to hand
as yet." Lieutenant Hoehne arrived on August 29. Sergeant
Major Reimann (flying the Albatros) and another noncommis-

sioned officer, Max Muller, came on September 1, as did Lieutenants Hans Riemann and Manfred von Richthofen. That day,
Boelcke, who had been trying to scrape up airplanes as quickly
as possible, brought in two new Fokker biplane scouts from a
nearby air park, where they had been held for consignment.
When the Albatros and the Fokkers had landed, the cubs had
something tangible to look at, and they began licking their
chops. Lieutenants Viehweger and Boehme showed up on the
8th, making all present and accounted for, and Boelcke could
go to work. He had used one of the Fokkers to shoot down his
twentieth and Jasta 2's first victim on September 2. The British
pilot, Captain Robert Wilson, was captured by German soldiers
when he crawled out of the wreckage. As was the case with
most airmen on both sides who survived being shot down, a race
developed over who would get to him first; the infantry preferred to throw fliers into prisoner-of-war camps as quickly as
possible, while their victors liked to entertain them in their
messes. There were many reasons for making a "guest" of a
vanquished opponent. First, it appealed to the victors' senses of
chivalry, which, if it could not exist while they were fighting for
their lives, at least could be extended over a glass of wine on
the ground. Second, the host pilots thought they could get more
useful information out of another pilot than could the infantry,
or even the intelligence people. Third, pilots on both sides found
pleasure in chatting and comparing notes with their opposite
numbers, with whom they often felt more in common than they
did with their own armies. Fourth, they liked to have their
photographs taken with their opponents, which was a civilized
form of trophy-collecting and which the newspapers back home
could use to show that they were, after all, as chivalrous as they
were said to be. Wilson was brought to Lagnicourt and entertained in Jasta 2's mess. His presence accomplished something
else, which Boelcke noted when the cubs saw the English
prisoner. Wilson was the living proof that the enemy could be
shot down, and he was just what the cubs needed at that

moment. Boelcke watched his pilots become noticeably more eager to get into the air and begin hunting.

Germany had had thirty-four small flying units when the war started. Each was equipped with six airplanes, used for observation, photography, and artillery spotting. The designation "squadrons," which had traditionally been used for the cavalry, was an indication that the "eyes" of the army were shifting to the air. Later, when armed Allied airplanes began shooting at the German observers, each unit was given two armed biplanes to escort the others. The units had been under the administrative control of the Inspectorate of Aviation Troops, which with the Inspectorate of Airship Troops and its Zeppelins made up the Air Service. Berlin's opinion of their importance when the war started could be judged by the fact that both inspectorates were, in turn, controlled by the army's Commander of Railways and Transport.

The Inspectorate of Aviation Troops had been subdivided into thirty-four parts only because it was too large for effective use in the field. Each unit was assigned to a large army group, usually of corps size, and was headed by a captain or major who reported to the commanding general of the army group and took orders from him. The orders were simple: observe enemy troops and artillery and report back. When that had been done better than it had ever been done before, the infantry and artillery generals quickly adapted to their new "eyes." The system of long-range observation worked well for both sides until they began trying to put out one another's "eyes." Hand-waving turned to occasional pistol shots, then to the use of rifles and, finally, machine guns. Some airmen tried to drop small bombs and hand grenades into enemy cockpits, others fired rockets tied to their wing struts, and a few British pilots even tried dropping tomato cans filled with dynamite on their opponents. General Trenchard told his Royal Flying Corps that it should make use of the Allies' vast stockpiles of men and matériel to carry the war to the enemy, to seize and maintain the offensive in the air at any reasonable cost. The French and British therefore began seeking out and attacking German observers, the Germans attacked back, and air-to-air fighting began. Many pilots on both sides began to enjoy fighting in the air so much that they often forgot that they were doing it to help their countrymen on the ground. They developed a taste for hunting for its own sake. The infantry and artillery generals did not really understand, at least at first, why their observation planes were being shot down, and when told, showed little sympathy. All they knew was that they were not getting the information they needed for their soldiers to win the war and, they continuously reminded the aviators, it *was* the infantry and artillery that would win the war, not the airmen. Reasons for failure did not concern the "ground" generals. But they had to concern someone. Furthermore, raids against enemy countries by Zeppelins and Large Battle Planes were being considered, and such missions would obviously be well beyond the scope or interest of infantry and artillery commanders. That was when a movement began among a few Air Service officers to bring more autonomy to their service.

The first concrete step toward making the Air Service a separate branch of the army came in October, 1915, when captains and majors in charge of the small units were given more responsibility for planning missions and countering enemy air opposition. In March, 1916, an Imperial Order in Council was issued providing the Air Service with control of its own administration. That order had then to be considered for ratification by the German high command. If approved, its provisions would also establish co-ordination between the Air Service and antiaircraft gunners on the ground. That would be useful to scout pilots, who needed on-the-spot confirmation of their victories. But there was still the British air offensive to worry about.

On November 9, 1915, Boelcke, who was already a national hero, was called from the front to meet Major Hermann Thomsen, the leader of the men who finally convinced the high command that reorganization and some autonomy was necessary for the Air Service. The two men, one concerned with over-all reorganization and strategy, and the other, with combat tactics, began a collaboration that was to have profound effects on the air war—even, for that matter, on future air war. Boelcke tutored Thomsen in all he knew about air fighting and explained how he thought Trenchard's air offensive could be turned back. The key, he said, was not to chain armed scouts to infantry and artillery groups. That was necessary for observers, of course, but not for scouts. Scouts were hunters and must always be allowed to search for prey where it was most abundant, wherever the Allied offensive was most threatening. Scout squadrons would have to be mobile enough to be shipped anywhere along the front, not in days, but in hours. They should be moved by road or rail, Boelcke said, and if there were no accommodations when they arrived, wall tents would be erected. Thomsen agreed. He gave Boelcke the responsibility of organizing *Jagdstaffeln,* or hunting squadrons, and of hand-picking the pilots he wanted. *Jagdstaffel* was soon abbreviated to *Jasta.* The small fighting groups were numbered consecutively from one upward. The first seven were formed in August, 1916. Numbers 8 through 15 followed that September, and eighteen more were created by the end of the year, bringing the total to thirty-three. Jasta 1 was formed on August 23. Jasta 2 was born at Lagnicourt on the 27th, and Boelcke decided to lead that one himself. But before he would allow his cubs off the ground, Boelcke decided to synthesize what he had learned in two years of combat flying, and feed it to them. It was the first time that the theory and practice of killing in the air was codified, and it eventually became known to war pilots everywhere as the "Dicta of Boelcke."

To begin with, Boelcke said, the Albatros was the best fighting airplane in the world.* He repeated that at regular intervals to

---

* He was right. Albatros D I's and D II's, which were eventually replaced by improved D III's and D V's, were superior to French and

build their confidence, but warned, looking at Richthofen, that it had to be understood to be used most effectively. That meant knowing the general construction of its wings, fuselage, and engine, and of understanding its wire rigging to the point where simple splices could be made after forced landings. That knowledge, Boelcke added, could make the difference between continuing to fight and spending the rest of the war in a prison camp, like Captain Wilson.

Next came the Albatros's handling characteristics. If it was to perform to its utmost, the cubs would have to memorize its top speeds at all altitudes, its absolute speed limits in a variety of dives, in order not to push it past its maximum tolerances and risk losing a wing or the tail, its highest altitude, turning radius, rate of climb to every altitude, and its stalling speeds, under which they could not go without falling. They would also have to learn how to put it into controlled spins and sideslips, and many other maneuvers, which could save their lives in tight situations. Then, there was shooting. Max Immelmann had once shot down two airplanes with twenty-six bullets, Boelcke said, and they must each try to better that.* It was no good maneuvering into kill position if they could not hit what they were shooting at when they got there. They must know how to clear jammed guns quickly, which meant understanding how the Albatros's two Spandaus worked, he added, again looking at Richthofen.

British scouts in almost all respects except maneuverability. The D I's, which Jasta 2 started with, had 160 h.p. Mercedes engines that pulled them at up to 109.4 m.p.h. The scouts weighed 1,976 pounds loaded, and could climb to 9,840 feet in a respectable 15½ minutes. They were 24 feet 3 inches long, and had wing spans of 27 feet 11 inches. Flight duration was an hour and a half.

* Immelmann was one of the first German scout pilots, and at one time was a squadron mate of Boelcke's. He invented the so-called Immelmann turn, which is a long, fast dive at the enemy, firing at him while in the dive, and then passing, climbing, turning, and repeating the dive for another machine-gun burst. Immelmann died on June 18, 1916, after sixteen victories, when his Fokker monoplane, apparently because of engine vibration, broke up in mid-air.

The pilots who lived to build the highest victory scores, or, for that matter, who lived at all, were the ones with the best eyes. Seeing the enemy before he sees you, Boelcke said, was crucial, and pilots who did not learn to use their eyes were as good as dead. He added that he understood that because the cubs were new to Albatroses, and, in some cases, to scout flying in general, they would be more concerned at first with watching their instruments and their airplanes. But, he warned, they had better learn to spot and identify distant airplanes as fast as possible.

On fighting: Get above the enemy, without being seen, if possible, and wait there until the most advantageous moment for attack. Then dive quickly and from behind. If the opponent is an observation plane with a rear machine gunner, come up at it from behind and below, but always from its blind side, where you cannot be seen. If it is a scout with a machine gun pointing forward, come in from behind and above, so the enemy pilot cannot shoot at you. Always attack when least expected. The best time is when the enemy is occupied with ground missions, such as bombing, strafing, photographing, or artillery spotting, because he is not thinking about you. Remember that your first task is to destroy observation planes, not scouts. Attack scouts only to get at the observers, because the observers help the enemy armies, not the scouts. Do not fire until your target is well within range. Point-blank range is preferable, but fifty yards will usually do. Not only will you not hit anything from 500 or 1,000 yards, but also you will be warning your intended victim that you are there, and the surprise will be lost.

On tricks: The French and some of the English love aerobatics, which, admittedly, are fun, but are also stupid. They stunt to dazzle their opponents in fights or when trying to escape. Remember that every time you turn, your airplane slows down a little, so zigzagging and looping to escape means only that if your opponent flies straight, he will catch you. Do not run. Turn on him. Using your guns head on will always give you a better chance than exposing your defenseless tail. Do not be fooled by tricks. Watch your opponent carefully after you think you have hit him. If he seems damaged and falls out of control, follow him down only to the point where you can see him crash, and keep looking behind all the way. Black smoke could mean he is burning, but it could also mean that he is deliberately releasing it to look like he is burning. Watch for fakers, and fake yourself, if you have to.

Finally, said Boelcke, the squadron hunts and attacks as a team. Exhibitionism and needless heroics bring death, not only to you, but also perhaps to your friends. Protect each other and obey your leader's signals. Boelcke had his Dicta transcribed and sent to other scout squadrons, with copies held for those not yet formed.

The man who was known throughout Germany as its greatest Teutonic knight had taught his pupils that to survive, and much less to pile up victories, they had to sneak up on their opponents and kill without warning. That was the reality of air fighting, and, for that matter, any other kind of fighting. What he taught his cubs that September was being learned by their French and British counterparts on their own. There was no reason why enemy prisoners could not be treated with the respect due to officers and gentlemen. That was safe enough. But no quarter could be given in the air, because killing was, after all, preferable to being killed. It was as simple as that. Now the cubs could try their wings.

There was still only the Albatros and two Fokkers, so Boelcke and his pupils took turns in them. Sometimes they flew close to the front and watched Boelcke attack the British, which he knew would whet their appetites, but they mostly practiced far enough behind their own lines so there was no chance of prematurely running into an enemy. They practiced formation flying, pouncing as a team, and made simulated attacks against each other. A Royal Flying Corps D.H. 2—the first to arrive in France—had been brought down behind their lines a year ago that August.

It was patched up and used by the cubs to acquaint themselves with its characteristics, because, to Boelcke's relief, the British were still using them. Boelcke knew that Lanoe Hawker's No. 24 Squadron had D.H. 2's, for example, and knew his pupils would be sure to tangle with it. Their chances would be much better after testing their opponents' airplane. When Boelcke and his cubs landed, there would be more lectures. The flight leader would usually see the enemy first, he said, because he had almost nothing else to do but look around, while the rest of the pack tried to keep formation near him and look to their sides and behind. When the flight leader saw the enemy, he would signal to the pack, and they would hold their positions until the attack started. Then each man would pick a target. If a pilot other than the leader saw the enemy first, he would pull forward, rock his wings until he attracted the leader's attention, and then turn toward the enemy while slowing so everyone else could catch up. An air battle meant burning, smoking airplanes and bursts from antiaircraft guns, Boelcke said, which would attract other scouts like blood attracts sharks. The flight leader would therefore try to stay a little above the fight, where he could watch for new arrivals and, to a limited extent, direct his flight by leading some of them, pointing with his hands, or shooting colored flares from his flare gun.

Early every morning, Boelcke would climb into one of the Fokkers and fly alone toward the British lines. The cubs waited for him on the flight line and looked closely at his face when he had landed and taxied to a stop. If there were black powder smudges on it, he had fired his machine guns, and that meant he had probably made a fresh kill. Then they would go with him to breakfast, where he recounted the battle in second-by-second sequence over eggs and coffee. The stories always ended with the mistakes made by his victims—a kind of moral.

On Saturday morning, September 16, when his score stood at twenty-eight, Boelcke got word that six new Albatroses and some Halberstadt scouts were waiting to be picked up at the air park.

He and the cubs collected the airplanes and brought them back to Lagnicourt. Boelcke told them later that they would fly their first combat patrols the next morning. Hoehne could not wait. He shot down an Englishman early in the evening while supposedly on a familiarization flight in one of the Albatroses. Boelcke looked around the mess after dinner and saw men who reminded him of schoolboys who had the right answer and were trying desperately, but silently, to be called on. Some of them, he said in his customarily low, matter-of-fact voice, would fly with him. He smiled. The tension was breath-taking. Reimann . . . Boehme . . . and Richthofen were the first named. They would be specially briefed in the morning. Richthofen would fly on Boelcke's right, Reimann next to Richthofen, and Boehme on Boelcke's left. Then the mentor said good night and advised them to retire early. Far from being too excited to sleep, Richthofen's discipline took hold, and he quickly fell into a deep, contented slumber.

Sunday, September 17, was a beautiful early-autumn day. Jasta 2's scouts climbed toward the west with a bright, warm sun coming up behind them. Richthofen, feeling like a hungry young eagle, worked hard at staying exactly where Boelcke wanted him while looking everywhere, including straight down, and seeing nothing to pounce on. He would have liked to have impressed Boelcke by being the first to spot the enemy, but the master saw them first. Twenty minutes after taking off, he spotted fourteen airplanes, flying in two groups, and heading toward the railway station at Marcoing. There were eight British B.E. 2 bombers, each carrying a 112-pound bomb and four twenty-pounders, and an escort of six F.E. 2 scouts. Boelcke knew that since the British were headed far behind German lines, time was on his side. He signaled for a slow climb behind the British formation. They would stalk the British all the way to the target. Boelcke could have attacked before the British dropped their bombs, which was, of course, the idea behind air defense. If, on the other hand, the British were allowed to make it all the way to Marcoing, they would be low on fuel and would have to fight a stiff head wind to get home. That would be the time to attack. Boelcke had to choose between the railway station—the men on the ground—and his pilots. He chose the latter, so they kept on stalking.

Then the British were dropping their bombs. Boelcke looked down on them while they looked down at the rail yards to see whether their bombs were taking effect. Jasta 2 flew east of Marcoing and patiently circled as bombs continued to fall and antiaircraft shells exploded like puffs of cotton around the attacking force. When there were no more bombs, the British turned for their lines, with a few columns of smoke rising from under where they had been. Jasta 2 broke its circle and unwound after the British, with Boelcke and each of his cubs trying to get their scouts' shadows on the airplanes ahead of and below them. Some of the Englishmen were still looking at debris in the rail yard when Boelcke signaled for a dive.

Richthofen picked out an F.E. 2, which he mistook for a Vickers fighter, and closed on it at more than a hundred miles an hour. He had been taught how to attack a Vickers but not an F.E. 2, which looked similar. His heart quickened as the large red-white-and-blue circles on its wings grew larger. Then he could make out cables and two men inside the fabric fuselage. He sighted on the center of that brown box. He did not notice the melee around him, as Albatroses plunged through the bomber formation, firing as they passed, and the British fighters tried to stave off the attack by returning fire as the fast Germans went by. Some of the F.E. 2's tried to catch the Albatroses, and this exposed their bombers to ferocious attacks from their blind undersides. It was anything but the systematic fight Richthofen had expected. He saw a free-for-all, with airplanes flying around him in all directions and the earth, thousands of feet away, absolutely forgotten. He did what he had been taught, and waited until he was fifty yards from the F.E. 2 before opening fire at what looked to him like a mammoth target. As he squeezed the trigger,

Lieutenant T. Rees, the F.E. 2's observer, stood up in his cockpit, swung around a swivel-mounted Lewis gun, and fired back. Richthofen continued to press his attack, but without seeing his bullets go in. Unlike Richthofen, the F.E. 2's pilot, Lieutenant L. B. F. Morris, was not on his first air-combat patrol in a scout. He skillfully swung his clumsy airplane around to give Rees the best possible shots. Richthofen was by that time so close to the British fighter that he thought he was going to collide with it. He put the Albatros into a sharp roll and spun away, with Rees still firing at him. The Prussian angrily flew into a cloud, calmed himself, and came out again determined to get that Englishman if it was the last airplane he ever shot down.

He was then below and behind the F.E. 2, whose pilot and observer, unaware that the Albatros was again stalking them, flew in a straight line toward their airdrome. Richthofen slowly pulled up under the enemy fighter's belly and settled into a blind spot where neither of its occupants could see him. He pulled the Albatros's nose up, and when he could see the stitching that held the fabric to the wooden frame—at thirty yards—he squeezed the trigger for a long time. He watched his bullets make holes in the fabric midway between the fighter's tail and engine. The holes began to move forward in two parallel lines, and he could not take his eyes off them. He tried to imagine what they were hitting after they tore through the linen belly. He saw them hit the engine area, and then, realizing that he was seconds away from another near-collision with the F.E. 2, quickly rolled away. The Albatros straightened out a few hundred yards from the British fighter, out of effective machine-gun range, and slowly, cautiously moved back in like a cat watching a mouse it has crippled. The F.E. 2's propeller stopped turning. Richthofen nearly shouted with joy, and moved in closer. Rees had apparently slumped in his seat, because Richthofen could see only his Lewis gun, dangling over one side of the cockpit. Then the F.E. 2 nosed up, sideslipped, and fell. Morris was mortally wounded, but he fought with his riddled airplane as it spun down almost

10,000 feet, with Richthofen right behind. The Englishman straightened his fighter just before it hit the ground and pancaked it onto a bumpy field behind the German lines, smashing its landing gear and crumpling its tail and lower wing. Richthofen's only thought was that no one was going to deny him credit for this kill. He landed near the wrecked fighter, and almost crashed his Albatros in the process, as German infantrymen rushed toward his victims.

Both Morris and Rees had several bullet wounds. Rees died a moment after he was pulled out of the cockpit and laid down. With Richthofen looking on, Morris was put on a stretcher and rushed to a field hospital. He died soon after he was brought in.

There was a celebration in Jasta 2's mess after the evening meal. Richthofen had already written a short combat report, in which he claimed his victory, and he now chattered with his squadron-mates. Everyone who had been at breakfast was at dinner, and the realization of that achievement made them laugh nervously. Boehme, Reimann, and Boelcke had also made kills. Boelcke announced the day's tally over clinking glasses and excited whispering: thirteen separate flights and five combats, of which four were successful. That day, Boelcke said, the sharks attracted to the blood were German—seven of the Kaiser's scouts, not belonging to Jasta 2, had seen the fight and joined in. All six F.E. 2's and two of the eight bombers had been destroyed. The British formation had been mangled. Someone made a sarcastic remark about Trenchard's air offensive. Boelcke stood and said he was presenting engraved beer mugs to his three freshly blooded pilots. He was, he said, very proud of them. Richthofen was even prouder of himself, and the beer mugs gave him an idea. He would present himself with a two-inch-high silver trophy cup for his day's work, and for every kill thereafter. They would make a fine display in his quarters, and he could look at them at night and remember the battle each stood for. He wrote out specifications that night, which he sent to a jeweler in Berlin the next morning. The first cup would read: "1 VICKERS 2   17.9.16."

The first number stood for his first kill (which he still thought was a Vickers) and the second, for the men in it.

"Dear Mama," Richthofen wrote that night, "You will have wondered at my continued silence, but this is the first chance I have had to sit down and take up a pen. I have been busy constantly of late.

"I had to fly a reserve plane with which I could not do much, being beaten in most encounters;* but yesterday my new plane arrived and, just think, when I was giving it a tryout, I sighted an English squadron right over our lines.

"Making for them, I shot one down. Its occupants were an English officer and a petty officer. I was rather proud of my tryout. Naturally, I have been credited with the downed plane.

"Boelcke is a mystery to everybody. Almost every flight sees him bring down an enemy. I was with him when he accounted for his twenty-fourth, twenty-fifth, twenty-sixth, and twenty-seventh, and took part in the fight.

"The battle on the Somme is not quite what you at home think it to be. For four weeks the enemy has been attacking us with superior forces, most notably artillery. And there are always fresh troops thrown into the battle. Our men fight excellently.

"During the next few days we will probably move our hangars farther back. The whole looks very much like an open battle. I suppose you know that my friend Schweinichen has been killed. I had just made up my mind to visit him because he was stationed nearby. That same day they got him."

Richthofen was bragging to his mother. He centered himself in the fight, omitting the facts that both Englishmen died and

---

* On a few occasions before Jasta 2's first full-scale combat patrol, Boelcke took one or two cubs close enough to the front in Fokkers to watch him "jump" lone Allied airplanes that came their way. This was done on the theory that they would learn more if they could watch actual battles to supplement target practice and formation work far behind the lines. They were absolutely forbidden to join the fight, however.

that he was not the first to spot the British, and then going on to link himself with Boelcke, his hero. He also neglected to mention that Boehme and Reimann had made kills. The letter was typical of many he sent to her, which, far from trying to soothe, seem to have been written to show her the mortal danger he faced and, with superior skill, survived. He wrote to his father infrequently.

Boelcke was not only the commander of Jasta 2, but also its mentor, so the battle was analyzed the next day, when the weather was too bad for patrols. He had stayed above the battle long enough to catch glimpses of what his men were doing, yet he had also found time to make his own kill, which, raked by bullets, crashed into an observation balloon while making a forced landing, and burst into flames. He explained to each of his cubs what they had done wrong and gave solutions. Richthofen described his fight to Boelcke, who listened silently and did not take his large contemplative eyes off the cub. An interrogation started. Did Richthofen carefully deliberate the circumstances before he went after the two-seater? Did he not, in fact, make a series of wild charges, instead of a controlled attack? Had he checked from time to time to see whether anyone was on his tail? Why had he made wide sweeps around his victim, thereby inviting an enemy to approach him unnoticed? Why, for that matter, had he stayed in the combat area so long, and, above all, why had he landed and wasted time *and almost an airplane?* Boelcke did not want to embarrass Richthofen in front of his fellows, so he praised the final attack, which, he said, seemed well judged. He decided to have a talk with Richthofen in private.

The Baron's landing to take a close look at his victims robbed him of one of the more grisly incidents in the air. Boelcke and the rest of Jasta 2's patrol were on their way back from the battle when a British two-seater suddenly came out of the clouds in front of them and headed straight for the startled Germans. One of the cubs dove to avoid a head-on collision. The others, their reflexes and muscles already strained from the battle, scattered.

Then they regrouped and attacked. They shot at the British plane from all sides and were mystified when no fire came, back. Its pilot and observer were visible, but they did not even look at the Germans, and their airplane kept droning toward the west. Boelcke signaled the others to stop attacking and went in for a closer look. Yes, there was a pilot and an observer. He dived on the enemy's tail and from point-blank range fired his twin Spandaus into the fuselage. Nothing happened. He pulled closer, and flew with the British plane until he was fifteen feet above its cockpits, where he remained ready to respond in case this was some new, diabolical trick. Then he looked down and saw two bloodstained aviators, their bodies chewed by bullets, still strapped upright in their seats. They were obviously dead, and their airplane, its controls locked in neutral, was flying home by itself. The cubs came in for a closer look at the "ghost" airplane, and then pulled away at their teacher's order. They watched Boelcke escort the Britisher, as though in a funeral procession, toward the Allied lines. Then he dipped his wings in salute and turned back for Lagnicourt. He said that he believed the two Englishmen had been dead when they came out of the cloud. No one in Jasta 2 took credit for the kill, nor did any other German aviator that day, and, to the best of Boelcke's knowledge, none ever did. The ghost airplane probably flew until its engine stopped, and then fell or glided down, with those finding it attributing the incident to a typical battle occurrence. But it was named "Boelcke's derelict," the way they name a comet after its discoverer, and Richthofen could only add that the Englishmen had had a "glorious death"—they had fought to their last drop of blood and gasoline.

Richthofen ordered his second trophy cup six days later. "2 MARTINSYDE 1 23.9.16." The Martinsyde Elephant had been designed as a large single-seat fighter, but it was so clumsy that its size and long range were utilized by converting it into a bomber. At least, its pilots could reflect, it was one of the few airplanes that had been honestly named. A Lewis gun was attached to the wing above the pilot's head and another was clamped to the side of his cockpit. They almost required a contortionist to operate them. For that reason alone, an Elephant was no match for an Albatros. Richthofen had little trouble moving in behind one of the bombers and shooting it down, although one of his squadron-mates collided with another Elephant and crashed, while the damaged English bomber limped back to its airdrome. It was, as its manufacturers pointed out, a sturdy airplane. Richthofen's third victim came on September 30, and was the first to go down in flames, which rattled him a little.

"Dear Mama," he wrote on October 5, "On September 30th, I brought down my third Britisher. His plane was burned when he crashed to the ground. One's heart is beating a bit more quickly when the adversary whose face one has just seen goes down enveloped in flames from an altitude of 12,000 feet. Naturally, nothing was left either of the pilot or his plane when they crashed. I picked up a plate as a souvenir.

"From my second Britisher, I have kept the machine gun, the breach block of which jammed by a bullet.

"The Frenchman I brought down before Verdun is not on my record, as unfortunately, we forgot to report him to headquarters.*

"Formerly, a pilot was decorated with the Order Pour le Mérite after he had brought down his eighth plane.† Now they have

---

* That was untrue. As has already been mentioned, the kill could not be confirmed because it came down on French territory.

† The Pour le Mérite medal, popularly known as the Blue Max, was Imperial Germany's highest award for individual gallantry, and was roughly equivalent to the U.S. Congressional Medal of Honor and the British Victoria Cross. It was given *only* to living officers, however, for continued meritorious service, rather than for single acts of heroism. The medal was a Maltese cross made of blue enamel edged in gold with gold eagles between the arms of the cross. It was worn at the throat on a black ribbon trimmed in white with silver threads. The Pour le Mérite was first authorized by Frederick the Great, who, because he had been tutored in French, made it his court language and named the medal accordingly. It was awarded to 83 aviators and slightly more than 1,000

discontinued that practice, although it always becomes more difficult to shoot one down. During the last four weeks, since the formation of the Boelcke squadron, we have lost five planes out of ten."

Richthofen started souvenir-hunting in earnest. After landing, he would take a staff car to the scene of his victim's crash and sift through the wreckage until he found something to remember it by. Guns, fabric serial numbers, name plates, bits of propeller, pistols, and, later, even an engine were brought back to the airdrome, carefully packed, and shipped to Schweidnitz, where they were put in his room until he came home on leave to arrange them. Meanwhile, he began to look forward to his Pour le Mérite, which he now wanted more than anything else. But so many pilots were on the verge of winning it that the number of kills needed to get the decoration had been changed from eight to sixteen. It made Richthofen furious.

The British pilots and observers sent over the lines in the great air offensive were, for the most part, going into battle with antiques. They lost 25 per cent of the almost 800 airplanes they had in France during the Battle of the Somme (July 1–November 18, 1916) to German scouts. Having ranged nearly unchallenged over France less than a year before, they were now running into speedy, well-armed Albatroses, Fokkers, and, to a lesser extent, Halberstadts. They grumbled about it in their combat reports, which were sent back to London. So, even as the German high command was joyously dangling the Pour le Mérite higher for its hungry scout pilots to jump for, airplanes were being designed and tested in England that would, once again, reverse the situation. There was the S.E. 5a, a sturdy scout that could flat out at 120 miles an hour at 15,000 feet, stay up

---

army and navy officers during the 1914–18 war, and then discontinued. The British never awarded the Victoria Cross to fighter pilots for shooting down specific numbers of airplanes, since it was felt that such a policy would hurt the morale of observers and bomber pilots, who took equal, if not greater, risks, but who had less opportunity to score kills.

for three hours, and had a respectable ceiling of 19,500 feet; the Sopwith triplane, which could fly at 108 miles an hour and turn so tightly, because of its three wings, that Anthony Fokker would be ordered to copy it for Germany. There was also a scrappy little biplane with an exceptionally good combination of speed and maneuverability that was passed by the Sopwith Company's experimental division three days before Christmas, 1916. They called it the Camel.

As the winter of 1916 approached, however, the German Air Service, spearheaded by its new hunting squadrons, reigned in the cold skies above the Somme. Richthofen began to average a kill a week, which, considering the weather, was good. His fourth victim was a bomber pilot whom he killed by putting one of 400 bullets in his head. Later he drove to the scene of the crash and cut the B.E. 12's serial number from its tail. He pinned the brown fabric on his wall. His fifth kill, another B.E. 12, went down three days later over Ypres, and a sixth followed on October 16. He claimed still another B.E. 12 on the 25th—the day Boelcke shot down his fortieth—but it was contested. A pilot of Jasta 5 claimed to have brought down the British bomber from 1,000 yards, which was almost impossible, as Richthofen noted in a sharply worded letter to Boelcke. It did not really matter to Boelcke, however, because Richthofen was becoming a fair scout pilot, which was more important than the kill list. The Saxon leader of Jasta 2 never hungered for recognition of his kills. They just came. But Boelcke showed obvious pride in his cub's accomplishments. He knew that Richthofen was good, but worried because he knew that Richthofen had an as yet undeservedly high opinion of himself. Such premature conceit could get him killed.

October 28 was cold, gray, and rainy. Boelcke went on four patrols that morning and on a fifth late in the afternoon. He returned showing deep exhaustion, built up under the strain of leading Jasta 2, which had a few days earlier prompted his superiors to order him on leave. He had refused. No sooner had he returned from that fifth patrol than a call came from the infantry, pinpointing two British scouts that were over their heads. Boelcke, Boehme, Richthofen, and three others climbed into their Albatroses and flew west as the light began to fade and the cold air became heavier with moisture.

When the Germans saw the British, silhouetted against thick dark clouds, they set up an ambush, and pounced. The British were outnumbered three to one, but decided to fight anyway and turned to meet the attack. Boelcke, with Boehme next to him, dropped on one. Richthofen, racing ahead of his wingman, went after the other. The British pilots changed their minds and dove away from the Germans. Richthofen, with wind whistling through the crossed wires on his wings and a pleasant blast of warm air rushing back from the engine over him, caught up with his intended victim and began firing. Boelcke and Boehme, a couple of hundred yards away and slightly higher, were both shooting at the other British airplane. Richthofen's Englishman suddenly swerved, pulled out of his dive, and cut across Boelcke's and Boehme's path. Both rolled sharply to avoid a collision. Boehme felt a dull thud under him. The master evidently had turned a little more tightly than the pupil, and the latter's landing gear had struck the upper left wing of his leader's Albatros. Boehme, forgetting the fleeing Englishman, looked down at Boelcke's wing. Its tip had broken off, exposing shattered spars and making the fabric flap. Richthofen broke off from the Englishman who had caused the accident and began circling around Boelcke's falling Albatros. He and Boehme, now horrified, saw the crippled scout disappear into a dark cloud and followed it. When they came out, it seemed as if Boelcke still had some control over his fluttering airplane. They watched, slightly relieved, as the Albatros appeared to respond to its pilot's manipulations. Then they saw its upper wing tear off and float away, half tumbling, in another direction. Boelcke fell straight down and landed in a heap near the infantrymen who had summoned him. The cubs circled the wreckage, disbelievingly, and then headed back to Lagnicourt. The two British pilots were forgotten. Boehme swore all the way back that he would commit suicide if Boelcke was dead.

Boelcke was dead. The funeral, which Richthofen told his mother might have been for a reigning prince, was held in the Cambrai Cathedral on November 3. The Baron carried a pillow with Boelcke's decorations, but had almost missed the train to Cambrai, because he could not resist shooting down another victim the morning of the funeral, whether it was Boelcke's or not. The occupants of his seventh kill crashed near the front lines and were bombarded by German artillery, which did so thorough a job that there was nothing left for a souvenir. 7 F.E. 2 3.11.16, thought Richthofen, remembering that he would at least have another cup. Flowers for Boelcke, the first great German scout pilot, came from all over his country and beyond. A Royal Flying Corps airplane flew over Lagnicourt to drop a wreath. The attached note read: "To the memory of Captain Boelcke, our brave and chivalrous foe." Another wreath was dropped later: "To the officers of the German Flying Corps in service on this front: We hope you will find this wreath, but are sorry it is so late in coming. The weather has prevented us from sending it earlier. We mourn with his relatives and friends. We all recognize his bravery." Another wreath was brought to the funeral by a British prisoner of war—an aviator—and was signed by Captain Robert Wilson, the officer Boelcke had entertained in Jasta 2's mess and who was then in a prison camp at Osnabrück. Boelcke's body was taken to Berlin for burial.

"It is a strange thing," Richthofen later wrote in his memoirs, "that everybody who met Boelcke imagined that he alone was his true friend. I have made the acquaintance of about forty men, each of whom imagined that he, alone, had Boelcke's affection. Men whose names were unknown to Boelcke believed that he was particularly fond of them. It is a curious phenomenon which

I have not noticed in anyone else. Boelcke had not a personal enemy. He was equally pleasant to everybody, making no differences.

"The only one who was perhaps more intimate with him than the others was the very man who had the misfortune to be in the accident which caused his death.

"Nothing," Richthofen concluded, "happens without God's will. That is our only consolation, which we can put to our soul during this war."

Boelcke's death, devastating as it was, had to be dismissed. The Battle of the Somme was still going on, British airplanes, even in worsening weather, were still coming, and the Germans had to try to stop them. Boehme did not commit suicide. He was cleared of guilt by an examining board and returned to duty. Lieutenant Stephan Kirmaier, a senior pilot, was given command of Jasta 2, which, by imperial decree, was renamed Jagdstaffel Boelcke. Kirmaier led the squadron to twenty-five more victories in November, but fell before the month was over.

Richthofen had made friends with an eighteen-year-old fellow pilot named Hans Imelmann (no relation to Max Immelmann), who had shot down five airplanes, and a friendly rivalry started between them. They took off together on November 9, with Richthofen looking for his eighth kill. After searching the Somme River area for some time, they saw a large bomber formation, escorted by three groups of fighters, apparently headed for Jasta 2's airdrome at Lagnicourt. Two miles short of the base, however, the British changed direction and bombed an ammunition dump at Vraucourt. Assorted German scouts had attacked them as soon as they passed over the lines, and by the time the British reached their target they were being picked at by about thirty defenders in what was turning out to be the largest air battle of the war to that date. While two British fighters, chased by Germans, went by under them and were shot to pieces, Richthofen and Imelmann surveyed the scene, which looked like a swarm of hornets, and decided to go after the bombers. Imelmann attacked a lagging bomber, whose pilot had no observer, and who was therefore forced to use his own Lewis gun while flying the airplane. When Imelmann started firing from behind at almost point-blank range, the Englishman turned to get out of the line of fire. The German shot into the side of the bomber, cutting control wires and forcing it to turn over. The Lewis gun fell out of the upside-down airplane, which spiraled from 6,000 feet down to 800 before straightening out. Imelmann followed his enemy down and kept firing. The bomber pilot had no choice at that altitude but to land. He overshot a large grass area in Vraucourt and finally came to a sliding stop beside a dirt road cluttered with picks and shovels. Members of a German work party, followed by soldiers, came running to the dusty bomber and peered into its cockpit. *"Guten Morgen!"* said the Englishman, smiling. *"Guten Morgen,"* said the German soldiers as they pulled him out and led him away.

Richthofen, meanwhile, was attacking another bomber and sending streams of bullets into it. It crashed near Lagnicourt, not too far from Imelmann's victim. When the Germans landed, they took a car and sped toward their kills, hoping there would be enough left for souvenirs. If downed enemy airplanes did not burn to cinders, there was always the possibility that soldiers would pull them apart before the aviators arrived. Infantrymen found a certain gratification in scavenging through wrecked enemy airplanes, probably because carrying away bits of cloth and wood proved that the flying machines were not so invincible, so out of reach, as they seemed from the trenches.

Richthofen's bomber was too far in the brush to be reached by car, but since it was a relatively mild day, he opened his tunic, threw his cap in the back seat, and walked through deep mud to the crash site. He was covered with grease, oil, and perspiration when he started across the field, and was spattered by mud as he continued. There were several people clustered around his bomber, including a group of immaculately dressed officers, so Richthofen began buttoning his collar as he neared the wreckage.

He walked toward the officers a little self-consciously ("I looked like a tramp," he said later), saluted, and asked them if they could tell him about the battle. He was told that the British had been on a bombing raid, and that the airplane in front of him had been shot down before it could drop its bomb, which was still attached under it. The officer who gave him the information then took Richthofen by the arm and led him to the other officers. "I was introduced to a personage who impressed me rather strangely," he recalled. "I noticed a general's trousers, an order at the neck, and an unusually youthful face and undefinable epaulettes. In short, the personage seemed extraordinary to me." During the conversation, Richthofen, while trying, as unobtrusively as possible, to button his shirt and adopt "a somewhat military attitude," mentioned that he had shot down the bomber. He did not find out who the officer with the undefinable epaulettes was until later that night, when he was notified by telephone that it had been the Grand Duke of Saxe-Coburg-Gotha, and that His Royal Highness requested the Lieutenant's presence. After they were introduced, the Grand Duke told the Baron that the downed bomber had been trying to hit his personal headquarters, and would have except for Richthofen's flying skill. Richthofen ended the day with the Saxe-Coburg-Gotha Medal for Bravery. Apparently, no one had told the Grand Duke that the British were after an ammunition dump, and not his headquarters. Richthofen, who by that time would have known, certainly did not. "8 B.E. 2 9.11.16," he wrote to the jeweler. Two days later, he was awarded the Order of the House of Hohenzollern with Swords, which, with the Grand Duke's medal, mollified him a little. But they were not, he continued to reflect, the Pour le Mérite.

After a week of fruitless hunting, Richthofen went into the air on November 20 and shot down numbers nine and ten. It was his first double victory, which presented a delightful problem: whether to order one large cup or two regular-sized ones. A large cup commemorating both victories would defeat the purpose of the collection, he decided, so there would be two, but the tenth (which made him an ace by German standards) would be twice the size of the others. In fact, he thought optimistically, every tenth cup would be twice normal size.

Three days later, on November 23, Richthofen, out on a regular patrol, shot down Major Lanoe Hawker with what was by that time an almost surgical skill. He found out who his victim was later that evening. At first, he thought he had somehow avenged Boelcke's death by killing England's counterpart. From that, he slowly recounted every second of the difficult fight, and came at last to the conclusion that if he could bring down England's greatest air fighter, who could he *not* bring down? He began to think that he might, after all, be even better than anyone imagined. He wrote to his mother, telling her about his eleventh victory (and mentioning that, according to British prisoners, Hawker had been the English Boelcke), and then ordered another cup: "11 VICKERS 1 23.11.16." Although he had test-flown a D.H. 2, he mistook Hawker's for a Vickers. Then his orderly came in with the serial number from Hawker's airplane and his Lewis gun, which had been dug out of the ground, and was covered with dried mud. Richthofen stared at the gun for a long time. December was a week away. The weather was already terrible and would become worse, restricting his chances for kills, but no more so than anyone else's. He thought about December, and then beyond to 1917, and wondered what it would bring. While he contemplated the coming year with more anticipation than he had ever known, and pondered the laurels he was certain would come, high-ranking General Staff officers were contemplating him.

PART II  THE HERO

SIX · THE BLUE MAX

"Good propaganda must keep well ahead of actual political events. It must act as a pacemaker of policy and mold public opinion, without appearing to do so."   —LUDENDORFF,
Ludendorff's Own Story

"It is a curious sidelight on Boche psychology that the [British] aviators may drop bombs which may fall on women and children, and yet be treated by the Germans with all the honors of war, but if caught dropping words, they will be promptly shot."
—CAPTAIN HEBER BLANKENHORN, U.S.A.,
*Adventures in Propaganda: Letters
from an Intelligence Officer in France*

Relations between the German General Staff and the workers who made its guns and biscuits had never really been good, but as the "quick" war approached its third Christmas, they became terrible. The British naval blockade was strangling the Fatherland along a dozen trade routes and in the waters around its home ports. It was reducing the flow of war materials, like the Chilean nitrates used to make explosives, to disastrously low levels. That angered and frustrated the General Staff. But the blockade was also cutting off consumer goods, which caused long lines in front of shops, which raised prices, which angered labor, which strengthened trade unions, which threatened strikes and violence, which infuriated the Prussian generals even more. In the old days, they reflected with nostalgic sighs, the workers in factories could be ignored. Not any longer. The war had settled into a massive stalemate, a siege, that was feeding on hundreds of thousands of men in order to stay alive. The men, in turn, had to be supplied with mountains of guns and biscuits, not to break the stalemate, but just to maintain it. If the stalemate *was* to be broken, advanced technology would have to do it, and technology, too, was made usable in the factories. So the generals begrudgingly admitted that they needed the workers.

But the workers were beginning to wonder whether they needed the generals. Prussian officers, bundled against the cold in regulation gray woolen mufflers and greatcoats, saw their worst nightmare coming true on the streets of every large city in Germany that December of 1916—the icy whirlpool surrounding them was turning red. Communists, appearing in growing numbers, were haranguing the people who produced the guns and biscuits with words like "exploitation" and "bloody revolution." The Russian and the German proletariat, as well as all others, had more in common with one another than with their governments, the Communists told people on the food lines. It was a war between capitalist businessmen, not between workers, so let the capitalists spill their own blood and the workers keep their bread. The ordinary citizens might not have listened if it were only a matter of bread. But it was also a matter of blood—the blood of their children. The first, heady days of the war were a fading memory. It was now an old war, and it had gotten that way by chewing up and digesting their sons, which put the fathers and mothers in an ugly mood. An economic solution, "War Socialism," modified the country's traditional profit system to give the workers an increasingly greater share of less and less. It was not a good solution and, anyway, had no bearing on their sons.

Then there was propaganda. When the war started, the military had only one man handling press relations. An "Information Department" had to be built from scratch. It had been a slow process, and one not looked on too kindly by Prussian officers who felt that soldiers should have better things to do than cater to journalists. As the war continued, however, the old guard had to change its mind. Not only did Allied propaganda have to be counteracted (especially where the United States and other neutral countries were concerned), but the "forces of upheaval" at home had to be thwarted. The idea of having to make their case with words did not come easily to men schooled on the theory that it was more effectively made with guns. But their enemies' words, which could not simply be shot at and killed, began to rankle to the point where they had to be dealt with. Besides, the other departments in Berlin were doing it, so the General Staff would, too. There were, by December, 1916, information departments in the War Ministry, General Staff, Navy Department, Food Ministry, Colonial Office, Post Office, Interior and Treasury departments, Foreign Office, and even among the district military authorities. A press conference was held two or three times a week, with its chairmanship rotating among the represented departments, and co-operation held to a minimum. An extensive press service was developed to report operations in the field, edit and censor journalists at the fronts, and control the reading material, including German newspapers, that was sent to the Kaiser's armies.

The Information Department of the General Staff, which was headed by a Prussian, saw its main function as the creation of heroes, and it was therefore always looking for them. Finding heroes among the ground soldiers was not easy because they always fought in groups, and groups could only be heroic in the most general ways. Furthermore, soldiers were seldom heroic more than once. Individual, Wagnerian heroes, who would keep doing brave things, were needed, and there was no better place to find them than in the sky. All the elements were there. Flying was still new enough so that most people thought just going up in an airplane was death-defying. Since the aviators thought so, too, they respected each other and were even chivalrous to their enemies, provided their lives did not depend on it. They were modern knights. Their airplanes were their steeds, the ground crewmen who fixed their steeds were squires, and the clumsy, insulated flying clothes, which made walking awkward, were even reminiscent of armor. Best of all, aerial combat—man against man—was jousting, and the fliers would keep choosing to joust until they were killed. This was perfect. Immelmann and Boelcke had been such knights, and, fortunately, both fell in mortal combat defending their homeland, rather than off a cliff or down a flight of stairs. Not content with recounting their epic battles in newspapers, the Information Department had them photographed for postcards, called Sanke cards after the company that printed them, and sold all over Germany. They were also filmed (climbing confidently onto their steeds, which were pointed toward the western sky) for segments of silent movies that circulated to theaters in the larger cities and towns. But Immelmann and Boelcke were dead, and the people were losing their will to fight, so the search for new heroes was pressed. That was why the Information Department of the General Staff took particular interest in Lanoe Hawker's death, and in the newcomer who killed him. Lieutenant Manfred von Richthofen, a young baron from a good Prussian family, would bear watching, especially since Hawker had been his eleventh.

Richthofen was also being watched by Captain Walz, the officer who inherited Jasta 2 after Kirmaier was killed, and was rewarded for his performance by being made a flight leader. Each squadron was divided into two flights, or *Ketten*, of five or six airplanes. (There were three flights of six airplanes each in British units.) Combat patrols were alternated between flights during daylight. Pilots not in the air remained at the base in case so many enemy airplanes entered the squadron's sector that a second flight had to be sent up. They could go anywhere they pleased at night, however, provided they were not listed for administrative duties. Richthofen, now believing implicitly that he was a pilot on the way up, applied himself with more determination than ever. He rarely left the airdrome for wine in nearby towns and, instead, took the wine to his quarters, where he planned voluntary patrols. He was allowed to lead those, too, which would better his chances for kills, because the leader attacked first and had his rear protected. And because of a new order, he could look for those kills over the front lines, rather than behind them.

The strategy of keeping scouts in defensive positions well behind the lines had a twofold purpose. First, it helped draw Allied airplanes so deep over German-held territory that their fuel ran low, and they then had to turn and run the gantlet of wind and German interceptors. Second, it helped prevent one of the new scouts from falling behind Allied lines. The British had captured a scout carrying a synchronized machine gun a few weeks after the mechanism made its debut. The interrupter gear was, of course, sent to London for copying, and the Germans were afraid more secrets would be lost if other airplanes were examined. But there was a new rub. The German soldiers in the trenches hardly ever saw their airplanes. They saw French and British formations passing over in waves, apparently unchallenged, and suffered the indignities of being photographed and the casualties of bombing and strafing by what seemed like any Allied airplane that cared to do so. They wanted to know where *their* aviators were, and began coining sayings like "God punish the English, our artillery and our air force." Ground commanders noticed that morale was being affected by rumors that the aviators spent all their time carousing. (Richthofen was to be put on a project the following May designed to dispel those rumors.) For the time being, it was decided to send scouts to the front lines in a show of strength for the men on the ground. Unfortunately, the weather at the end of December was so poor that Maltese crosses could rarely be seen from the ground.

Richthofen was nevertheless able to put on a show for soldiers on both sides of the barbed wire on December 11, when he shot down his twelfth victim, a D.H. 2. But the weather closed in again and all but grounded Jasta 2. When it cleared, five days before Christmas, he led his flight to a near-massacre of a third of the Royal Flying Corps' No. 29 Squadron. Flying in front of and slightly below a V formation of five Albatroses, he led it against six D.H. 2's. Five of the British were shot up. One crashed into the trenches and another, Richthofen's, broke up well behind German lines. He went up again that day and, with the same V strung behind him, pounced on an F.E. 2. He sent about 200 rounds into the British fighter, as did some of his squadron-mates, but Richthofen was up front and thought the kill belonged to him. He reported it that way, and was credited with his fourteenth victory, as well as his second daily double.

Sitting alone in his quarters that night, Richthofen looked at the red-white-and-blue roundels and serial numbers on his wall, at the line of little silver cups, and at himself. What he saw made him feel good. He would soon be his country's leading war pilot, its ace of aces. Furthermore, his father, who had volunteered for service despite his disability, and who was now the military mayor of an occupied town not far from Lagnicourt, was coming to Jasta 2 to spend Christmas with him. So was Lothar, who had left the cavalry for the same reasons as he had and who was now also in the Air Service. It would be a fine reunion, if only a partial one. Evergreen branches and a Christmas tree had been put in the mess to make it more festive. It would be the last Christmas without a Pour le Mérite, he promised himself, drifting into a mood of unbounded happiness. It was then that he decided to fly a scarlet airplane.

Toward the end of 1916, German airplane manufacturers began to paint their products in standardized camouflage color schemes, as stipulated by Berlin. Early Albatroses had the upper sides of their wings and tail painted in irregular patches of khaki and dark olive green. Undersides were light sky blue and fuselages were just varnished over their natural plywood color. But pilots, in their never-ending search for individuality, wanted their own trade-marks, and therefore "modified" parts of their scouts—usually the engine cowling and tail—by painting them varying colors. Boelcke had had his scout's nose painted red, and members of the squadron began to associate that color with their group. Richthofen wanted a distinctive airplane. He wanted friend and foe alike to know he was present, but, he reflected, there was no point in continuing to dab colors here and there. It was almost impossible to differentiate between different-colored noses and tails in the blur of a fight, so why not paint the whole thing? And what better color than red, which was Boelcke's and which, he thought, was the easiest to see and the most flamboyant? He therefore had almost all of his Albatros painted scarlet. Its tail fin and a square on each side of the fuselage remained white, to show the black crosses more clearly. He half expected an official reprimand. It never came; possibly because his superiors were trying to encourage his blatantly aggressive spirit and because they considered the Boelcke Squadron elite enough to warrant some splashes of color if that enhanced morale. If Richthofen kept shooting down Englishmen, and was proud enough of his work to want the whole world to know about it, his comrades might emulate him, his enemies might be intimidated by him, and the men in the trenches might see him. A gaudy, conspicuous airplane was a small price to pay for all those possibilities.

Richthofen showed his father and Lothar around the airdrome on Christmas Day, introduced them to his commander and friends, and took them to dinner in the squadron's mess. Albrecht was impressed by everything he saw and was fascinated by the neat line of Albatroses. He told his oldest son that he was proud of him. Lothar, looking eagerly around, informed Manfred that he expected to solo at any time, and would then like to be posted to a scout squadron on the western front. Manfred, who felt closer to Lothar than to any of his other contemporaries, smiled and said he would see what could be done. It would be good to have Lothar with him, he thought, and he would be able to give his brother the kind of personal instruction that would help when he went into combat.

Lothar had been commissioned a second lieutenant when war broke out, was put into a heavy cavalry (dragoon) regiment, and sent to France. Contrary to Manfred's fears, Lothar was doing anything but charging into Paris and staggering under the weight of medals. When, in the autumn of 1914, it was discovered that horses were useless against barbed wire, trenches, and machine guns, Lothar's Fourth Dragoon Regiment was sent to the wide expanses of the Russian front. He had his first taste of a Slavic winter there, but in spite of a hatred for it, which he shared with his comrades, he performed with traditional Prussian honor and courage.

On one occasion, he had a chilling encounter with a river, as had his father soon after Lothar was born. One night, the Russian and German armies confronted each other on opposite banks of the Warthe River, in western Poland. Lothar decided to swim across it alone to find the enemy positions. When he reached the other side, he crawled along the bank, memorized the Russian positions, and then swam back. His uniform froze while he was returning to camp, but he stayed on duty that way all through the following day, and did not catch so much as a cold.

Eventually, the cavalry began to bore him, so when Manfred suggested that he try for the Air Service, he took his brother's advice, the way he generally did. He was never sorry about the change, because not only did flying come more naturally to him than it had to Manfred, but also it better suited his disposition, in a way opposite from the effects it had on Manfred. But then, Manfred and Lothar were different in many ways, which caused minor clashes between them.

"Lothar treated war," said Lieutenant Walter Kreutzmann, a friend and fellow pilot, "like a huge cosmic joke to which he personally had the obligation of contributing some of the best laughs." The description was accurate, and it applied not only to war, but also to almost everything. Lothar was lean, like Manfred, but three inches taller, had a more angular face, and a totally different personality. Where Manfred was quiet and often brooding, Lothar was boisterous and forward. Where Manfred was fond of sitting by himself for hours, Lothar was prankish, ebullient, and very much one of the boys. Where

Manfred had a highly developed sense of his place in history and tried mightily to attain it, Lothar was more content with life's everyday pleasures and what he considered a necessary balance of work and play. Where Manfred drank in moderation, considering drunkenness dulling and undignified for a Prussian officer and noble, Lothar was an undignified devotee of wine- and beer-drinking bouts, and was free with the cash they required. Where Manfred stayed away from women, saying either he had no time or he did not want to make some girl a widow, Lothar made plenty of time and never thought about widowhood because he never thought about marriage, at least not during the war. His boyish face, strong body, and happy-go-lucky charm brought him enough conquests to earn the good-natured jibes of his many friends. Manfred, who hated discipline as a child, grew into it, began to see its virtues, and rigidly imposed it on himself and his underlings. It almost seemed as though he were clinging to discipline for the mental and emotional security it brought. Lothar had accepted his parents' and teachers' discipline with happy resignation, but then went off on his own, rebelled, and became a free spirit—at least as free a spirit as a Prussian officer was likely to become. The brothers' differences showed in battle, too.

Like Manfred, Lothar started flying as an observer, but did not particularly like its passive nature. He was observing at Verdun and along the Somme in the summer of 1916 when he was posted to a bombing unit, which overjoyed him, and he became very good at releasing bombs at exactly the right moment. He did not care for daylight bombing, because the high altitudes, often in excess of 10,000 feet, prevented him from seeing the damage he had done, although flying high offered more protection against antiaircraft fire. To judge by his attitude, which was similar to Manfred's, dropping bombs had its own visual gratification, the way shooting down airplanes did. Night bombing was more fun because it was done at low altitude, and Lothar took an almost childish delight in peering over the side of his airplane and watching the explosions and flames, which, he said, reminded him of fireworks. The biggest "fireworks" display came the night his squadron bombed a large French ammunition dump, sending flames thousands of feet and rounds of glowing ammunition in all directions, like Roman candles. When he returned to the target the next day, it was still burning, which prompted Lothar to comment: "Manfred will be proud of me."

Lothar was observing and bombing in the same sector where Max Immelmann and Boelcke were making celebrities of themselves, and he occasionally saw them in action, which whetted his appetite for scout flying. He wrangled permission for pilot training and began the course about when Manfred started at Jasta 2. Lothar had less difficulty learning to fly than Manfred, and was spurred on during the autumn of 1916 by his brother's growing string of victories. He politely told Manfred as much on Christmas Day, and when he added, finally, that he was supposed to solo the next day, Manfred decided to come and watch. The flight went well, and Lothar was greeted on landing with congratulations and assurances from his instructor and his brother that he was on the way to becoming a fine scout pilot. The final examination—the third, testing cross-country ability—was tentatively scheduled for March, depending on his progress.

The day after the younger Richthofen soloed, the older shot down his fifteenth Englishman. He returned to Lagnicourt filled with the tingling excitement that comes to men who approach glory, are thwarted, and then are poised on the brink of it again. Eight kills had brought the Pour le Mérite when Richthofen had started trying for it. Halfway there, the number was changed to sixteen, and thus the coveted medal was yanked almost from his grasp. Now he had fifteen. The pilots who were even close to that could be counted on one hand, he thought, so they would not change the number again.

Richthofen was grounded by miserably cold, turbulent weather during most of the last week of the year, and he spent hours prowling around his quarters, the mess, and the hangars like a caged tiger smelling blood. He went up whenever the weather permitted, but always came back hungry. On the morning of January 4, 1917, Flight Lieutenant A. S. Todd of the Royal Naval Air Service ventured alone into Jasta 2's sector. He flew a new Sopwith Pup, the predecessor of the Camel. The Royal Flying Corps had taken such a severe beating during the Battle of the Somme that it had to be reinforced by No. 8 Squadron of the Royal Navy, which was moved into Vert Galand and made ready for operations on November 3. The unit had started with three types of fighters, but, through combat testing, decided that the Pup was the best of them and was outfitted accordingly. During November and December, the Pups, which were easy to fly, relatively fast, and more maneuverable than Albatros scouts, accounted for twenty German airplanes. Richthofen had his first look at a Pup when, leading two Albatroses on a routine patrol, he was attacked by Todd. While the British naval officer was gamely going after one of the German scouts, another—a scarlet one—came in from behind and shot the Pup out of the air, killing Todd and showering a field near Metz-en-Couture with pieces of wood, wire, and canvas.

Richthofen landed and immediately drove to the crash site, cut serial number N 5193 from the Pup's tail, and returned to Lagnicourt to write his sixteenth report and order another cup. The cloth serial number on his writing table was the Pour le Mérite. It gave him unbounded satisfaction and was a new source of confidence. It should not have been either, because although it might have reaffirmed Richthofen's ability, it also represented the shape of things to come in British fighters—airplanes that would not be as easy prey as D.H. 2's and F.E. 2's.

A week passed, and no medal came. Richthofen began to sulk. News that he had been selected to command Jasta 11, at Douai, not only failed to cheer him up, but it also made him angrier. He would have to leave his friends in the Boelcke Squadron, where he had run up that magic sixteen kills, and take the responsibility for a group which, although in existence for several months, had yet to score a victory. Being made the commander of a scout squadron, even one like Jasta 11, was an honor. But it was no substitute for the Pour le Mérite, thought Richthofen. He accepted everyone's congratulations with thinly concealed irritation. Then word came that he had been awarded his medal. On that day—January 16, 1917—Lieutenant Manfred Freiherr von Richthofen officially became a hero. With sixteen kills, he also became the highest-scoring German alive—the ace of aces.

Richthofen was headline news. Reporters, directed by editors who attended the Information Department's press conferences in Berlin and at command headquarters on the Rhine, scrambled from other assignments along the front and came to Lagnicourt by the carload. RICHTHOFEN—the name appeared above and below his photograph in newspapers and magazines throughout Germany. Over and over again, the photographers asked him to mount his Albatros and look confidently toward the western sky for an enemy. Then he was asked to dismount, smiling, as if he had just made another kill, or stand beside his airplane with a sincere, boyish face pointed forthrightly at the cameras. He was interviewed and asked his opinion on the merits of German aviators versus their opponents, on German airplanes, on tactics, and on the outcome of the war. He told the reporters exactly what he knew the General Staff expected him to, but not in long-winded detail, because he was not really a talker. He enormously enjoyed being photographed and interviewed, but hated to make speeches and was as brief as possible. This was wonderful. The journalists said he was shy. A blue-eyed Prussian noble, twenty-four years old, who was deadly behind the guns that defended the Fatherland, but who was certainly no braggart. He was quietly dignified and modest, the articles said.

Sanke cards of Richthofen were bought and his photographs cut out of newspapers by hundreds of girls, who kept them in secret places and wrote him adoring letters. Mail came by the bagful. Perfumed letters proposing everything from marriage to less formal arrangements poured in, and all were shared with his squadron-mates, who delightedly read them aloud by turn and laughed at the mushiest. Photographs came with some of the letters, and were lined up for judging, with Richthofen always advised with mock seriousness to "take" the day's winner. He accepted his comrades' joking good-naturedly, if with some embarrassment, and agreed that when the right time came, he would look up such and such a winner. But he did not answer those letters, because, he said, the war left no time for romance. When the Pour le Mérite actually arrived, he slowly, meticulously, fastened it at his throat and began looking in the mirror whenever possible. A week after he received the decoration, however, the mirror-watching stopped. It was time to go to war with Jasta 11, *his* squadron.

When Richthofen arrived at Douai, he went through his pilots' records, and found them much better than average. Yet there had been no victories. The missing factor, if Boelcke's squadron was any indication, had been leadership. When he had satisfied himself that he had the material to work with, he resolved to set his men a good example—which would not hurt his score, either. First, though, he met with his pilots, whom he called "my gentlemen," and, trying as hard as he could to judge them the way Boelcke would have, determined who had the most potential. Two pilots stood out immediately; a third was to arrive in March. The two were Lieutenants Kurt Wolff and Karl Allmenroeder.

Wolff was so thin that he looked emaciated, and a dislocated shoulder that never healed properly added to his frail, awkward appearance. He was born in Pomerania in February, 1895, and orphaned soon afterward. He was raised by relatives in Memel, eventually joined the army, and received his commission with the 4th Railway Regiment in April, 1915. He transferred to the Air Service in July of the following year, but got off to an almost disastrous start when the airplane in which he was taking his first flight crashed, killing his instructor and dislocating Wolff's shoulder. He went on to earn a pilot's badge and was then sent to Jasta 11. Richthofen saw tenacity and obvious courage under Wolff's gentle, bashful appearance, and decided that if a noticeable reckless streak, which reminded him of Zeumer, could be curbed, Wolff would become an excellent scout pilot. He was to learn that Wolff was as dedicated a souvenir collector as his squadron leader.

Karl Allmenroeder, who was called Karlchen, or Little Charles, was the son of a Rhineland pastor. He was at medical school in Marburg when war came, and left to join the 62nd Field Artillery Regiment at Oldenburg. The unit was eventually sent to the Russian front with Mackensen's army. There Allmenroeder won the Iron Cross (Second Class) and the Friedrich August Cross (First Class) for outstanding service. But big guns bored Karlchen, so he and his brother, Willi, entered the Air Service and took pilot training at Halberstadt. Karl arrived at Jasta 11 in November, 1916.

Karl Emil Schaefer was to become Richthofen's best pupil, because he, too, had an instinct and appetite for hunting. He was born in Krefeld on December 17, 1891. After graduating from high school, Schaefer entered the army and was put in the 10th Jager, a hunting battalion. *Jägern* were snipers, and therefore expert marksmen, which appealed to Schaefer, as it would have appealed to Richthofen. When his enlistment was over, Schaefer went to England and France to study languages, and returned home only three days before the war. He was recalled, put into another sniper battalion, and sent to Belgium and France. During the attack on Maubeuge, Sergeant Schaefer, with eighty men temporarily under his command, captured 2,800 Allied soldiers. Soon after that exploit, he was wounded in the thigh and sent to a hospital, from which he emerged six months later with one leg shorter than the other. He was sent back to the front in May, 1916, and was then made a second lieutenant. But, like so many other ground soldiers, he became bored with the motionless war and sought a faster one in the Air Service. He was accepted in spite of his crippled leg.* Though he crashed during training, he was not hurt. He graduated and was sent to the Russian front with a bomber squadron. The group was moved to France in January, 1917, and given the protection of a scout squadron, which Schaefer transferred to when he realized that the scouts did almost all of the hunting. It was from that squadron that he came to Jasta 11 in March.

Richthofen tried hard to be equal to the demands of his new job and made no secret of following the example of Boelcke. He started by outlining the Dicta, illustrating with descriptions of his own fights, which was in no way boasting. He seems to have been almost overwhelmed with a sense of responsibility to his men, and leadership, which was new to him, was taken at least as seriously as combat. He went up with Jasta 11 for practice sessions. Most of his men were unblooded, but they were not new pilots, so the practice flights were kept short and concentrated on attacking.

Deciding that his pilots had to apply Boelcke's theories to combat, on January 23 Richthofen took his class up for a practical demonstration of air fighting. They saw a flight of F.E. 8 fighters over the lines near Lens. Richthofen signaled for the standard pouncing attack, sun behind, and dropped on the Englishmen with his pack right behind. He picked a plane, closed to within fifty yards, and shot 150 bullets into it. The fighter burst into flames and went down. At 1,000 feet, its pilot either fell out of his cockpit or, more probably, chose smashing into the ground, rather than burning alive, and jumped. It was Richthofen's seventeenth kill and Jasta 11's first.

---

* Although there has apparently been no study of the "physically unfit" men who flew for both sides during World War I, the number seems extremely high. The major reason for this was the notion that flying was not as physically taxing as running or riding horseback. Many men who were not up to the rigors of the ground army took to the air because, among other things, they thought it would be less strenuous. They were right, but only so far as legs were concerned. Violent maneuvering could sweat off up to five pounds an hour.

The next day, Richthofen and one other member of the squadron took off at noon and spotted a flight of F.E. 2's. Instead of attacking the large formation, they stalked it until the lead airplane, with Captain O. Greig at the controls and Lieutenant J. E. MacLenan at the machine gun, got far ahead of the rest of the group. As soon as Greig heard Richthofen's guns, he put his fighter into a tight bank, but it was too late. Bullets hit and stopped the F.E. 2's engine and tore into its pilot's legs. Even before the propeller stopped, MacLenan was firing at Richthofen, who by that time was circling for advantage. The other F.E. 2's had caught up by that time, and while Richthofen was making another firing run at Greig and MacLenan, a second British fighter was shooting at him. His victim glided toward British lines, but Richthofen, determined to force it down before it got there, pressed his attack in spite of bullets coming at him now from two directions. Then his wing cracked.

He pulled back on the throttle to reduce speed and pressure on the airplane's wings, and brought it—a new Albatros D III—down to a gentle landing near where his victim had by that time also landed. While Richthofen was coming down, MacLenan pulled Greig out of their fighter and touched a match to the gasoline leaking out of its fuel tank. The airplane caught fire before German infantrymen arrived to collect the airmen. Richthofen later politely questioned MacLenan. He got no military information out of the prisoner, but was pleased to learn that his Albatros was being called *Le Petit Rouge* by his opponents. Its color was accomplishing what he had intended, and that—the evident respect of enemy pilots—overjoyed him.*

When he returned to Douai, he learned that two pilots in Jasta 2 had been killed that day because of structural failures in the

---

* Richthofen was not so overjoyed when, on meeting another captured pilot, he was told that the English thought he was a girl. The red Albatros was handled so deftly, the Royal Flying Corps pilot said, that his squadron's pilots thought it was flown with a girl's touch. The other Germans in the room laughed. Richthofen stiffened and scowled.

wings of their Albatroses. One of them was Hans Imelmann, with whom he had competed for the most victories. The thought of working so hard and risking his life so often to become his country's ace of aces and then being killed because of some designer's shortcomings angered Richthofen. He decided to fly a Halberstadt, which he did not like as well as the Albatros, until the wing problem was corrected. He also decided to begin February by announcing an unofficial competition between Jasta 11 and Jasta 2 for the most kills. The Boelcke Squadron was about a hundred kills ahead of his group. Jasta 11 was going to have to try harder, and Richthofen coldly put it to them just like that.

SEVEN · BLOODY APRIL

". . . the four-year campaign in France saw several marked fluctuations in the air fighting as one side and then the other was able to put into the line new aircraft of performance superior to those of the enemy. It was a matter of ups and downs, and for the Royal Flying Corps the spring of 1917 was the worst 'down' we experienced in that war."

—AIR MARSHAL SIR JOHN SLESSOR,
The Central Blue

While Lieutenant von Richthofen embraced his war—chasing Englishmen and immortality in a scarlet scout, describing each new victory to his mother with deep pride, wearing his country's highest military decoration, even under his flying suit, ordering more silver cups, sending serial numbers and other souvenirs back to Schweidnitz, and trying to mold Jasta 11 into his image—Kaiser Wilhelm was having considerable trouble with the same war. While postcards of Richthofen were being sold across the street from the Imperial Palace, the Admiral Staff was informing the sovereign inside that the war could not be won on the sea. The General Staff, smarting from massive beatings at Verdun and the Somme, was intimating that it could not be won on land, either. Not even the most junior officers in the Air Service thought that it could be won in the air, but they understood that they were helping the army, and were not told that they were not, and could not, help it enough to make a serious difference. They also were not told that their

Chancellor, Theobald von Bethmann-Hollweg, had sent a secret note to the Allies offering to make peace on Germany's terms, and that it had been rejected as "empty and insincere" by politicians and generals thirsting for the vengeance they knew was coming. Finally, they were not told that the straw being clutched by the General Staff was not the red airplane they saw in the newspapers, but anonymous black submarines.

The old struggle between the Kaiser's civilian and military advisers continued to boil during the winter of 1916–17. Faced with a common enemy they thought was even more dangerous than the Allies—the Berlin liberals—the army and navy reluctantly joined forces and agreed that only unrestricted submarine warfare could break the deadlock that was sapping Germany's strength at a catastrophic rate. If the war could not be won on land, sea, or in the air, they told the Kaiser, it would be won underwater. Admiral von Holtzendorff, the Chief of the Naval Staff, went so far as to tell him that five months of unrestricted U-boat attacks would finish Britain. On December 23, 1916, while Richthofen was having his Albatros painted red, General von Hindenburg telegraphed an ultimatum to Wilhelm: "The diplomatic and military preparations for unrestricted submarine warfare should begin now, so that it may for certain commence at the end of January." Wilhelm obediently signed a formal order on January 31 for his U-boats to be turned loose the following day, despite warnings by the liberals in the *Idiotenhaus* that they would bring the United States into the war. "Submarine warfare is the last card," warned a beaten and disgusted Bethmann-Hollweg as the first of the Fatherland's 111 U-boats put to sea in search of almost anything to torpedo.

Richthofen, of course, knew nothing of all that. He did know that long lines of wounded were being brought back to Germany, increasingly large formations of Allied airplanes were lapping at German positions like the rising tide on a beach, and that morale among the soldiers in the trenches was dangerously low. Richthofen saw most of the war more vividly from 10,000 feet than his generals did from their two-dimensional rear positions. He could not have misinterpreted what he saw in the beginning of 1917, especially in view of the pessimism he expressed to his mother in mid-1915, but the censors would have taken care of any thoughts he put down on the matter. Yet the waves of British airplanes that contributed to the sense of impending doom in Berlin were welcomed by Richthofen as so many more objects to hunt and destroy. They were so many more cups and serial numbers and bits of propeller that represented the victories marking his progress through an increasingly personal war, made more personal by publicity. He began to wait for the British airplanes the way a drought-stricken farmer waits for rain, because there could be no sustenance, no real life, without them.

The day, February 1, that the first U-boats slid furtively out of their berths and disappeared into the dark choppy North Sea with full loads of torpedoes and virtually unlimited hunting licenses, Richthofen shot down his nineteenth victim. It was a lone B.E. 2, whose pilot and observer were so intent on spotting targets for their artillery that they did not see him and Allmenroeder drop from 5,000 feet and approach to within fifty yards. When the number in the little adding-machine-like window at the back of Richthofen's gun reached 150, indicating the number of rounds fired, the B.E. 2 went down in large curves to the right and crashed into barbed wire strung in front of the first line of German trenches. Twenty minutes after the pilot and his observer, both mortally wounded, were dragged from their airplane, a Canadian artillery battery blew it to splinters to deny it to the Germans. Its crew died the next day.

The weather closed in again during the next two weeks, with thundershowers and snow squalls, prohibiting air patrols, but not a five-mile advance up the muddy and then frosted Ancre Valley by the British Fifth Army. Hindenburg had been for some time considering a demand by Crown Prince Rupprecht, the commander of the armies facing the British, that they be allowed to fall back to prepared positions that were easier to defend than where they were. The British advance, supplied by piles of matériel that the Germans could not match, made Rupprecht's case more urgent. He summarized it to the Kaiser on January 28 this way: the German positions were poor, the troops were exhausted and badly supplied, and it was doubtful that they had the stomach for another major battle like the Somme. There *would* be another Somme, however, unless German soldiers fell back; and that would be a calamity, because morale and munitions were at an all-time low. Wilhelm agreed to Rupprecht's proposals and signed an order on February 4 authorizing them to be carried out. The plan called for a zone, in some areas twenty miles deep, between the existing and the proposed front lines, and sixty-five miles long, to be made into a wasteland. So far as possible, every village was to be destroyed, every well polluted or filled in, every tree and other obstacle cut down, and every resident removed, until the area had been turned into a flat, exposed belt of devastation that could easily be watched and heavily bombarded. The operation was to be completed on April 5, when the twenty-nine German divisions between Soissons and Arras had dug into their new trenches, wearily strung new barbed wire, and set up new machine-gun, mortar, and artillery positions. Then they would look out at the advancing British and French armies from what they called the Hindenburg Position and wait for the next onslaught.

The army might be on the defensive, and the Air Service, too, but not Richthofen. He spent the first two weeks of February going over tactics with his squadron and meeting with its members one at a time to discuss their mistakes. He was developing Boelcke's ability to see almost everything around him during a fight, even when he was engaged, and he remembered what he saw. There was no excuse for not continuously looking behind, he warned Jasta 11, and any pilot returning with holes in his tail had to have a good explanation. There was no truth, however, to stories circulated later that even a single hole in a scout's tail was reason for Richthofen to have its pilot transferred. He was nonetheless taken at his word. Returning from one fight, a Jasta 11 pilot with a generous scattering of bullet holes faked engine trouble and landed at another squadron's field, where the holes were patched before he continued home. Pilots did not generally adore Richthofen the way they had Boelcke, and he knew it. But he also knew that they respected him, and his schooling told him that that was enough. He made it a rule never to ask pilots to do something that he would not do, and he took satisfaction in knowing that they knew that, too.

Der röte Kampfflieger, or the Red Battle Flier, as he was then being called by the German press,* scored his twentieth and twenty-first kills on February 14, and that night ordered a regular trophy cup and a second double-sized one. He shot down the first at noon while returning from a staff conference at Jasta 2, in which plans for a telephone warning system were discussed. Since German interceptors were at that time outnumbered two to one by French and British intruders, a system was being worked out by which observation posts could telephone the positions of enemy airplanes to central switchboards, which would in turn send up the scout squadron nearest to the sighting. With limited numbers of scouts, and gasoline far from limitless, such a system would be preferable to having scouts waste time patrolling areas where there was no action. If a large enemy formation was spotted, a second, and even a third, interceptor squadron could be called to help the group that got there first. That, in theory, was supposed to prevent the defenders from being overwhelmed.

---

* Richthofen was *never* called the Red Baron by the Germans. British pilots called him the Bloody Red Baron, the Jolly Red Baron, and *Le Diable Rouge*—the Red Devil. Some British infantrymen called him the Red Falcon or the Red Devil.

Richthofen had been at 6,000 feet when he saw his noon kill, another of the plodding B.E. 2's, flying alone west of Loos. Again he dropped down, pulled to within fifty yards of the unaware pilot and observer, and sent several hundred bullets into their airplane. He said in his report that the pilot had been killed in the air and the observer seriously wounded when the B.E. 2 crashed into German trenches. The opposite was true. Second Lieutenant H. A. Croft, the observer, was probably killed instantly. But the pilot, Lieutenant C. D. Bennett, fractured the base of his skull in the crash, erasing all memory of his encounter with Richthofen. He eventually became a London businessman, but forever lost the events of February 14, 1917.

The day's second kill came at 4:45 P.M. southwest of Mazingarbe, when Richthofen led a full patrol against five more B.E. 2's. He silenced one airplane's observer with a hundred rounds, and then sent enough additional bursts into the bomber to cause smoke and uncontrolled circling. For once, though, the wind was on the side of the British. It blew the B.E. 2 over the lines, which Richthofen did not want, because airplanes forced down were not credited unless captured. He went after the floundering bomber, firing a series of bursts until its wing came off. It dropped straight down and landed in the snow on the British side. Richthofen's squadron-mates had already started back to Douai, to beat the darkness that was quickly coming over the front, so there were no witnesses, and the airplane obviously could not be captured. His claim was accepted anyway.

More than two weeks passed before he scored again, but when he did, on March 3, it was the beginning of his greatest run of victories—kills that were, in large part, responsible for the Royal Flying Corps's remembering the following month as "Bloody April."

His victims on March 3 were two men he caught doing artillery spotting in another B.E. 2. It, too, crashed on its own side of the lines, which delayed confirmation. He shot down still another B.E. 2 the next morning, but only after being seen by the airplane's pilot, who tried to make it back to his lines by going into a steep dive. Richthofen started firing at 7,500 feet, but could not keep up, and the last he saw of the British bomber was as it passed 3,000 feet, still diving. German infantry reported that it never came out of the dive and crashed into no man's land, killing both crewmen. At 4:20 that afternoon, Richthofen led five of his men into a fight with a patrol of No. 43 Squadron. He sent so many bullets into his victim's wing that it broke off. The airplane then disintegrated and came down over several acres.

Richthofen scored again on March 9, but on that day he also found out what it was like to be shot down. Leading a flight of five Albatroses,* he attacked nine lumbering F.E. 8's that were photographing trench positions, spotting for artillery, and doing light bombing. During the thirty-minute fight, which was long as air battles went, four F.E. 8's were shot down, one in flames, while the rest tried to twist away. D.H. 2 pilots of No. 29 Squadron saw the battle, however, and joined in. Richthofen later described, in a narrative that offers some insight into his thinking, what happened when the D.H. 2 formation entered the fight:

"I watched whether one of the fellows would hurriedly take leave of his colleagues. One of them was stupid enough to depart alone. I could reach him, and I said to myself, 'That man is lost!' Shouting aloud, I went after him. I came up to him, or at least was getting very near him. He started shooting prematurely, which showed that he was nervous. So I said to myself, 'Go on shooting. You won't hit me.' He shot with a kind of am-

---

* He had gone back to an Albatros, apparently satisfied that the wing problem had been corrected. He preferred it to the Halberstadt. Besides the Albatros's better performance, it had twin machine guns, whereas the Halberstadt had only one, which was placed to one side of the cockpit. The Halberstadt D II's top speed was 95 m.p.h.

munition that ignites.* So I could see his shots passing me. I felt as if I were sitting in front of a gigantic watering pot. The sensation was not pleasant. Still, the English usually shoot with this terrible stuff, and so we must try to get accustomed to it. One can get accustomed to anything. At the moment, I think, I laughed aloud. But soon I got a lesson. When I approached the Englishman quite closely, when I had come to a distance of about 300 feet, I got ready for firing, aimed, and gave a few trial shots. The machine guns were in order. The decision would be there before long. In my mind's eye, I saw my enemy dropping.

"My former excitement was gone. In such a position, one thinks quite calmly and collectedly and weighs the probabilities of hitting and of being hit. Altogether, the fight itself is the least exciting part of the business, as a rule. He who gets excited in fighting is sure to make mistakes. He will never get his enemy down. Besides, calmness is, after all, a matter of habit. At any rate, in this case, I did not make a mistake. I approached my man up to within fifty yards. I fired some well-aimed shots and thought that I was bound to be successful. That was my idea. But suddenly I heard a tremendous bang, when I scarcely fired ten cartridges, and presently, something again hit my machine. It became clear to me that I had been hit, or rather my machine. At the same time I noticed a fearful stench of gasoline, and I saw that the motor was running slack. The Englishman noticed it, too, for he started shooting with redoubled energy, while I had to stop it.

"I went right down. Instinctively, I switched off the engine, and, indeed, it was high time to do this. When one's gasoline tank has been punctured and when the infernal liquid is squirt-

---

* He was referring to tracer bullets, which left smoke trails so gunners could follow their trajectories. The Germans used them, too. This narrative, which has been taken from Richthofen's memoirs, seems to have been heavily edited (see Chapter Eight).

ing around one's legs, the danger of fire is very great. One has in front an explosive engine of more the 150 horse power, which is red hot. If a single drop of gasoline should fall on it, the whole machine would be in flames."

Richthofen had actually fired about a hundred rounds, sending the D.H. 2 down, but he had no time to follow it. He saw a white cloud of gasoline vapor which, judging by what he had seen coming from some of his victims, meant an imminent explosion. With his engine turned off, he glided down to 1,000 feet and looked for a place to land. His descent was made all the more frightening by a flaming British airplane that passed him on the way down. The Albatros was bumpily, but safely, landed in a meadow. After seeing that both gas tanks had been punctured and the engine hit, Richthofen dangled his legs over the side of the cockpit and waited to be driven away.

"In a moment," he later wrote, "I was surrounded by a large crowd of soldiers. Then came an officer. He was out of breath and terribly excited. No doubt something fearful had happened to him. He rushed toward me, gasped, and asked: 'I hope nothing has happened to you? I followed the whole affair, and am terribly excited. Good Lord, it looked awful!' I assured him that I felt quite well, jumped down from the side of my machine, and introduced myself to him. Of course he did not understand a particle of my name. However, he invited me to go in his motor car to Hénin-Liétard, where he was quartered. He was an engineer officer.

"We were sitting in the motor car and commencing our ride. My host was still extraordinarily excited. He jumped up and asked: 'Good Lord, but where is your chauffeur?' At first, I did not quite understand what he meant. I probably looked puzzled. Then it dawned on me that he thought I was the observer in a two-seater, and that he asked after the fate of my pilot. I pulled myself together and said in the driest tones: 'I always drive myself.' Of course the word drive is absolutely taboo among flying men.

"An aviator does not drive, he flies. In the eyes of the kind gentleman, I had obviously lost caste when he discovered that I 'drove' my own airplane. The conversation began to slacken. "We arrived at his quarters. I was still dressed in my dirty and oily leather jacket, and had round my neck a thick scarf. On our journey he had, of course, asked me a tremendous number of questions. Altogether, he was far more excited than I was.

"When we got to his quarters, he forced me to lie down on a sofa, or at least tried to force me because, he argued, I was bound to be exhausted after my fight. I assured him that this was not my first aerial battle, but he did not, apparently, believe it. Probably, I did not look very warlike.

"After we had been talking for some time, he asked me the famous question: 'Have you ever brought down a machine?' As I said before, he had probably not understood my name. So I answered nonchalantly, 'Oh, yes. I've done so now and then.' He replied: 'Indeed! Perhaps you've shot down two?' I answered: 'No. Not two, but twenty-four.' He smiled, repeated his question, and led me to understand that when he was speaking about shooting down an airplane, he did not mean shooting *at* an airplane, but shooting *into* an airplane in such a manner that it would fall to the ground and remain there. I immediately assured him that I entirely shared his conception of the meaning of the words 'shooting down.'

"Now I had completely lost caste with him. He was convinced that I was a fearful liar. He left me sitting there where I was, and told me that a meal would be served in an hour. If I liked, I could join in. I accepted his invitation, and slept soundly for an hour. Then we went to the Officers' Club. I was glad to find when we arrived at the Club that I was wearing the Pour le Mérite.

"Unfortunately, I had no uniform jacket under my greasy leather coat, but only a vest. I apologized for being so poorly dressed. Suddenly, my good officer discovered the Pour le Mérite. He was speechless with surprise, and assured me that he did not know my name. I gave him my name once more. Now it seemed to dawn on him that he had heard my name before. He feasted me with oysters and champagne, and I did gloriously, until my orderly arrived at last and picked me up.

"In the evening, I could assure my kind host of Hénin-Liétard that I had increased my 'bag' to twenty-five."

Although the weather remained poor during the rest of the month, Richthofen's "bag" continued to fill up. He shot down another B.E. 2 on March 11, an F.E. 2 and a B.E. 2 on the 17th, a B.E. 2 on the 21st, a SPAD VII on the 24th, and a Nieuport 17 on the 25th. The last two, victims thirty and thirty-one, were not as easy pickings as were the F.E.'s and B.E.'s. They were French-built scouts, and much better than the British-built reconnaissance and bombing planes, which Richthofen noted in his report when he described the SPAD as "fast and handy."

His score rose, in spite of the weather, for two reasons. First, the Royal Flying Corps continued to send observation flights forward, this time to survey the new Hindenburg Position and Arras, which the army was supposed to attack. Second, the telephone warning system was put into operation, which allowed Jasta 11 to be sent directly into the lumbering British formations. The ground observers were also responsible for directing antiaircraft fire, which the British called "Archie," and for recording and confirming kills made by their scout pilots. Many German aviators began painting their airplanes gaudy, distinctive colors and patterns to help ground observers credit them correctly.

Richthofen rarely saw his victims' bodies. Orderlies were sent to the crash sites to get information necessary for reports and to collect souvenirs. Several days after his double victory of the 17th, however, he received a photo postcard showing the contorted body of the F.E. 2 pilot, Lieutenant A. E. Boultbee, lying in the debris of his airplane. The inscription on the other side read: "Sir: I witnessed on March 17, 1917, your air fight, and took this photograph, which I send to you with hearty congratulations, because you seldom have occasion to see your prey. *Vivat sequens!* [Here's to the next!] With fraternal greetings, Baron von Riezenstein, Colonel and Commander of the 87th Reserve Infantry Regiment."

Richthofen seemed pleased to have the photograph, which he showed around and then kept in his room. He was more than pleased to learn on March 22 that he had been promoted to full lieutenant, which for a twenty-four-year-old was rare in the German military. His official score at the end of March was: thirty-one airplanes officially shot down, thirty-two men killed, and another thirteen men wounded or made prisoner.

Lothar had meanwhile passed his final examination, and joined Jasta 11 in the middle of the month. True to his word, Manfred had pulled some strings, which would not have been easy for a lieutenant, but being a Pour le Mérite winner and the Red Battle Flier was something else. Manfred gave Lothar two weeks of practice before taking him on his first serious patrol. The younger Richthofen, although spoiling for his first fight in a scout, spent the last half of March learning about his Albatros, the Dicta of Boelcke, and the geography of Jasta 11's sector. Then he started flying combat patrols, always in Manfred's flight, and always with a warning to stay out of the shooting. Remain on the edge, Manfred told him, and watch everything. Lothar obeyed until he could not stand it any longer. His patience gave out on the third patrol when he saw what looked like an easy kill and attacked. It *was* an easy kill. Manfred watched, first with deep concern, and then with pride, as his brother sent the Englishman down. But the differences between them, which were so evident in their personalities, also showed in their fighting. Manfred considered Lothar a "shooter," rather than a "sportsman," and often made his feelings known to Lothar and others.

"My father discriminates between a sportsman and a shooter," he later wrote. "The latter shoots for fun. When I have shot down an Englishman, my hunting passion is satisfied for a quarter of an hour. Therefore, I do not succeed in shooting two Englishmen in succession. If one of them comes down, I have a feeling of complete satisfaction. Only much, much later I have overcome my instinct, and have become a shooter.*

"My brother was differently constituted. I had an opportunity of observing him when he was shooting down his fourth and fifth opponents. We were attacking in a squadron. I started the dance. I had settled my opponent very quickly. When I looked around, I noticed my brother rushing after an English machine, which was bursting into flames, and exploded. Next to it was another Englishman. My brother, though following No. 1, immediately directed his machine gun against No. 2, although his first opponent was still in the air, and had not yet fallen. His second victim also fell after a short struggle.

"When we met at home, he asked me proudly: 'How many have you shot down?' I said quite modestly, 'One.' He turned his back upon me and said, 'I did two.' Thereupon, I sent him forward to make inquiries. He was to find out the names of his victims, etc. He returned late in the afternoon, having found only a single Englishman.

"He had looked carelessly, as is usual amongst such shooters. Only on the following day I received a report as to the place where the second had come down.

"We all had seen his fall."

Manfred was also upset by Lothar's flying technique, which, by frequent use of stunting, showed a basic love of being in the air, an exhilaration, that Manfred did not have. Airplanes, and particularly scouts, were gun platforms for Manfred. They were vehicles that allowed him to get his guns on the enemy.

---

* This was evidently a concession that, despite his naturally sportsman-like tendencies, the pressure of war forced him, too, to become a shooter. The fifteen minutes of "satisfaction" after a kill is one of the most revealing admissions Richthofen ever made, and has startled many observers, who have attached Freudian sexual implications to it. The Air Service censor, unsurprisingly, was not a student of Freud.

The guns were the important thing, and the scout was only important because it brought him and the guns to the target. Lothar, on the other hand, enjoyed the giddy feeling of flying upside down and, with his hands and feet almost extensions of the airplane, twisting, turning, rolling, and slipping in a machine that seemed a part of him. Manfred became enraged the first time he saw Lothar turn over and drop into a fast, upside-down spin. The Englishman who was closely following him thought he had killed or mortally wounded him, and became careless. Lothar ended the ruse, straightened, counterattacked, and shot down his pursuer.

Lothar used his daredevil tactics to shoot down forty airplanes in seventy-seven days at the front, win the Pour le Mérite, and survive the war. Almost from the day he came to Jasta 11, he made no secret of aspirations to equal and then pass his brother's record, which Manfred reacted to with good-natured disdain, at least outwardly.

By April 1, Jasta 11 had become the chief topic of conversation at the mess tables of Royal Flying Corps squadrons in the Somme province. Scout pilots, with bravado typical of young flyers who prowl for prey, assured each other that they were better than the Hun and, with flattened hands zooming over coffee cups, debated the best techniques for destroying their counterparts. The men who flew observation, bombing, and photo missions over German lines were more than satisfied just to get home, however, because they knew they were Jasta 11's prey and were getting torn to pieces. They did not talk about seeking the enemy. They talked about defending themselves, and finally borrowed a technique from wagon trains in the old American West, for use against red scouts, instead of red Indians. As soon as the Germans pounced on them, the rickety F.E.'s and B.E.'s would form a circle and "play ring-around-the-rosie" while covering each other with concentrated defensive fire. The technique worked fairly well, until the Germans began drawing them out by offering lucrative targets and then attacking the airplane that broke the circle, flying into the hole it left, and attacking the others from inside.

But Jasta 11, or, rather, its leader, also had a problem. Although Richthofen was not yet known by name to British pilots, his distinctive red scouts were, and they became prized targets. He and his pilots began to notice disproportionate numbers of enemy scouts coming after him, and although these were not yet a serious problem, because they were unequal to his Albatros, intelligence reports said that the quality of British scouts could change at any time. The pilots of Jasta 11 therefore asked Richthofen to change the color of his airplane. They became insistent when they heard a rumor that London had put a price on their leader's head. The rumor was started in Berlin for propaganda purposes, and was totally untrue, as was another charging that the British had organized an anti-Richthofen squadron to kill him. At any rate, Richthofen saw their point, but he flatly rejected giving up his trade-mark. Instead, he suggested that red become the squadron color. Each pilot would have parts of his scout painted red, too, in combination with whatever other color he chose. Jasta 11 pilots liked the idea. Lothar, who had served in a cavalry regiment known as the "Yellow Dragoons," had his scout's ailerons, elevator, and parts of its fuselage painted that color; the remainder was red. Schaefer followed the same general scheme, but used black, while Allmenroeder chose white, and Wolff, green. When they flew together, red was the predominant color. This not only relieved the pressure on the leader, but also helped them to recognize each other. Since each man had a different style after the initial attack turned into a free-for-all, Jasta 11 pilots could now quickly determine who their immediate partners were, and use compatible tactics. The resulting teamwork was so effective that other squadrons adopted the recognition system, and soon every scout squadron on the western front was painting a distinctive color on its airplanes.

April, 1917, was the happiest and, by air-war standards, the most productive month of Richthofen's life. In spite of unusually heavy rains and snowfalls, the British kept coming, and Richthofen shot down twenty-one of them, including four in one day. He was promoted to *Rittmeister,** or cavalry captain, during Easter, and by the end of the month had passed Boelcke's forty victories to become the leading ace of the war and his country's paramount hero. General Ludendorff was to proclaim that the Red Battle Flier was worth two whole divisions, and while the effect of that remark on the infantry can only be imagined, it did wonders for the Air Service's morale.

Morale in the Royal Flying Corps came as close to disintegrating in April, 1917, as it ever would. The new scouts were on their way, but that was as good as nothing at squadron level. British commanders had to continue sending large numbers of obsolete scouts to protect observers and bombers on the assumption that at least some would get back. Some did.

Another way of trying to offset German successes in the air was to bomb them where they lived. No. 100 Squadron, which was the first in the Royal Flying Corps to be trained for night bombing, was moved to northern France on March 21. The plan was to have them bomb several German scout squadrons, and Jasta 11 had by that time come to the top of the list. Eleven F.E. 2's took off on the night of April 5 and, under a full moon, which provided excellent visibility, attacked Jasta 11. Richthofen and Wolff stood at the entrance to a bombproof bunker and watched as the first "prehistoric packing case," as the Rittmeister contemptuously called them, was picked up by searchlights while it made its bomb run. One after another, the bombers followed their leader, sometimes coming in as low as 150 feet to release their twenty- and forty-pounders. The Germans put up no defense that first night, but Richthofen likened an F.E. 2 flying past at 150 feet to a game bird, and decided that if they

---

* *Hauptmann,* or captain of infantry, was the other designation for that rank, and still is. *Rittmeister* has been dropped.

returned the following night, he would try to shoot one down from the ground with a machine gun, because "on a moonlit night, I think I can hit a wild pig at the chosen spot from 150 feet with a rifle. Why, then, should I not succeed in hitting an Englishman?"

Damage from the first raid apparently was light, with only four sheds set on fire, according to No. 100 Squadron's own records. The British did not return the next night, but Jasta 11 was ready for them—or at least it thought it was. Since German machine guns were in short supply, the squadron mounted captured Lewis and Vickers guns on piles, and probably noted in doing so that there was, after all, a useful side to souvenir-hunting. Men not assigned to machine guns were given carbines, which made Schaefer, the sniper, very happy.

Richthofen and his pilots were in the messroom on the night of April 7 when an orderly rushed in shouting, "They're here! They're here!" Everyone ran to his post, and the attack of two nights before was repeated. The first F.E. 2 skimmed over the barracks, was picked up by searchlights, and when within 400 yards of the guns, was fired on. It flew slowly through the ground fire, still lighted by beams from the German positions, and dropped its bombs. Richthofen and the others dove for shelter and then emerged, firing, as it lumbered past. Schaefer thought he scored a hit. The other F.E. 2's again followed and again did no serious damage, although one bomb exploded near enough to the all-red Albatros to send a few small pieces of shrapnel through it. Richthofen, disgruntled, went to sleep. Sometime later, he dreamed that he heard gunfire, and awoke to find that it was real. No. 100 Squadron had refueled, reloaded, and returned. "One Englishman flew at so low an altitude over my quarters that in my fright, I pulled the blanket over my head. The next moment, I heard an incredible bang just outside my window. The panes had fallen a victim to the bomb. I rushed out of my room in my shirt in order to fire a few shots after him. They were firing from everywhere. Unfortunately, I had overslept my opportunity." The primary target that night had not been Jasta 11, but the nearby railway station, which was where the British assumed Jasta 11's ammunition was unloaded at night. One of the nine airplanes on that raid was shot down, and its crew taken prisoner, again with negligible results for their effort. They were new at night bombing and would get better.

The following night, No. 100 Squadron bypassed Jasta 11, for a mission over the town of Douai, which they repeated on the nights of the 13th and 17th. The men of Jasta 11 convinced themselves that they had frightened away the British, which, in view of the losses the Royal Flying Corps was always prepared to take, was unlikely. The Germans' record in the air that April left no room for doubt, however. Royal Flying Corps records list 151 airplanes as "missing" for that month, while the Germans recorded thirty of their own lost between March 31 and May 11.

Richthofen's tally was as follows: April 2, one B.E. 2 and one Sopwith 1½ Strutter; April 3, one F.E. 2; April 5, two Bristol F2A's; April 7, one Nieuport 17; April 8, one Sopwith 1½ Strutter and one B.E. 2; April 11, another B.E. 2; April 13, one R.E. 8 and two F.E. 2's; April 14, one Nieuport 17; April 16, one B.E. 2; April 22, one F.E. 2; April 23, one B.E. 2; April 28, another B.E. 2, and April 29, Manfred von Richthofen's greatest day, one SPAD VII, one F.E. 2, one B.E. 2, and one Nieuport 17.

In the three months from January 23, when Richthofen made Jasta 11's first kill, to April 23, his squadron officially destroyed one hundred Allied airplanes. Eighty-three of them went after April 1, with Richthofen accounting for twenty-one, Wolff for twenty-one, Lothar for eighteen, Schaefer for fifteen and Sergeant Major Sebastian Festner for eight. The British had lost five airplanes to one against the Germans, with Richthofen claiming an all-time high of fifty-two by the end of the month. That was why the Royal Flying Corps called it "Bloody April."

EIGHT · COMMANDING

"The spirit of the people at home rendered action imperative. We had the best prospects of winning the war, but it was not over, and what we had won had to be kept. The popular state of mind jeopardized everything." —LUDENDORFF,
Ludendorff's Own Story

"The importance of patriotic instruction, or, as we first called it, the 'work of enlightenment among the troops,' was summed up in the following sentences: 'The German Army, owing to the spirit which animates it, is superior to its enemies and a powerful support to its allies. . . .'" —LUDENDORFF,
Ludendorff's Own Story

Richthofen was tired. It showed in the deepening wrinkles around his eyes, in the slower way he walked, and in the sighs that now punctuated every sentence. And there were fewer sentences. Richthofen had become quiet, even for Richthofen. While still with the Boelcke Squadron, he had written to his mother that six pilots were killed and one wounded in six weeks, and that two others had "suffered a complete nervous collapse." The others' "bad luck," he continued, "has not yet affected my nerves." That was in November. It was six months, forty-six kills, and a couple of hundred fights later. In April alone, he had led Jasta 11 to eighty-nine confirmed kills. Its closest competitor, Jasta 12, scored twenty-three, and Jasta 2, the Boelcke Squadron, eighteen. General Staff headquarters, which kept statistics on its pilots' victories, also kept them on their ailments, and it was clear that Richthofen needed a rest. He was therefore ordered on six weeks' leave. There were more than medical reasons behind the order, however, because the Information Department of

Manfred von Richthofen. A popular postcard showing his Pour
le Mérite (*Jagdgeschwader 71 Richthofen*)

Richthofen at seven—four years before the Wright brothers flew at Kitty Hawk—and with his sister, Ilse, in a goat cart on their father's estate (*Both from Jagdgeschwader 71 Richthofen*)

ABOVE: Albrecht Baron von Richthofen with his sons, Lothar (left) and Manfred (*Jagdgeschwader 71 Richthofen*)
RIGHT: Lothar von Richthofen, who shot down forty planes in seventy-seven days of combat (*Jagdgeschwader 71 Richthofen*)

BELOW: Capt. Oswald Boelcke, who taught Richthofen air-combat tactics *(Imperial War Museum, London)*   RIGHT: Lieut. Werner Voss, Richthofen's friend and competitor, who scored forty-eight kills *(Jagdgeschwader 71 Richthofen)*

ABOVE: Lieut. Ernst Udet, who, with sixty-two kills, became Germany's top surviving World War I ace *(Imperial War Museum, London)*   RIGHT: Lieut. Kurt Wolff, who permanently dislocated his shoulder while learning to fly but who later claimed thirty-three kills *(Jagdgeschwader 71 Richthofen)*

Richthofen with Nurse Katie Otersdorf, and chatting with a fellow officer while a mechanic prepares his Albatros for a patrol (*Both from Jagdgeschwader 71 Richthofen*)

Richthofen im Lazareth

ABOVE: Postcard of Richthofen and superiors Major Hermann Thomsen and General Ernst von Hoeppner (*Jagdgeschwader 71 Richthofen*) RIGHT: "Jinx" photograph taken of Richthofen playing with his dog, Moritz, five minutes before his last flight (*Imperial War Museum, London*)

Capt. Arthur R. Brown, who the Royal Air Force claimed killed Richthofen, and Maj. Lanoe G. Hawker, Richthofen's most famous victim *(Both from Imperial War Museum, London)*

British D.H. 2 "Spinning Incinerator," an antique by 1916, and British Sopwith Camel, fast and scrappy, but dangerous for inexperienced pilots *(Both from Imperial War Museum, London)*

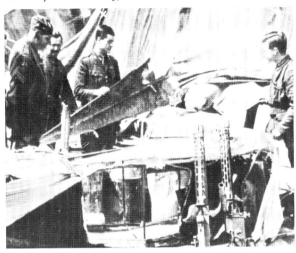

LEFT: Richthofen with his fur coat unbuttoned to show the Pour le Mérite *(Jagdgeschwader 71 Richthofen)* BELOW: Capt. Brown and Australian soldiers inspect Richthofen's cannibalized triplane *(West German Defense Ministry)*

Lieut. Werner Voss's Fokker triplane, one of the first two that reached the front; Richthofen flew the other *(Imperial War Museum, London)*

Col. Horst D. Kallerhoff, leade of today's Richthofen Wing sits under picture of Richtho fen and behind model of hi World War II Bf-109G *(Wi liam E. Burrows)*

RIGHT: Jasta 11 Albatros scouts lined up in the summer of 1917 *(Jagdgeschwader 71 Richthofen)*

BELOW: Albatros D III, fast, maneuverable, well-armed, and a favorite with Richthofen *(Imperial War Museum, London)*

BELOW: American-designed F-104G Starfighter of the Richthofen Wing. Inset: the unit's insigne, a red R over the NATO star on a white shield *(Jagdgeschwader 71 Richthofen)*

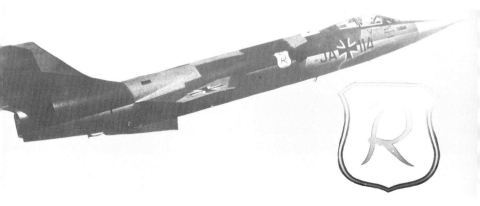

ABOVE: Richthofen's war trophies, including serial numbers from his kills, displayed in his room at Schweidnitz (*West German Defense Ministry*)

BELOW: Richthofen's grave in East Berlin's Invaliden Cemetery. The tombstone, pockmarked by bullets, stands a few feet from the Berlin Wall (*William E. Burrows*)

the Air Service, among others, had plans for Germany's champion air fighter.

Jasta 11 threw a farewell dinner for its leader on the night of April 29; appropriately, it was the day he put the most airplanes into his "bag." At eight o'clock, in the middle of the meal, and with his father again present, an orderly called Richthofen to the phone. It was high command headquarters, which passed on the following telegram: "I have just received the message that today you have been the victor of an air battle for the fiftieth time. I heartily congratulate you upon this marvelous success with my full acknowledgment. The Fatherland looks with thankfulness upon its brave flier. May God further preserve you. [Signed] Wilhelm." News of his fiftieth kill, which had been made only seven hours before, wasted no time in getting to the Imperial Palace. He repeated the message to the men looking at him from around the large table. There were cheers. His father, no longer able to suppress Prussian pride with Prussian modesty, told Manfred that it was all the more wonderful considering that the Kaiser must have more important things on his mind than sending telegrams to his fliers, even to his best fliers. Albrecht was right. The United States had entered the war twenty-three days earlier.

The high command now knew it could probably expect millions more enemy soldiers and tons of matériel at any time. At least one peace feeler had already been spurned by the Allies, raw materials were almost gone, Bolshevism was apparently taking hold in the streets, and some army and navy units seemed on the verge of mutiny. It was clear, even to the General Staff, that something had to be done quickly and decisively to prevent disaster. That day, April 29, the French army had the beginning of its own mutiny, which was not to be put down until July 5. Soldiers in several French units refused to relieve others at the front, sang revolutionary songs, waved red flags, threw stones at their own vehicles and depots, set fire to equipment, interfered with trains, and, in a few instances, attacked officers. When it was over, 110 instances of "grave indiscipline," affecting fifty-four divisions, had been brought before the courts-martial, which issued death sentences to 432 of 23,385 soldiers found guilty. Only fifty-five were shot. The rest were sent to penal colonies. Knowledge of the trouble on the French side of the trenches did nothing to make the Germans feel better, because rebellion was in the air, and could strike the Fatherland next. Communists *could* be used, however, if it was done in the right way. That was why Lenin's return to Russia was facilitated, and his reappearance accomplished what it was intended to: the revolution came on March 12, and Czar Nicholas II abdicated three days later. If the Russian army refused to continue the war, which was expected, German divisions tied down in the east could be moved west for a great offensive.

The Air Service had a plan, too. The day before Richthofen left for Germany, April 30, four scout squadrons—3, 4, 11, and 33—were sent into combat for the first time as a single unit. Since that unit had four times the firing power of one squadron, it was thought that Allied observers and bombers would be stopped more effectively. True, the larger units would be spread more thinly, leaving some sectors less protected than others, but if the telephone-alert system continued to work, it would not be a serious problem, the staff planners thought. The important thing now was to smash the growing formations of enemy airplanes with large, quick assaults. Individual squadrons' kill ratios, even Jasta 11's, were not proving sufficient to turn back what amounted to an aerial inundation. On that first day of the experiment, the four combined squadrons shot down six British airplanes in exchange for five of their own—not exactly an auspicious beginning. They tangled with new S.E. 5a's, Sopwith triplanes, and the reliably vulnerable F.E. 2's, which took the beating, the way they always had. But there was some consolation for the British. Many of their artillery spotters and bombers were able to work unmolested above the Battle of Arras, which had started on April 9, while a limited number of their comrades bore the brunt of the concerted German attacks. "Bloody April" would never come again.

Richthofen received another phone call on the night of April 30, this time to inform him that a briefing at General Staff headquarters, another at Air Service headquarters, lunch with the Kaiser, and a meeting with the Empress had been arranged for the beginning of his leave. He was expected at Air Service headquarters in Cologne at noon the next day. Richthofen planned to fly there in the back seat of a utility plane piloted by Lieutenant Krefft, who was also going on leave. After formally leaving Lothar in charge of the squadron,* and probably warning him not to do anything impetuous with it, Richthofen and Krefft took off into what looked like the start of a beautiful May Day. Clouds soon appeared, however, forcing Krefft to "feel" his way along the 200-mile route to Cologne by passing over Namur and Liége, in Belgium, and using the towns as geographical checkpoints. A straight line from Douai to Cologne passes over the southern tip of Holland, which was then neutral. The possibility of the Red Battle Flier's being interred for the duration of the war because of a forced landing there was too ridiculous to chance. The flight went perfectly, though, with Krefft and his passenger setting down at Cologne before noon. News of Richthofen's arrival had been announced the day before, along with his fifty-second victory, so he was greeted by city officials, screaming girls with flowers, entranced schoolboys, and some workers who had gotten the morning off to help welcome their hero. He saw and heard the cheering crowd before his airplane stopped. Situations not covered by the Prussian officer's code of manners tended to shake him. He pulled himself out of the cockpit, looked at the mob for a minute, and then, before the civilian dignitaries had gotten far into their speeches, said he

---

* Wolff, Allmenroeder, and Schaefer were all senior to Lothar, so it may be assumed that someone in the chain of command wanted another Richthofen in charge of Jasta 11 while Manfred was away.

was exhausted and begged a rest. He was taken to a nearby officers' club, where he slept for a while, trying to regain his composure. The man who had relentlessly pursued fame backed off, startled, when he finally caught up with it for a direct confrontation. He was genuinely embarrassed. After lunch, and still wearing the only uniform he had brought, he was taken to Air Service headquarters.

He met with General von Hoeppner, commander of the Air Service, for an exchange of information about scout tactics and the war in the air generally. It was undoubtedly at that meeting that he was given his first full briefing on the new system of grouping four scout squadrons into larger units. Each new group would be called a *Jagdgeschwader*, or hunting wing, and abbreviated as J.G. He was told that he would command the first of them. Jagdgeschwader 1 would be composed of Jastas 4, 6, 10, and his own 11. J.G. 1 would be given ample lorries or railroad cars so that its men, equipment, and corrugated metal huts could quickly be moved to within fifteen miles of whatever part of the front they were required to cover. The collection of assorted trucks and boxcars, the time spent "on the road," and J.G. 1's gaily painted and often outlandishly striped and polka-dotted airplanes were to prompt Royal Flying Corps pilots to nickname their opponents "Richthofen's Traveling Circus." It was a term of respect.

After the meeting with Hoeppner, Richthofen toured almost every department in the building, including "Airplanes," which recorded air victories, kept track of personnel, systematized the structure of all units, handled supply requirements, and dealt with technical problems, such as the Albatros's weak wing. One way or another, Richthofen touched on the interests and responsibilities of almost everyone in the building, and all of the "ink-spillers," as he called them, were anxious to meet or at least see him. The small staff of Department B of the Adjutant General's branch was particularly interested in meeting him, because they were responsible for intelligence and press, and they had a project for him. He was going to write his memoirs. A publisher had made the suggestion, and the Air Service thought it was a fine idea. Richthofen, by his own admission, had never been a good student, much less a man of letters. But he was assured that he would not have to produce a masterpiece, that his fellow countrymen simply wanted to know more about him, and that he could complete the small book at Schweidnitz before his six-weeks' leave was over. He would, in addition, be given a stenographer to speed along the manuscript. It would be sent to Department B in small sections for editing and censoring, and would then be published in magazine installments. Finally, it would all be put together in book form, a small paperback, to be sure, but it would nonetheless be *his* book—the memoirs of the world's greatest air fighter. Richthofen liked the idea because, among other reasons, proceeds would go to his family in case he was killed. If the war turned out badly, they would need that money.

Richthofen met Hindenburg the following morning at General Staff headquarters in Kreuznach. The Chief of the General Staff, the living symbol of the Prussian military caste, had a bull neck, heavily creased face, and eyes set above such large bags that they called for immediate sympathy. The mouth, almost hidden by four-inch-long white mustache tusks pointing optimistically upward, slowly uttered trivia for a few moments, and then reminded Richthofen that he was to lunch with the Kaiser. The newly promoted Captain was then led out of Hindenburg's office and into Ludendorff's anteroom. He felt uncomfortable again. Sitting in his wrinkled, field-gray uniform, he looked around the room at the small groups of generals and industrialists engaged in what he took for granted were conversations of supreme importance, and squirmed. He saw Balin, the shipping magnate, talking with a General Staff officer. Bethmann-Hollweg, the liberal Chancellor whose frustrating, losing battle with the military was to cause him to resign seventy-two days later, walked stolidly out of Ludendorff's office. After waiting an hour, Richthofen was led through another thick wooden door. The man behind it, looking anything but paternal, the way Hindenburg had, quickly asked him to sit down.

Ludendorff, a balding man who also wore an optimistic mustache, but one considerably shorter and darker than Hindenburg's, was officially the Quartermaster General of the army. Less officially, he was Hindenburg's assistant. Actually, he was the brains behind his country's war effort, and Hindenburg was its figurehead. Richthofen, slightly lulled by Hindenburg's benevolent chatter, and perhaps by that time thinking such was the way with the Fatherland's highest officers, found himself being sharply interrogated. "How is air activity over Arras?" asked Ludendorff, prefacing a series of direct, probing questions that instantly followed answers. Richthofen at first liked Ludendorff's businesslike manner, and was happy to be able to talk about something he was an expert on. He was also glad not to have to respond to more congratulations and say that yes, he felt fine and was anxious to return to the front for the Fatherland. He had the impression that such talk would have bored Ludendorff and, as a matter of fact, that the Quartermaster General was not overly impressed with his air victories. To illustrate his answers, however, Richthofen began wandering to personal anecdotes. He thought they would make his descriptions more interesting and easier to understand. They did the opposite. When he wandered too far, Ludendorff interrupted with a wave of the hand, and with obvious impatience brought him back to the subject. Half an hour later, Richthofen was mentally flinching, and was immensely relieved when he found that he had told Ludendorff as much as he wanted to hear. He was then politely, but quickly, dismissed.

Promptly at noon, Richthofen was presented to Kaiser Wilhelm II, who looked him over as though buying a horse. Standing in front of his emperor, and with his back to more glittering generals than he had ever seen, Richthofen remembered his wrinkled uniform and leather puttees, and was embarrassed again. Wilhelm was rather good-looking, with close-cropped gray hair and a shorter mustache than either of his top generals. He was about Richthofen's height and had a good physique, although he bulged in the middle, which may have been why he poked Richthofen's ribs and told him that he looked fat and happy. The Kaiser then congratulated Richthofen on his fifty-two kills, and on his twenty-fifth birthday, which was that day. He told Richthofen that he thought him a great asset to the Fatherland, and expressed the hope that he would live to more than double his kills and birthdays. The Captain thanked the Kaiser and added that nothing would make him happier than to return to the front and fight for the Fatherland. Wilhelm then presented a life-size bronze and marble bust of himself to Richthofen as a birthday present. Although it was not exactly what the future commander of the Flying Circus most needed, it was a souvenir of sorts, and could therefore be sent to Schweidnitz. After lunch, Wilhelm spent half an hour telling Richthofen about the newest types of antiaircraft guns, which bored the flier and even annoyed him. Scout pilots on both sides often felt that antiaircraft gunners claimed to destroy more airplanes than they hit and that most of their claims really belonged to the pilots. The meeting with the Kaiser finally ended, somewhat to Richthofen's relief, and he was off on another tour.

Hindenburg gave a dinner for him that night. The old gentleman, then sixty-nine, became nostalgic when he learned that he and Richthofen had both lived in Room 6 at the Wahlstatt cadet school. He told the pilot that he had recently given a picture of himself to the school in remembrance of the wonderful times he had had there playing at soldier. Richthofen must have groaned inwardly. Hindenburg also compared notes with him on the average number of shots necessary to kill a bison. Ludendorff was not present.

The next day, Krefft flew Richthofen to Bad Homburg, where the Empress waited on the royal estate's private airdrome to welcome him. He apologized for his leather flying suit, but she put him at ease and asked for a flying demonstration. He posed with the Empress, who wore a full-length dark dress with a fur collar and carried a matching parasol, while photographers took pictures. Then, while Her Highness watched from below, Richthofen flew the utility plane around the estate, landed, showed her how its engine worked, and then posed for more pictures with the ladies of the court. They went to lunch, where his hostess presented Richthofen with another birthday present—a gold cigarette case, trimmed in white enamel and inscribed with her name. He liked the Empress, whom he considered a grandmother type, and was actually sorry when she took her leave. The formalities were over. Krefft departed for his home. Richthofen, saying that his nerves were a little raw, flew to Freiburg for some hunting in the Black Forest.

No more official congratulations, formal dinners, awkward conversations with stuffy generals and their ladies, and no more tours of pale-green offices that smelled of varnish and were insulated against the real war by stacks of filing cabinets. Secure in the knowledge that no more bullets or trivia would come his way for weeks, Richthofen happily roamed through the thick trees and over the spongy leaf beds of a forest so dense that it blocked out the bright May sun. Alone, with rifle on his arm, he prowled over the dark hills that rise to the southeast until they become the Alps. The only sounds were those of the forest, and they were the music that Richthofen relaxed by in his splendid isolation. He stopped every once in a while to sit on a log, have a cigarette, look up at the branches that covered him, and listen to the subtle sounds—sounds that were a soothing change from the Albatros's 160-horsepower engine and Spandau machine guns. He was content to be alone with the small animals, game birds, and his thoughts.

While he was shooting in the Black Forest, Lothar was being

shot at—and down—over Vimy Ridge. On the evening of May 7, he dueled with the Royal Flying Corps's Albert Ball, who, like Lanoe Hawker, had the Victoria Cross and the Distinguished Service Order. Unlike Hawker, Ball had never flown for fun and had only one ambition—to become the greatest ace of the war. He preferred to fly alone, liked to strike quickly and daringly, and spent most of his free time working on his S.E. 5. When he was not flying it on patrols, he was testing it, and liked to throw newspapers out of the cockpit and shoot them full of holes as they drifted down. When he was not flying the fighter, he was tuning its guns, which he took to his room and cleaned as meticulously as game hunters like Richthofen cleaned prize shotguns. Ball's letters home usually mentioned other aces, British, French, and German, and how many more kills he needed to pass them. On the evening of May 7, 1917, with forty-four, Ball seemed well in contention for the title he wanted. He had Manfred von Richthofen's cold ambition and used tactics similar to Lothar's to try to make that ambition a reality.

May 7 was cloudy, which was why Lothar split Jasta 11 into three flights, instead of trying to keep everyone together as they wove through valleys walled with dark fluff. Ball, flying in a ten-scout patrol belonging to No. 56 Squadron, had the same idea, and also divided his group into three flights, which soon lost contact with each other in the fading light. Lothar's and Ball's flights ran into one another head on at about 7,000 feet, and after the first rushing attack, everyone picked an opponent and went into a free-for-all. A quarter of an hour later, during which the battle was joined by a SPAD from No. 19 Squadron and triplanes from the Royal Navy's No. 8 Squadron, Ball was seen fighting a lone Albatros. Both disappeared into low clouds and mist as the day became too dark for fighting and pilots on both sides began breaking off for home.

News broadcasts on German radio that night reported that Lieutenant von Richthofen had shot down an English triplane, killing its pilot, Captain Albert Ball. Lothar was officially credited with the victory, which made page one all over Germany the next day. Ball was indeed dead. But he had been flying a biplane, not a triplane, which could only have belonged to the Royal Navy. A German machine-gun crew positioned in a church steeple also put in a claim for Ball, but they were ignored. Lothar himself was unable to give a clear account of what happened after he flew into the clouds, because he, too, was shot down. After becoming lost in the mist, he was shot in the hip—probably by ground fire as he darted through the overcast—and, seeing his own blood, barely managed to land his Albatros before fainting. He was never thoroughly convinced that he shot down Ball, although his superiors seemed to be, and they authorized the press release accordingly. Although he claimed the English ace in his combat report, he questioned prisoners of war when he got out of the hospital in an effort to piece the battle together, but without success. Baroness von Richthofen had meanwhile received a telegram saying that Lothar was wounded, but not seriously, and Manfred was also notified.

After finishing his hunting, the older Richthofen spent three days at Adlershof, the airdrome near Berlin used for testing new airplanes, and then went home. Schweidnitz was proud of its war hero. He graciously accepted official welcomes, including one by the local Boy Scout group, and the respects of almost everyone in the town. Visitors, including many of his mother's friends who brought their unmarried daughters, came in a processional. Little boys followed the Red Battle Flier whenever he stepped outside, and Karl Bolko, home on vacation from Wahlstatt, found friends he never dreamed he had. Sanke cards were brought for autographing, and Richthofen gladly obliged all requests except one. He angrily refused to sign a pile of one hundred left by a woman who, he found out, planned to sell them for a mark apiece.

The stenographer came to help him with the book. She was

young, single, and attractive. Word quickly spread among the town's elderly ladies that Richthofen's interest in his house guest, whose work they were ignorant of, was romantic. His mother even chided him about the rumors, though with a tinge of genuine curiosity, but he laughingly denied them. He told his mother the truth. While walking with the stenographer one day, Germany's most eligible bachelor was stopped by two elderly women who showed more curiosity than Richthofen liked. Angry at being delayed and offended by the obvious prying, he suddenly smiled shyly, looked adoringly at his companion, and confided to the busybodies in mock seriousness that she was his bride. Then he pledged them to secrecy. Richthofen's "bride" acted her part as though she believed it.

There was little else to joke about during that leave. In a long conversation with his mother, he repeated what he had told her in May, 1915, about Germany's military position, and went so far as to say that it would probably lose the war. The Baroness was no longer surprised. She had been receiving letters from her sons for some time that praised the courage of German fighting men against overwhelming odds, but she had never read of any hope for victory. She coupled what she read between the lines of those letters with the growing scarcities of food and other domestic goods, and came to the right conclusion. But Manfred confirmed it in so many words. He would, of course, fight to the end, as would Lothar and, in his own way, their father. It was not a complicated decision. In fact, there was no decision. The politicians, the General Staff, and the Kaiser made the decisions affecting war and peace. The Richthofen men, and the thousands of other junior officers like them on all sides, would do as they were told. Everyone seemed to be doing as he was told, and there was never an alternative, since there was always someone above giving orders. The Richthofens would fight for their country until someone told them to stop, just the way everyone else would, and would try to make it a good war. The war *had* been good to the Richthofens, especially to Manfred, who was fulfilling his compulsion to hunt in its most dangerous, but rewarding, form. He had once confided to a friend that his greatest ambition was to become the most renowned scout pilot in Germany. He had done that. The decoration he most wanted, the Pour le Mérite, had come. The medals, captured fabric, and admirers attested to his prowess. The popular adulation, which he had never really thought about before it came, was a mixed blessing, because while it testified to his skill, it also violated the privacy he had always cherished. Worst of all, though, was the realization that glory had to be paid for, that he was suffering from more serious battle fatigue than anyone knew, and lived with the probability of dying in a lost war.

He would fight to the end. He had been taught to do that by the tradition into which he was born, and the lesson had been reinforced every day of his life. Being a soldier was not enough. There would be no soft instructor's job, no "ink-spilling." He had a title to defend, and the pride that was bred into him, in addition to his liking combat flying more than anything else, would drag him back into the dangerous skies over France, even though he knew that each time he went into a fight the odds of his coming out alive were less. He believed in his ability, but knew that Ball had had ability, too, and what happened to Ball could happen to him. There would be a time—on the thousandth or ten thousandth patrol—when having ability would not matter any more.

Richthofen drove to the Pless Estate, not far from Schweidnitz, on May 26, in acceptance of an invitation to hunt bison. He brought down his animal from eighty yards by grouping three bullets close to its heart. He would have liked to stay longer, but his leave had to be cut short and a planned tour of other fronts, such as Boelcke had made, canceled. Jagdgeschwader 1 was forming and needed him. He went from the Pless Estate to Adlershof, where he looked over the Albatros D V, an improved version of his D III, and from there, to Karl Schaefer's funeral in Krefeld.

The Sniper had been given command of Jasta 28 five days before Richthofen went on leave, and received his Pour le Mérite, after shooting down his twenty-fourth airplane, the day Richthofen flew to Cologne. Sixteen kills were still required for the decoration, but Bloody April's high scores had slowed their coming, since more pilots qualified than the high command had expected. Schaefer took a short leave to visit his parents after he received his decoration. On June 5, after thirty victories, he was killed in a fight with F.E. 2's of No. 20 Squadron. His loss deeply saddened Richthofen and undoubtedly added to his increasingly morbid view of the war. He flew from the funeral back to General Staff headquarters, where he was given a medal by the King of Bulgaria, and then started final planning for J.G. 1 with Colonel Thomsen.

Richthofen returned to Douai on June 14. That day, Karlchen Allmenroeder became the fourth member of Jasta 11 to receive a Pour le Mérite. Richthofen's pleasure in seeing Allmenroeder get his decoration was dampened four days later when he learned that his old flying companion Zeumer, "the Lunger," had been shot down and killed. There was little consolation in knowing that it was the way Zeumer had planned to go. Sergeant Major Festner, with twelve victories, was killed at about the same time.

The British assault on Arras had by then come to a halt. Many British squadrons were shifted north to support other army operations. Furthermore, the large Gotha long-range bombers, stationed near Ostend, had finally become operational. The day before Richthofen returned to Douai, seventeen of them bombed London's East End, killing 162 people, injuring 432, and doing more than £129,000 worth of damage. None of the Gothas were shot down, and the raid caused such a public outcry that S.E. 5's of No. 56 Squadron and Sopwith Pups of No. 66 Squadron had to be withdrawn from the front for home-defense duties at Calais and near London. The pickings around Douai therefore became lean, and, for once, the Germans outnumbered the

British in the air. Richthofen shot down an R.E. 8, killing both crewmen, on June 18, for his fifty-third victory. He then asked for permission to look for the British on northerly patrols toward Ypres, but the request was unnecessary. Jasta 11 was moved north, to just outside Courtrai, anyway, in preparation for the birth of J.G. 1. Richthofen used the occasion to switch from his Albatros D III to a D V. The newest model disappointed many pilots who thought it would be a great improvement on the D III. It was in some respects better—it could climb faster at low altitude—but it developed an evil reputation because of a lower wing that tended to break during long fast dives. Almost as disgruntling, it was not a mile an hour faster than the D III, although it weighed about a hundred pounds less.

Richthofen claimed his fifty-fourth airplane after a fight over the front lines near Ypres on the evening of June 23. He said it was a SPAD, and, since neither the British nor the French reported losing a SPAD that day, it is presumed to have been Belgian. Official confirmation of J.G. 1's existence came the following day in a telegram from Crown Prince Rupprecht's headquarters, saying that Jastas 4, 6, 10, and 11 would, from that day on, constitute Jagdgeschwader 1. A telegram the next day officially gave command to Rittmeister Manfred Freiherr von Richthofen. Another telegram came on the 26th, affirming that J.G. 1 was a self-contained unit under orders to maintain air supremacy wherever it was directed to do so. The Flying Circus, which was to become one of the most formidable and widely known air-combat groups in the world, was officially born on June 26, 1917. Its four squadrons ringed Courtrai, with Jasta 4 at Cuene, Jasta 6 at Bissegem, Jasta 10 at Heule, and Jasta 11 at Marcke, where Richthofen's headquarters were set up. He chose his subordinates carefully, and they reflected his growing ability to judge the best men for given jobs. Karl Bodenschatz, whom he had known in the Boelcke Squadron, was made adjutant, to handle Richthofen's paper work. Krefft was appointed the wing's technical officer, to be responsible for care of the airplanes, whose number varied, but averaged about forty-eight. Lieutenant Kurt von Doering, who had only three kills but showed cool leadership ability, was given command of Jasta 4. Lieutenant Eduard von Dostler, a Bavarian with a reputation for strict military discipline and courage, got Jasta 6. Jasta 10 was given to another baron, Ernst von Althaus, a Pour le Mérite winner and the son of the adjutant to the Duke of Saxe-Coburg-Gotha. Immediate command of Richthofen's Jasta 11 went to Kurt Wolff, one of the last of the old-timers, and another holder of the Pour le Mérite.

Allmenroeder shot down his thirtieth and last victim on June 26, and was killed the next day by a long-range burst from the guns of Raymond Collishaw, the Royal Navy ace. Allmenroeder's last days were bitter ones. His brother, Willi, had earlier in the year forced down an English pilot who, after surrendering, shot up at the circling German and wounded him so badly that he was unfit for further flying. Karlchen was so angry at what he considered a violation of the code of chivalry that he began to fly with a vengeance and died despising the English.

Richthofen led Jasta 11 into a clear sky on the morning of July 6 after a report came in that six F.E. 2's were observing over the German positions. The British airplanes quickly formed a circle when the Germans arrived, setting up a wheel of fire that kept the Albatroses at a distance. Then more German scouts entered the fight, followed by Royal Navy triplanes, and a melee developed. Four Germans were shot down, along with two F.E. 2's, as the British tried to get back to their lines. One of the British airplanes, piloted by Captain D. C. Cunnell, was about 300 yards from an all-red Albatros when its gunner, Second Lieutenant A. E. Woodbridge, began shooting at it. Richthofen saw that he was under fire, but, because he was well out of effective range, it did not worry him and he kept probing for an opening. Woodbridge, who said later that flying F.E. 2's against Albatroses was like sending butterflies out to insult eagles, stood up in his cockpit and kept firing at the red Albatros.

The F.E. 2 and the Albatros then came at one another head on. Woodbridge continued his steady fire, but the German was now firing back. Woodbridge could see his tracer bullets hitting along the barrels of the German's machine guns, and he knew that there was a head right behind them. Richthofen's bullets were also finding their target, however, and tore holes in the F.E. 2. Then Woodbridge saw the red Albatros suddenly nose down, pass under him, and slip into a spin. It turned over several times, apparently out of control, and fell. Neither Englishman knew that Richthofen was in the falling scout, but as they circled and watched it drop out of sight, they knew for certain that its pilot was not faking. Woodbridge thought he had hit the German in the head. That is exactly where he hit him.

NINE · IMMORTALLY WOUNDED

"Wounded vanity knows when it is mortally hurt; it limps off the field, piteous, all disguises thrown away. But pride carries its banner to the last."

—HELEN HUNT JACKSON,
Ramona

There was pain, and beyond the pain there was dark fog; beyond the fog, a spinning sensation that brought nausea, and beyond that, a single, flickering thought: "This is how it feels when you're shot down to your death."

The scarlet Albatros was not badly damaged, but it was uncontrolled, so it spun down from 12,000 feet like a dying autumn leaf. It spun around with the man slumped inside, but he did not care, at least at first. He knew he was badly hurt, but did not know how badly, because the wound was in his head. Besides, no matter how hard he tried, he could not see. The nerves between his brain and his arms and legs were paralyzed, and the blood in his eyes prevented him from seeing. He could think, however, so he thought about the Albatros's wings and wondered whether they would break off. If they did, the airplane would drop straight down and end everything in a pile of wood, wire, and red linen, like Boelcke. The Albatros kept falling, and the man inside felt absolutely alone in the air for the first time, which helped him to fight for his life.

Richthofen struggled to make his arms and legs move. He blindly reached for the gasoline valve, eased it back, and heard the engine stop. Then he tore off his goggles, forced open his eyes, and tried to look toward the sun. He saw nothing. His head felt wet, and he guessed that it was blood, but was still not sure. The Albatros came out of its spin every once in a while, only to start again within seconds, and he figured that it had already spun down 9,000 feet. "I must see," he told himself over and over again as he fought to regain control. Then he began to pick out black and white shapes, and when he looked toward the sun once more, he saw it as though through dark glasses. It did not hurt to look right at it. The blur in front of him slowly sharpened until it looked like an instrument panel. He focused on the altimeter, which showed about 1,000 feet. His arms and legs began to respond, and he worked them until the Albatros came out of its spin, and then looked for a place to land. He had to land quickly, because he knew he was in shock and was afraid of passing out. Hundreds of shell holes passed underneath him. He looked farther ahead, ignoring the blood that ran down his neck, soaking his scarf and the Pour le Mérite at his throat.

He recognized the shape of a small forest and knew he was on his own side of the lines. Two Jasta 11 pilots, Lieutenants Brauneck and Niederhoff, had seen the scarlet Albatros fall, and they circled around it all the way down. They continued circling their leader as his airplane tore through telephone wires and made a bounding, but right-side-up, landing beside a road. Richthofen climbed out of the cockpit and fell, half unconscious, into thorn bushes. He lay there, too weak to move, with his eyes closed and blood continuing to stream from a long hole in his leather helmet.

A lieutenant in an air-observation post about a mile away had seen Richthofen's fall through his telescope and rushed to the spot under the two circling scouts. When he and a corporal reached Richthofen, they found him unconscious. After opening his collar and taking off the soaked helmet, they applied a field dressing to the wound. Woodbridge's bullet had left a four-inch crease in Richthofen's head, furrowing deeply enough so that, after the blood was washed off, his skull was plainly visible. So were several bone splinters. While the enlisted man ran for a field telephone, more soldiers arrived. Richthofen regained consciousness and was offered cognac. He declined it in favor of water. By the time an ambulance came, the Red Battle Flier was deathly white, running a high temperature, and feeling successively hot and cold. When the ambulance reached Menin, the site of the nearest aid station, he asked where he was. The medical officer, junior in rank and knowing who he was, told him. Richthofen then insisted on being taken to the hospital in Courtrai, having weighed the superior medical facilities there against the time lost. The doctor shrugged compliance, and the ambulance was off again.

The best German army doctors in the area were waiting for Richthofen when he arrived at St. Nicholas's Hospital, which the Germans had taken over for their casualties. The attendant who shaved his head before surgery sliced off the ends of a cluster of thorns that had become imbedded when he fell into the bushes. They had to be pulled out, as well as the bone splinters, and contributed to what he called "a deadly headache" that lasted for days. He was given his own nurse, a pretty brunette named Katie Otersdorf, at least partly in the hope that she would help ease the Rittmeister's "headache." As his recuperation progressed, word spread around the hospital that the nurse and her patient, both of whom took short walks in the hospital's garden, were becoming serious about one another. The thought of the Fatherland's greatest war hero falling in love with the dark-eyed woman who nursed him back to health was a heart-warming rumor, and persists to this day, but it was untrue.

So, for that matter, was the even stronger rumor that Richthofen secretly corresponded with a girl he loved too much to marry for fear of making her a widow. As soon as he pulled in after a patrol, the story went, his orderly would rush up with one delicately scented letter taken from the dozens that came every day. He would then go off by himself and devour every word before pouring out his own heart by return mail. The mystery girl's letters were supposedly even routed to his hospital bed and gave him the will to fight more tenaciously for recovery. The couple's love was never consummated, the story said, because he did not want to dishonor his maiden or leave her with an illegitimate child. Their letters have never been found, those who believe the story say, because Prussian honor forbade Richthofen's family to identify his sweetheart, and she sank into obscurity rather than share his letters with the world. Still others say a son was born to the couple, who is alive today, but does not know his father's name.

Good friends of Richthofen's, like Lieutenant Hans Georg von der Osten, who joined Jasta 11 in August, 1917, and who now lives in Cologne, insist that the rumors were nonsense. Richthofen treated all women with profound respect, but was indifferent to them romantically and never had a sweetheart.

News of the Red Battle Flier's having been shot down was withheld from the public on the supposition that already sagging morale would be further affected when it became known that both Richthofens were languishing in hospitals at the same time. Lothar's hip wound was almost healed, however, and he was preparing to return to Jasta 11. Less than a week after he was admitted to St. Nicholas's, Manfred was able to sit up in frogged silk pajamas to be photographed (with publication officially embargoed) and sketched by an artist. Letters and telegrams wishing him a fast recovery came from family and friends, along with the usual fan mail, which was rerouted from Marcke. The Rittmeister, as he was called by his comrades, was visited by several members of the squadron, and was briefed on developments at the front by Lieutenant Wilhelm Reinhard and Doering, the leader of Jasta 4, who took over J.G. 1 hours after Richthofen was shot down. The members of J.G. 1's four squadrons were in a state of disbelief after they heard the news on the night of the

6th, but they had gone up in strength the next day and shot down nine Allied airplanes, which, they liked to think, was in revenge for what had happened to their leader. Kurt Wolff was given command of Jasta 11 when Doering moved up to take over the wing, and he had been the first to score on the morning of the 7th, bringing down his thirty-third plane. Four days later, he was shot in the left hand during a dogfight, and wound up in the bed next to Richthofen's.

The man who sat up in bed next to Wolff having his picture taken was vastly different from the one who had gone into that air battle on the 6th. He looked thirty-five, instead of twenty-five, and had become quieter. He stared blankly at the walls or out the windows from under his bandages and was moody and pensive. When he ordered his fifty-third through fifty-seventh cups from the Berlin jeweler, it was not with enthusiasm as much as because he thought he might as well finish what he had started so long before. Less than two months later, the jeweler would regretfully have to inform Freiherr von Richthofen that the sixty-first cup, representing a Sopwith Pup, would have to be made out of ersatz metal because of war shortages. Richthofen would take the opportunity to stop ordering the trophy cups, so his collection ended with the sixtieth, an R.E. 8 whose pilot was captured and whose gunner was killed. When his father came to the hospital, Richthofen put on his double-breasted gray tunic, fastened the right side's column of six shiny brass buttons, picked up his carved walking stick (walking sticks were in vogue then, along with holding small dogs in formal photographs) and went into the garden. Another picture was taken. More pictures were taken when members of the squadron came to present their leader with what they thought was a souvenir that would cheer him up —a seven-foot propeller from a downed observation plane. He also posed for photos with Katie Otersdorf, Lieutenant Reinhard, and others.

While he smiled confidently as the shutters clicked, his thoughts increasingly returned to the morning of July 6, and to his torn head. The wound had to be opened at least twice in the hospital and several times afterward for removal of splinters, leaving more headaches and reminders of that fight. The feeling of doom that he had hinted at while at home in Schweidnitz intensified. There could have been no doubt in his mind as he lay in that hospital that Germany was going to lose the war. British and French airplanes were being made faster than they could be shot down. And, he reflected, the chances of his being killed by any one of those thousands of enemy airplanes were becoming excellent. He began to feel vulnerable for the first time, and although he was still sure that he had the advantages of better training, more experience, and superior equipment than the men he fought, he began to think about the element of luck more than he had before. But, he concluded, as long as his equipment was better, luck would have to be pushed to its limit. On July 20, Sergeant Major Kurt Wustoff, the son of a Dresden orchestra leader, shot down one of five airplanes claimed by J.G. 1 that day, and noted in his report that it was a new Sopwith. The Camel had arrived.

Richthofen preferred the front to the hospital and, after losing a few arguments with his doctors, finally received permission to return to J.G. 1 on July 25. He was welcomed by his squadron-mates, who toasted and cheered him, and by his old friends in the Royal Flying Corps's No. 100 Squadron, who dropped a 230-pound bomb near some hangars that evening. The British did not know that the Jolly Red Baron had been wounded, though, and were merely resuming night bombing of the Circus, which was their favorite target. Earlier that evening, many separate dogfights had started along the front, until about a hundred airplanes were tangling over Polygon Wood in one of the biggest air battles of the war. Jasta 11 scored no victories and lost Lieutenant Brauneck. The British were hitting the Imperial Air Service as hard as they could in preparation for the Battle of Ypres, which was to start on July 31. No. 56 Squadron's fighters went after the Germans in the air during the day, and No. 100 Squadron's bombers went after them on the ground at night. After

Ypres began, No. 56 Squadron also attacked J.G. 1 on the ground, and for the first time strafed the airdromes where the Albatroses were kept, on the reasonable assumption that the more Germans who could be prevented from getting into the air, the fewer British pilots would fall. The Circus spent the last week of July losing several pilots in combat and scoring erratically. That was why, when Althaus was sent to be an instructor in scout school after three years of combat, Richthofen replaced him as leader of Jasta 10 with Lieutenant Werner Voss, the son of a Krefeld dye manufacturer and an old friend from the Boelcke Squadron, which he had joined when he was nineteen. Voss and Lieutenant Ernst Udet, another future Circus star, who at that time commanded Jasta 37, not far from Ostend, were born pilots who became among the most skilled in the Air Service. Richthofen, on the other hand, was not a superb pilot and was never inclined to "mix it up" in fights. He preferred to go by the book—Boelcke's book—and scorned everything else as trick flying. Going by the book meant making almost surgical kills: a pouncing, slicing attack, flying quickly out of enemy machine-gun range if the pounce was beaten off, and then regrouping and pouncing again. The idea behind scout flying, he kept telling newcomers, was to shoot down as many airplanes as possible, and not to fly upside down because it was fun. He was, of course, right. Nonetheless, he tended to use the Dicta of Boelcke to mask a certain lack of imagination in new situations.

Not so with Voss, who became a pilot in May, 1916, and who also studied under Boelcke. Richthofen and Voss had been friends since those formative days in the autumn of 1916, and Richthofen occasionally went to Voss's home in Krefeld for short leaves, while Voss at other times was put up at Schweidnitz. There was even talk of a romance between Voss's sister and Richthofen, but, like the other rumors, it was unfounded. If the two pilots were friends, they were also scoring rivals, so the friendship was tinted by professional jealousy. Voss became convinced that he was better than Richthofen after an incident that happened in the beginning of that past April. Captain Walz, the leader of the Boelcke Squadron, was supposed to have flown to Richthofen's squadron for a meeting. He was ill that day, however, so he delegated Voss to go in his place. When the meeting was over, Richthofen offered to fly back to Jasta 2 with Voss, and, glad for the company, Voss accepted. The two aces saw a flight of Sopwith 1½ Strutters at 3,000 feet, and, without signaling to Voss, Richthofen dove to attack. Since Voss thought that Richthofen would make the kill quickly, and since the other observation planes scattered, he circled above and watched. He saw Richthofen hit the Sopwith's gunner on his first pass and then shoot the airplane's fuel tanks, controls, and even the instruments in the pilot's cockpit, but apparently without being able to hit the pilot. Richthofen eventually shot down the Britisher, but not without difficulty, as Voss watched the repeated attempts with growing amazement. From then on, Voss believed he was a better pilot than Richthofen, which was true, and thought he was a better marksman, which was not true. Richthofen was ordinarily an excellent shot, but had had a bad day.

Voss landed between the trenches the next day to pull the machine gun out of a B.E. 2 he had shot down. He threw the proof of his kill into the cockpit of his Albatros, burned the British airplane, and took off between large shell holes. He was awarded the Pour le Mérite on April 8, 1917, and on May 20, after having scored twenty-eight kills, was given command of Jasta 5. He was made leader of Jasta 29 on July 7, and a week before Richthofen selected him for the Circus had been sent to Jasta 14 to lead it to some badly needed victories. Werner Voss, the young ace and prodigy, was building a reputation surpassed only by the Rittmeister. He wore old clothes around the airdrome, but always flew in a silk shirt and his best uniform, explaining that if he was taken prisoner, he wanted to look his best for the ladies he would meet. The Albatros he used in Jasta 5—his most famous—had a beige fuselage, purple-and-green upper wings, and a white tail and underwings. It also had a red nose and a red heart on each side of the fuselage. Voss had green laurel wreaths, symbolizing victory, painted between the hearts, which were under his cockpit, and the black Maltese crosses near the tail. The insides of the wreaths were decorated with white Greek crosses, bent at the ends, which were also used by American Indians and are believed to have been ancient sun symbols. The insigne, as a German symbol, was to outlive Voss.*

The first week of August, 1917, was wet. Flanders' fields, both trenches and airdromes, were too muddy for operations. Richthofen caught up on administrative work and went back to St. Nicholas's to have more splinters taken out of his head. He had frequent spells of dizziness and nausea, but by the end of the second week in August wanted to get back into the air. The weather cleared enough by the 14th for patrols to be sent up, and Reinhard shot down his third and fourth that day. Voss scored the following day, and again the day after that, bringing his official kill list to thirty-seven. Only two men had shot down more airplanes than Voss by August 16, 1917, and one of them, Oswald Boelcke with forty, was no longer in competition. Richthofen not only wanted to see whether he had kept his touch, but also felt Voss pressing him for the ace-of-aces title, and therefore he took off on the morning of August 16 for his first patrol since July 6. No sooner had he gone into the air than the sick feeling returned, but he overcame it and continued hunting until he saw a lone Nieuport. After stalking for several minutes, he eased into firing position, squeezed the trigger, and watched his fifty-eighth victim falter, spin away, and crash into the slime below. The nausea came back, but he returned to Marcke consoled that he was still able to score.

There was a party the next night for Lieutenant von der Osten, a newcomer to Jasta 11, who had shot down his first enemy that

---

* An Albatros flown by Lieutenant Billick, of Jasta 12, was decorated with a large swastika, as was at least one of the Gotha bombers in the England Squadron. Voss's reason for choosing the insigne is not known, nor are those of the others.

evening. Parties for first kills were practically unheard of, but Jasta 11 made an exception for the happy fledgling, because his victim was also the squadron's 200th. Ludendorff came to review Jasta 11 the following day, the 18th, and congratulations poured in. It was a morale booster that Jasta 11 and its parent wing, J.G. 1, needed, because, although they were outscoring every other unit in the Air Service, opposition was improving in quantity and quality. But there seemed to be an answer for that, too, and it arrived on August 28. The first two production models of Anthony Fokker's triplane were delivered that day, with one going to Richthofen and the other to Voss. The Rittmeister had his painted scarlet, of course, while Voss had his streaked with blue over silver and had a mustached face painted on its flat nose. The face looked like Hindenburg frowning.

Pilots who thought they finally had a scout that could fly faster than the S.E. 5a's 120 miles an hour were disappointed. The new Fokker's maximum speed at 13,000 feet was 102½ miles an hour, which was even slower than the Albatros's. But it could climb to 10,000 feet in eleven minutes, as opposed to the Albatros's twelve and a half, which was vitally important for an interceptor that had to take off and quickly reach its prey. Best of all, the Fokker triplane's three wings grabbed the air so well that it became the tightest turning scout at the front, with the possible exceptions of the Sopwith triplane and the Camel. Several pilots in Jastas 10 and 11 test-flew their leaders' triplanes within hours of their arrival and were impressed with the stubby scouts' maneuverability. Richthofen came to prefer the Dr. I * for its handling qualities but never liked it as much as many writers have said. He still leaned toward the Albatros D V for its speed and diving characteristics. Voss made a hobby out of caring for his triplane, and often helped his mechanics tune its engine, tighten cables, test and zero-in its two Spandaus, and patch holes. He shot down his thirty-eighth victim in the Fokker on August 30, and

---

* Dr. stood for *Dridekker,* or three-winger.

was followed three days later by Richthofen, who pulled up close to an R.E. 8 and fired only twenty rounds into it at point-blank range before it fell. The British observer had seen Richthofen coming, but apparently mistook the Fokker for a Sopwith triplane, and never got off a shot.

Jasta 11, still flying Albatroses except for Richthofen's Dr. I, shot down ten British airplanes on September 3, for one of its best days since Bloody April. The Rittmeister shot down his sixty-first, a Sopwith Pup, and Voss got his thirty-ninth, another Pup. On September 5, the day before Richthofen left Marcke for convalescent leave, Voss shot down another Pup at 3:50 P.M. and a French Caudron at 4:30. Five days later, while the ace of aces was hunting elk at Gotha, Voss destroyed three British airplanes in thirty minutes, bringing his score to forty-five. The last month of Werner Voss's life was, by his standards, the best. Richthofen, meanwhile, stayed at the new, large Schloss Hotel, which he used as a base for his elk-hunting. He wrote the following to his mother on September 30:

"I was extremely glad to hear of Lothar's sudden recovery. On my return from leave, we can go up together and show the English a few tricks. We will be in the same squadron.

"My bag during the last two weeks has been far from bad—a large elk, three excellent stags, and a buck. I am rather proud of my record, because Papa has only shot three stags in all of his life. I am leaving for Berlin today and will be with you in less than a week."

Richthofen spent a week in Berlin. He visited Adlershof to look over new scout designs, and created excitement wherever he went in the capital city. Girls stared more wistfully than ever, boys followed him, and people were always pushing and shoving to shake his hand or get autographs. He tolerated the show of adulation but did not like it. He visited "hospitality" suites set up by airplane manufacturers for airmen on leave. There, in Berlin's best hotels, the aviators were supplied with free wine, women, and music. The Red Battle Flier would walk in and sit alone, sipping his wine. He stared icily at pilots with open tunics or unfastened collars, and many with girls on their laps had to button up before the Rittmeister's eyes left them to wander elsewhere. The music seemed to lessen while Richthofen was in the room, and decorum was put aside only after he had closed the door behind him. It was all very well for those aviators to lose themselves in hotel rooms, but Richthofen could not pretend to join them, not even if he had wanted to. He was a Prussian and a national hero and would therefore not do such things in public places. Furthermore, the wine and women could not ease the burdens of command, and certainly could not prevent death, so what was their use? In addition, he had been in almost daily contact with J.G. 1 since he left, and had had one piece of bad news after another. Kurt Wolff, with thirty-three victories, had been shot down on September 15 while flying Richthofen's triplane. He was ambushed by Camels of No. 10 Squadron, Royal Navy, and went down behind a flaming engine before Jasta 11's Albatroses could help him. The burning engine caused the red Fokker's gas tank to explode when it hit the ground, which Richthofen neglected to mention in the obituary he wrote for the newspapers.

Eight days later, Werner Voss was killed, after scoring his forty-eighth victory, in what has been called the most heroic air fight of the war. Late on the afternoon of the 23rd, he was looking for his forty-ninth as he neared Ypres at 18,000 feet. When he saw six two-man Bristol fighters, escorted by S.E. 5's, he picked one of the latter and dropped on it. As he started to fire, something made him look behind, and he saw that another flight of S.E. 5's, B Flight of No. 56 Squadron, was closing on him. The new arrivals were led by Captain James McCudden, who was soon to return to England with fifty-seven kills and a Victoria Cross, and comprised five more of the Royal Flying Corps's best fighter pilots. No. 56 Squadron, which was Jasta 11's long-time antagonist, had a galaxy of stars equivalent to the Circus pilots. Voss turned, dropped into a half-spin, and found himself surrounded. He had noticed a flight of Camels several thousand feet below, so flying in that direction was impossible. Instead, he decided to fight it out with B Flight, which by that time had formed a circle around him. Thinking that Voss was trapped, McCudden got on his tail twice, but before the English marksman could fire, the silver-and-blue triplane in front of him twisted away, broke out of the circle, turned, and came back in again, putting bullets through the S.E. 5's that it passed. When Voss returned to the center of the wheel, five fighters converged on him, all firing their machine guns. The triplane with the mustached face came out again, this time full of holes—it was a measure of its pilot's ability that it came out at all—and went back in. When Voss saw a flight of Albatroses, he flew toward them in an apparent effort to lead them back to the British, but all of the Germans except one sped in the other direction. The pilot who tried to help Voss was killed immediately. Another group of Albatroses appeared and tried to reach Voss, but they were cut off by SPAD's and Camels, again leaving him on his own. Seven British fighters and one German slowly drifted over Allied lines as Second Lieutenant A. P. F. Rhys-Davids, who had by then gotten under Voss, fired his wing-mounted Lewis gun up into the Fokker's belly. He had to empty two ammunition drums into the triplane before it stopped maneuvering violently. Then Rhys-Davids climbed above his crippled victim and shot into its cockpit. The Fokker slowed so much that he almost collided with it, but he kept firing until both airplanes reached 1,000 feet, when the triplane, torn to shreds, stalled and fell. Voss had, however, put holes in each of his seven opponents.

"As long as I live," said McCudden, "I shall never forget my admiration of that German pilot, who, single-handed, fought seven of us for ten minutes, and also put some bullets through all of our machines. His flying was wonderful, his courage magnificent, and, in my opinion, he was the bravest German airman whom it has been my privilege to fight." Voss was buried by the British with full military honors.

Wolff's and Voss's deaths weighed on Richthofen, who again looked tired and disheartened when he arrived at Schweidnitz. He told his mother that if Russia left the war, enough troops and airplanes could be sent to the western front to turn the tide, but she did not believe it any more than he did. It seemed to Baroness von Richthofen in October, 1917, that every time she picked up a newspaper, she read the obituary of one of the young pilots her son had brought home. And while Manfred slept among the serial numbers and pieces of propeller in his room or put the finishing touches on his book, she wondered if she would ever see him again after his return to the front. She thought frightening things that could not be discussed with Manfred, and the probability of his death was chief among them. Her oldest son's life, emotionally as well as physically, had been planted by his father. It was nurtured by a strict tradition that three years before had seemed infallible, but which was now crumbling to ruin, perhaps forever. Manfred had pushed his life to its climax on undercurrents of passion that were so strong they were almost animate, but which, strangely, she could not fully account for. She was proud of him, so proud, in fact, that she took her problems to him before consulting her husband. She relied heavily on his strength and wisdom, even concerning problems in the large white house, domestic problems. Father and son were equally far from Schweidnitz, but when the Baroness had a problem that seemed unsolvable, she wrote or telegraphed Manfred. A closeness had always existed between mother and son, but it was not close enough to allow the mother to make sense out of the forces that appeared to be leading her son to destruction.

Richthofen finished his book and sent it to the Intelligence and Press Department at Air Service headquarters. There, it was carefully edited and censored and prepared as magazine articles before being sent to the book publisher. It appeared in book form that winter as a 185-page, yellow-covered paperback, showing a red Fokker triplane victorious over a smoking foe, and

entitled *Der röte Kampfflieger* (*The Red Battle Flier*).* Parts
of Richthofen's passages dealing with his frailties, such as his
recollection of hiding under the blanket during the British
bombing attack at Douai, were left in to keep him as human as
possible. It is, in fact, remarkable that his reference to Lothar as
a "shooter" was left alone, especially in the context he meant it,
which equated with "butcher." Other passages, however, were
written either by Richthofen or his editors for pure propaganda.
The most outstanding example is this one: "I am not out for
breaking records. Besides, generally speaking, we of the Air
Service do not think of records at all. We merely think of our
duty." That passage, which is blatantly false, is all the more interesting because thousands of the 500,000 copies of the first print-
ing of *The Red Battle Flier* went to German soldiers in the
trenches, which may explain this: "Had I not become a professional chaser (scout, or pursuit pilot), I should have turned an
Infantry (support) flier. After all, it must be a very satisfactory
feeling to be able to aid troops whose work is hardest. The infantry flier can do a great deal to assist the man on foot. His is a very
grateful task." And: "I dare say many an airman has shouted
Hurrah! as, after an assault, he saw the hostile masses (enemy
infantry) stream back when our smart infantry jumped from the
trenches and fought the aggressors eye to eye. Many a time, after
a chasing expedition, I have fired my remaining cartridges into
the enemy trenches. Although I may have done little practical
good, such firing affects the enemy's morale." The General Staff
apparently thought that the men in the trenches should be
reminded that their air force *was* fighting an honorable and

---

* All of the quotations from Richthofen in this book dealing with his
childhood, training, and combat experiences, except those from letters
to his mother, are from his book, and were carefully judged for veracity
before inclusion. The letters were taken from Gibbons' *The Red Knight
of Germany*, because the originals were at Schweidnitz when the Red
Army overran it in 1944 and are apparently lost.

heroic battle, too. Copies of *The Red Battle Flier* turned up in London, where it was translated and published, with the title *The Red Air Fighter*, in mid-1918 by "The Aeroplane" & General Publishing Co., Ltd. A preface to the English edition, written by C. G. Grey, the editor of *The Aeroplane* magazine, said that while Richthofen's narrative was "extraordinarily interesting," it was obviously "touched up here and there for propagandistic purposes." But allowing for the propaganda, Grey continued, "which gives one the general impression of the writings of a gentleman prepared for publication by a hack journalist, one forms a distinctly favorable mental picture of the young Rittmeister Manfred Freiherr von Richthofen." Richthofen's own family was not as charitable, and insisted privately that Manfred's writing had been reworked and made into the diary of a killer. Hans Georg von der Osten says emphatically that Richthofen did not write any of the finished product, but he has no idea who did.

Toward the middle of October, when Richthofen was preparing to leave Schweidnitz and return to the front, he was warned by General Staff headquarters to take good care of himself and think about becoming an adviser, instead of continuing to fight. He was asked, but since his fighting talents were by that time needed as much as his aeronautical knowledge, he was not ordered. Furthermore, Richthofen was only headline news when he shot down enemy airplanes, and his practical and propagandistic uses accrued from that. No one at General Staff headquarters was upset, then, when Richthofen replied to their warning with this memorandum: "I should indeed consider myself a despicable person if, now that I have achieved fame and wear many decorations, I should consent to exist as a pensioner of my dignity and to preserve my life for the nation, *while every poor fellow in the trenches* [my italics]—who is doing his duty equally as much as I—has to stick it out." He returned to the front to take command of J.G. 1 on October 23. His memorandum to the General Staff was released to the press at about the same time.

Six days later, Lieutenant Heinrich Gontermann, nicknamed "The Balloon Specialist" for his attacks on observation balloons, and the leader of Jasta 15, was doing aerobatics at 1,500 feet when his triplane was seen to go out of control. Its upper wing broke apart. Thus the pilot who in ten months had destroyed eighteen balloons and twenty-one airplanes was killed in his second flight in one of the new Fokkers. The next accident came two days later at Jasta 11, which had received six triplanes in the middle of October. One of them, flown by Lieutenant Pastor, broke apart the way Gontermann's had, again killing its pilot. The triplanes were immediately grounded and examined. When the fabric covering the upper wings of Gontermann's and Pastor's scouts was cut away, it was seen that dampness had weakened the wings' structural joints. It was blamed on poor workmanship in Anthony Fokker's factory. The wings on existing triplanes were stripped and strengthened, those on Fokker's production line modified, and the scouts were put back in service at the end of November. Richthofen had meanwhile gone back to an Albatros and had, in fact, wrecked his second triplane the day before Pastor was killed. While flying with Lothar, who had only recently returned to combat, Manfred saw his brother suddenly drop into a steep dive. Since there were no enemy airplanes around, he followed Lothar low enough to watch him make an emergency landing, which, it turned out, was because of engine trouble. Manfred also landed, but caught a wheel in a hole, which brought his triplane to a crashing stop. The Rittmeister walked away, but his Fokker was a total loss.

The infantry's problems made Richthofen's seem small in comparison. German soldiers looking out of their trenches and into the mist at 6:30 A.M. on the morning of November 20 were horrified to see steel boxes rumbling toward them. They shot at the boxes without effect and then saw the barbed wire that separated them from the British flattened into the mud as the first tanks used en masse in war came at them. During the next four hours, almost 400 tanks rolled over the barbed wire and trench networks of the Hindenburg Position along a six-mile front, causing the Germans to abandon it and drop back three to four miles. The Battle of Cambrai was on. Since the British had not spent days pounding German positions to "soften" them before the assault, the way they usually did, the German army was caught off balance. The British, however, did not suppose that their tanks would be as successful as they proved, and were therefore also caught off balance by not having enough reinforcements behind them to continue the offensive. Three days later, the British had moved five miles—to within three miles of Cambrai itself—but that was as far as they were going to get. The Germans quickly assembled twenty divisions to plug the hole, and at 8:30 A.M. on November 30—the day Richthofen wrecked his triplane—they counterattacked. The British withdrew during the night of December 4-5 to the positions they had taken on the first day. But the German attack stalled, too, when Crown Prince Rupprecht came to the conclusion that he did not have enough men to push the British back any farther. Casualties on both sides during the two-week-long Battle of Cambrai came to about 45,000 men.

The day after the British attack, German army headquarters, in a state of panic, ordered J.G. 1 to Cambrai to provide support and air cover for its men in the mud. Other air groups were ordered to strafe the British. Since the three airfields that were supposed to be used by J.G. 1's four squadrons could not be made ready in time, the Circus moved to a training field at Valenciennes, about twenty miles from the front, and was flying on the 22nd. The next day—the first anniversary of Richthofen's victory over Lanoe Hawker—he forced down one British D.H. 5 out on a troop-strafing mission, and shot another out of the air. Lothar, leading a flight of Jasta 11 Albatroses, brought down a Bristol the same day. A week later, Manfred shot down his sixty-third plane, an S.E. 5 whose pilot was killed. Then air fighting slowed as winter set in.

Manfred von Richthofen thought about the hopes and plans

he had had as Christmas approached the year before. He had gotten everything he wanted in 1917, but, now that the year was almost over, his perspective on glory had changed, and he was not certain that it was worth the cost. Christmas, 1917, was going to be very different from the others. He would not find as much to hope for on his last Christmas.

TEN · PHOENIX FALLS

"What a man he was! The others, admittedly, were doing their share, but they had wives at home, children, a mother or a profession. And only on rare occasions could they forget it. But Richthofen always lived on the other side of the boundary which we crossed only in our great moments. When he fought, his private life was thrust ruthlessly behind him. Eating, drinking and sleeping were all he granted life, and then only the minimum that was necessary to keep flesh and blood in working order. He was the simplest man I ever met. He was a Prussian through and through. A great soldier."

—ERNST UDET,
Ace of the Black Cross

Major Albrecht Freiherr von Richthofen once watched through a telescope as his sons each shot down a SPAD. The kills, Manfred's forty-ninth and Lothar's eighteenth, were made on April 29, 1917. Bloody April was Imperial Germany's best month in the air and the worst Britain would ever have. It was a measure of the agony of the Royal Flying Corps that its airplanes could be shot down, almost for sport, in front of a prearranged audience. The patriarch of the Richthofen family had rubbed his short silver beard with pride while his oldest son's victim caught fire, broke apart in the air, and dropped into a nearby swamp. It was the first of four airplanes Manfred destroyed on that, his greatest, day, and Lothar's was the first of two for him. Between them, the Richthofen brothers wiped out the equivalent of a British flight, which delighted their father as much as it delighted them. It had been a good war, at least for the Richthofens, on April 29.

It was not a good war on December 25. The pilots who sat at

Jasta 11's Christmas table were mostly newcomers. They openly idolized their leader, which bored him, and referred to good old days they had not experienced, which saddened him. Their leader could go to the movies and see himself on the screen in a fragmented ten-minute film called "War Fliers on the Western Front." It started with an aviator hand-dropping a twenty-pound bomb, followed by bombs being released from under the wings of a large airplane, and then a climactic black mushroom explosion. The next scene showed an aviator leaning out of his cockpit and pointing a large square camera downward. When the photo had been taken, he pulled in the camera, pitched out a tiny bomb for good measure, and smiled proudly at the man filming him. Scene three showed a German scout attacking an observation balloon, setting it on fire, and turning away as the observer in the balloon's basket vaulted over the side and opened his parachute. People watching the movie would see that the British soldier's parachute did not save his life, though, because the flaming balloon came down on top of him as he touched the ground. "Balloon busting" was dangerous, but so was being "busted." *
Next, the heroes appeared. There was Max Immelmann and there was Boelcke, who looked almost indifferently into the camera

---

* Attacking balloons was, if anything, more dangerous than attacking airplanes. Both sides used so-called kite balloons, moored by cables to winches on the ground, for observation of enemy positions and artillery spotting. They were usually let out to altitudes of 500 to 1,000 feet, but sometimes went as high as 2,500 feet, depending on how close they were to the lines or how distant the object being observed. When attacked by airplanes, the man in the basket would jump out and open a parachute. It was at first easy to explode them, and many pilots did. Soon, elaborate clusters of antiaircraft guns were set up around the balloons, and scouts were occasionally kept above on circling patrols. Even without scout protection, it was unwise to attack balloons from above, because when they exploded, the ball of flame would rise and envelop the attacker. Balloons therefore had to be attacked by racing toward them just above the ground, usually through a wall of antiaircraft fire, shooting incendiary bullets into them, and then breaking sharply away to avoid the shock waves and heat from the explosion.

with his large sad eyes. There was also a relatively unknown, dandyish-looking pilot from Jasta 27 named Hermann Goering. Then Richthofen came on, with his head bandaged, and, standing next to an Albatros, tried to pull a cumbersome flying suit over his uniform. When the Red Battle Flier had it up to his waist, he lost his grip, and the suit fell in a thick heap around his fur boots. The suit fell faster in the film than it really had, and Richthofen, embarrassed, laughed hard. He patted Moritz, his dog, and appeared in Jasta 11's mess with a captured British aviator, who smiled nervously. Finally, there was an air battle, which showed a British plane going down in flames and an approving crowd later gathered around what was represented as its wreckage.

Walking down almost any street in Germany, Richthofen could buy several different postcards of himself—shown alone, with superiors, including Colonel Thomsen and General von Hoeppner, or with his men—and read about his exploits in magazines and newspapers. He could read the serialization of his book in magazine installments. When *Der röte Kampfflieger* was published in book form, it included two photographs purporting to show Richthofen's thirtieth and fortieth victims. Both pictures were of the same British R.E. 8, but taken from different angles and with its ailerons in the down position for number thirty and up for number forty. What went through Richthofen's mind when he saw these pictures is easily imagined.

He could even see his portrait on public display. One rainy day soon after Christmas, he found out that a portrait of him by Fritz Reusing, which he had sat seven hours for, was being shown with a drawing of him in a shop at the corner of Linden and New Wilhelm streets in Berlin. He took a cab there, got out, and, standing in the cold rain, looked at the painting of himself through the beaded window. He did not like the sketch and could not make up his mind about the painting. An old man walked up and also looked in the window. "Some people say I look like him," he said to the old man. "Do you think I do?" The man put on his glasses and looked carefully at the painting, then at Richthofen, and then at the painting again. *"I* don't think so," he said angrily, "and I think it's presumptuous of *you* to think so. That's Baron von Richthofen, the Red Battle Flier." He gave Richthofen a long, contemptuous look, and walked away. Richthofen's mind was made up. He did not like the painting either.

Medals? He could not wear all of them at the same time. Besides the Pour le Mérite, he had the Bulgarian Order of Military Valor, Iron Cross (First Class), Hungarian Order of the Holy Crown, Order of the Royal House of Oldenburg, Turkish Star of Gallipoli, Turkish Imtjaz Medal, Turkish Liakat Medal, Order of the House of Hohenzollern, Saint Henry's Military Order (Saxony), Saxe-Coburg-Gotha Medal, Austrian Military Service Cross, Order of the House of Ernestine (Saxony), Order of the Iron Crown, Cross for the Faithful Services, the Hanseatic crosses of Bremen and Hamburg, Griffen Cross, Hessian Phillips Order, Imperial Order of the Iron Cross, German Naval Pilot's Badge, and many others.

Trophies? A room full of them at Schweidnitz: his cavalry saber, a stirrup nearly cut in half by shrapnel, a Russian bugle, awards for horsemanship, Lanoe Hawker's machine gun, a bust of the Kaiser, dozens of fabric serial numbers, pieces of propellers, pistols, ammunition, serial tags from engines, compasses and altimeters from British cockpits, flare guns, plaques, photographs, roundels, sixty inscribed silver cups, mugs, flying caps, goggles, certificates, red-white-and-blue tail stripes, maps, albums, and, hanging from the ceiling as a chandelier illuminating it all, the front of an engine, each of whose nine cylinder heads was wired to take a bulb.

Manfred von Richthofen had achieved everything he set out to, including respect, if not close friendships. He was considered a superb leader on the ground as well as in the air and an excellent judge of pilots. Those he honored by picking for J.G. 1 almost always justified themselves. The exceptions were rooted out. Von der Osten was made leader of Jasta 4, for example, when his predecessor was found to have falsely claimed a kill. Punishment meant being posted out of the Circus, and that was enough.

Friendship was a different matter. Richthofen was never a good mixer and certainly not a party goer. He did not like music and did not have much patience for reading. Sports, which he did enjoy, were given up when war came. He settled for an occasional game of billiards instead. He smoked a few cigarettes a day, drank wine and champagne moderately, and hated idle talk. The head wound, which he once showed to von der Osten's mother by putting his head down on the table of a Berlin restaurant, changed his quietness to brooding. He began to spend more time alone, or playing with Moritz. He had the fame, medals, and trophies, but he also had dark thoughts that Christmas of 1917 and into the new year. There were thoughts of what now amounted to hundreds of pilots he had known who were gone, of waves of British and French airplanes that could not be stopped and were expected to double when the Americans came, of an ugly wound on his head which, unlike the medals, had to be worn forever, and of his being displayed by the General Staff like some prize horse. He had been told in December that he and Lothar would be given an extended leave, and found out that they were going to Brest-Litovsk, where negotiations were going on between Soviet Russia and the Central Powers. There they would be shown to the Russians as examples of Teutonic fighting champions, because no trick could be spared in bringing the Bolshevik rabble to terms so that German divisions could move west. Richthofen was also to speak to the workers in German factories. Communism was taking serious hold and threatened to undermine what was left of the war effort. Hindenburg's plan for drafting 123,000 workers for a planned March offensive had only made matters worse. So Richthofen, who hated public speaking, was going to have to tell the workers about patriotism and about how their country could not win the war unless they kept producing. He knew that Germany was doomed, but he could not tell them that. They knew it anyway, but the farce would have to be played out. The factory workers gave him a loud ovation when he finished his speech, even though they knew that what he told them was untrue.

The Richthofen brothers arrived at Brest-Litovsk in mid-January, and had their first look at real Bolsheviks, which was fascinating to the unworldly young Prussians. Contrary to the German officers, whose gray dress uniforms and black boots were immaculate, the people's deputies took great pride in wearing the symbols of their revolution—workers' and peasants' clothing, dirty and foul-smelling from having been worn on the farms and in the factories. It was not fun for the Richthofens to mingle with the Communists, but it was interesting, at least at first. Manfred became particularly fascinated by Madam Bicenko, undoubtedly because he was amazed to see a woman negotiate something as important as a peace treaty. He and Lothar also met Count Ottokar Czernin, the leader of the Austro-Hungarian delegation, with whom they talked about chivalry and air fighting. They soon tired of the pomp and politics, however, and, since their presence had been noted by most of the Bolsheviks (without noticeable effect), they were excused for bison- and elk-hunting in the snow-covered forest of Bialowieza, which had belonged to the Czar, but which was then held by the Germans. After that, Lothar visited Schweidnitz and Manfred went to Adlershof to look at new scouts.

Ludendorff thought negotiations with the Russians were going well enough to withdraw several divisions from the eastern front for use in France. The offensive of March, 1918, had first been discussed the previous November. It would require three and a half million men and would be a *Kaiserschlacht,* or emperor battle. It would, in other words, be a do-or-die attempt to end the war before the Americans came. But it was to be too late. The day the battle was to start—March 21—116,000 eager doughboys, itching for some of the glory before the war was over, reinforced French and British positions.

One of the many squadrons that were ordered to support the great offensive was Lieutenant Ernst Udet's Jasta 37. On March 15, Udet was told to move his group to Le Cateau and support General von der Marwitz's twenty-one divisions. When Jasta 37 got there, a few days later, Udet began helping his men erect tents beside a road while a heavy drizzle came down.

"I had pulled on a leather jacket, and was helping my mechanics to drive tent pegs when a motor car drove along the road," Udet wrote in his memoirs. "So many cars passed us that we took no notice of it. We continued our work, silently and doggedly.

"Then I felt a tap on the shoulder, and turning around saw— Richthofen. Rain trickled from the peak of his cap and ran down his face.

" 'How d'you do, Udet,' he said, negligently acknowledging my salute. 'Nice weather we're having today.'

"I looked at him and noted the calm expression and the big, cold eyes, half shaded by heavy lids. He was the man who at that time had brought down no fewer than sixty-seven machines—our best fighter.

"His car was waiting on the side of the road, and he had climbed down the embankment in the rain to speak to me. I waited.

" 'How many have you shot down to date, Udet?' he asked.

" 'Nineteen recognized, one waiting for confirmation,' I replied.

"He raked the mud with one point of his walking stick.

" 'Hmmm, twenty,' he commented. Then he raised his eyes and scrutinized me for a while.

" 'That about qualifies you to join us. Would you care to?'

"Would I care to? It was the most attractive suggestion any- one had ever made me. If it rested with me, I would have packed up and followed him then and there. There were many good squadrons in the German Army, and *Jasta* 37 was by no means the worst of them. But there was only one Richthofen squadron.

" 'Yes Sir, Captain,' I said.

"We shook hands and he left. I watched him—a tall, slender, fragile-looking man—as he climbed the embankment. He then jumped into the car and disappeared in the rain."

Udet was a good-looking, shortish, blue-eyed blond. He had Lothar von Richthofen's impish expression and the same taste for wine and women, although, like Lothar, he never let them interfere with his flying. Unlike either of the Richthofens, however, Udet was a born pilot. He had built model airplanes and a full-size glider while in high school. He started his military career as a volunteer motorcycle dispatch rider, but broke his shoulder in an accident and was not able to catch up with his unit when he left the hospital. He later pleaded with his father, a wealthy Frankfurt businessman, to send him to the Otto Flying School in Munich, so he could gain an edge for admission to the Air Service. His father agreed, against his better judgment, and not only paid Mr. Otto 2,000 marks for Ernst's lessons but also refurnished the flight instructor's bathroom. The younger Udet soloed quickly, which in no way mollified his father, and went on to win his pilot's badge. After two crashes, the last of which was into the side of a hangar, Udet was made a scout pilot. His climb in the Air Service had been steady. On the rainy day the Red Battle Flier touched him on the shoulder, he left the leadership of a squadron to become an ordinary pilot in the Richthofen Wing, which was a step up, and Udet knew it.

All leaves were canceled during the first week in March, so Manfred and Lothar joined the streams of men and equipment making their way across Germany to the front. New pilots and airplanes arrived from the east, and although aviators who had fought the underequipped and uninterested Russians were not prepared to fight the French, British, and Americans, they were much better than nothing. Morale among the Germans already living on French soil was as high as could be expected. Flying over their rear areas in the beginning of March, 1918, German airmen could see one trainload after another of men and munitions emptying, as if through an hourglass, onto a sixty-mile front between Arras and the Oise River south of Saint-Quentin. Roads were clogged with trucks and long lines of gray soldiers, stretching from the eastern horizon to where the sun went down. Barge traffic filled narrow canals, and new artillery pieces were brought up, swung around, and secured, until more than 5,500 of them faced the Allied trenches along forty of the sixty miles. New ammunition depots were built and expanded, more communications lines were laid and plugged into mobile command posts, observation balloons were readied, and thousands of mustard-gas cannisters were distributed. Three and a half million German soldiers—almost all of those left—prepared to go forward. The generals thought their plans were secret, but the Royal Flying Corps had been watching them prepare. The French and British massed their own armies to meet the attack.

Lothar von Richthofen shot down his twenty-seventh airplane on March 11 and the next day, flying with Manfred, shot down two more. Manfred got his sixty-fourth, a Bristol, that day. He sent its hospitalized gunner a box of cigars for the tenacious fight he had put up. Manfred shot down a Sopwith Camel the next day, but a Bristol disabled Lothar's triplane and he had to crash land. His Fokker came in sideways, ripping away its landing gear, crumpling the left wing, and smashing Lothar's face into the instrument panel and gun butts. He was taken to the hospital with a badly cut nose and jaw, a deep gash over his right eye, and the possibility of losing his teeth. Manfred visited Lothar every day, learned that his brother would keep his teeth, and notified the Baroness accordingly.

There was little time now for flying, and except for a Camel Richthofen shot down on March 18, most of his work was done on paper. Richthofen's Circus * would control Jasta 5 and Jasta 46 when the offensive began, and would be primarily concerned with bombing and strafing enemy soldiers, rather than dog-fighting with the Royal Flying Corps. The German high command decided that its air groups' mobility would give them a numerical advantage over enemy airplanes in the sectors they concentrated on, and that that advantage had to be exploited by shooting at everything in the path of the advancing infantry. People back home were not to be told that their airborne "knights" were going after ground soldiers. They *were* told that the French and British were strafing German soldiers, which was true, and that the Americans would do the same, which was also true. A minority of the "knights" on both sides, contrary to their images in the press, enjoyed shooting soldiers. Captain Eddie Rickenbacker, whose twenty-six kills made him America's ace of aces in World War I, had this to say about strafing: "This ground strafing is probably the most exciting sport in aviation and one that is attended with comparatively little danger to the pilot. The airplanes swoop down so swiftly and are so terrifying in the roar of their engines and the streams of bullets from two machine guns that an ordinary soldier always looks for a hole rather than a weapon of defense." And, "I have frequently dived down upon a highway filled with marching Germans and put them to flight with one swoop." † Rickenbacker's thoughts on strafing are strikingly similar to Richthofen's—at least when Russians were the targets—but were not shared by most other pilots, who found the "sport" more dangerous than they did. The majority of scout pilots preferred three dimensions of maneuvering room, not the two of low-level flying, and would rather have

---

* J.G. 1 proved so successful that the high command authorized a second wing, J.G. 2, which was formed on August 17, 1917. It was composed of Jastas 12, 13, 15, and 19, and was also called a "circus" by pilots who fought against it.

† Capt. Eddie V. Rickenbacker, *Fighting the Flying Circus*, Avon, New York, 1967, p. 44.

three or four enemy pilots chasing them than have to fly through what seemed like a wall of rifle and machine-gun fire coming from the ground. Richthofen came to dread strafing.

At 4:40 A.M. on March 21, German high explosives and gas shells started coming down through a thick mist on British artillery batteries, telephone exchanges, command posts, and living quarters. The noise was so deafening that when 2,500 British guns answered, no one really heard them. During the first fifty minutes of the heaviest concerted artillery bombardment in history, British positions erupted into hell. Hot shrapnel flew everywhere as Tommies staggered through collapsing trenches or out into the fog. They sniffed lethal gas, struggled frantically to get their masks on, and then stumbled through the darkness, unable to see more than fifteen feet, while more artillery rounds came down on them. The ground trembled. Many large British guns were torn into bloodstained shreds of metal. Wooden beams supporting tunnels cracked and gave way, dumping tons of earth on the frightened, screaming men underneath and burying hundreds alive. Ammunition dumps, preselected by the German gunners and carefully zeroed-in, went up in red-and-black mushrooms that sent more hot steel spraying out for hundreds of yards, catching silhouetted Tommies and cutting them down by platoons. Soon the explosions became routine, and numbed senses no longer fully responded to them. Coughing, vomiting men gathered around first-aid stations while looking apprehensively back toward the gas clouds.

During the last ten minutes of that first hour, the German guns moved their fire from the British rear areas to the front trenches, obliterating machine-gun positions, chopping telephone wires, ripping barbed wire, and tearing men apart. Then the big guns were turned on their original targets until 6:40 A.M., again pulverizing the British rear. A third of them began working over the front trenches once more. Slowly, the Tommies up front tried to regain their senses as they waited for German soldiers to come out of the mist. By 9:35 A.M., every mortar on the German side was arcing shells into the British trenches, which had almost disappeared. Five minutes later, the German infantry scrambled out of their trenches and ran forward into the lifting mist and the fire from the few British machine guns that were still working. Many Germans avoided pockets of British soldiers and just kept running forward, throwing stick bombs at the crazed Tommies as they passed. Others used bayonets in sudden hand-to-hand fights that ended as quickly as they started and left moaning, crying men in shell holes behind them. The advance went as planned.

Four days later, the Germans were still advancing, and it looked like they would separate the British and the French armies. In spite of continued morning fog, the Royal Flying Corps was ordered to "bomb and shoot everything they can see on the enemy's side of the line. Very low flying is essential. All risks are to be taken." Many British pilots obeyed their orders to the letter. The 8th German Grenadiers reported that an officer was run over by an S.E. 5.

The Richthofen Wing had been ready for take-off at 8:00 A.M. on the 21st, but the fog and smoke kept it grounded until noon. An hour later, pilots of Jasta 10 destroyed two observation balloons. J.G. 1 spent the next two days trying to pick out ground targets in the mist. When visibility improved on the 24th, Richthofen led twenty-five of his scouts into a fight with ten S.E. 5's of No. 56 Squadron, and shot one of them down for his group's only kill of the day. He shot down a bomb-carrying Camel the following day, again for J.G. 1's only victory, and watched its bombs explode before it hit the ground. He claimed his sixty-ninth kill on the 26th, made while flying for the first time with Udet. Later, on another patrol, he brought down his seventieth. To some of his squadron mates, and certainly to the German public, which was reading about him again, he seemed like his old self. No one except his adjutant, Karl Bodenschatz, knew that he had left a sealed envelope with Bodenschatz labeled: "Should I not return—Open."

J.G. 1 followed the army's advance and was ordered to a new airdrome at Léchelle, which had been vacated, almost intact, by the British. Flying from there on March 27, Richthofen shot down three airplanes, his best day since the previous April. The second and third burned all the way down. Ten other British airplanes went down in front of J.G. 1's guns that day, one of which was credited to Udet. Richthofen and Udet scored again the next day. Rain and clouds then limited J.G. 1's patrols until April 1, the day the Royal Flying Corps and the Royal Naval Air Service were amalgamated into the Royal Air Force. Before the sun went down, England's newest service had wrecked thirty-eight of its own airplanes, lost ten in combat, and four more under German bombs. Half of the R.A.F.'s air losses that April Fool's Day were claimed by Richthofen's Circus.

The ringmaster himself was flying alone the next day when he saw an R.E. 8 at 2,500 feet, and fired into it from ten yards. His victim burst into flames, and he was close enough to see its crewmen writhing in their cockpits, surrounded by fire, as the airplane dropped away. Kill seventy-six, a Camel, went down on April 6, also in flames. That day, a cousin, Wolfram von Richthofen, reported for duty in time to see the Red Battle Flier receive a telegram saying that he had been awarded the Order of the Red Eagle (Third Class) with Crown and Swords in honor of his seventy-fifth kill. It was the first time that the decoration had been given to someone other than a general, a high noble, or a member of the royal family. If Wolfram thought his famous relative was going to be the dashing aviator he had heard about, however, he was disappointed. Richthofen had begun to dwell on death by fire, on going down in an airplane that was being devoured by flames.

"Queer," Richthofen told a German correspondent later that week, "but the last ten I shot down all burned. The one I got today also burned." At first, he continued, there had been just a small flame under the pilot's seat. But when the airplane dived, he could see under it, and noticed that the pilot's seat had burned through. The flames were visible all the way down, he added, staring blankly through the doorway.

The Richthofen Wing had moved to two small forward airdromes after Léchelle, and at the end of the first week in April was ordered to move again, this time to Cappy, a small town on the Somme about twenty miles east of Amiens. Richthofen claimed two more kills on April 7, and was taken at his word by headquarters, although neither the British nor the French reported losing on that day the types of airplanes he reported destroying.

The German attack toward Amiens, which had kept J.G. 1 in the center of action, petered out around the outskirts of the city. The high command therefore decided to put pressure on the Lys area in front of Boulogne and the Strait of Dover, and launched an attack in that direction on April 8, first barraging the enemy with mustard gas and high explosives. At 8:00 A.M. on April 9, nine German divisions advanced on the Portuguese 2nd Division, which took off its boots, commandeered bicycles belonging to the 11th British Cyclist Battalion, and fled. The bicycleless Englishmen tried to hold the line until reinforcements came. General Haig, the British Field Marshal, then issued his famous order of the day, which ended: "There is no other course open to us but to fight it out. Every position must be held to the last man. There must be no retirement. With our backs to the wall and believing in the justice of our cause, each one must fight on to the end. The safety of our homes and the freedom of mankind alike depend upon the conduct of each one of us at this critical moment." Hindenburg had had to say things like that, but not in April, 1918. While the Kaiser was bestowing on him the Iron Cross with Golden Rays, which had not been awarded since 1814—even to a Kaiser—for the advance on Amiens, the Tommies in General Plumer's Second Army, their backs almost to the water, resolved to hold again.

Richthofen, meanwhile, became depressed at Cappy. The village itself was practically gutted, as was Péronne, about twelve miles to the east. Days of rain had washed down and spattered the broken buildings and made them look as though they were sinking back into the mud from which they came. Trees were uprooted and charred, the people were hostile, and the R.A.F. had mostly gone north for the Battle of the Lys, so air activity lessened around Cappy. Richthofen disappeared inside his quarters and, with a light cold rain pelting the roof, began updating the Dicta of Boelcke. He laid special emphasis on the organization of squadrons and their tactical use.

The rain continued through Saturday morning, April 20, but let up enough in the afternoon to allow patrols. Richthofen shot down his seventy-ninth and eightieth kills—two Camels—in three minutes that evening. The old "packing cases" and "flying pianos" used by the British had given way to S.E. 5's and Camels, which were easily a match for the Albatroses and Fokkers. Making kills had therefore become more difficult, and although he had been criticized by some Allied pilots for always picking easy meat, that was not really fair.* Almost all British "meat" had been easy through the winter of 1916–17, but Richthofen's score had, in the past six months, become increasingly sprinkled with Camels. His job was still to put out the eyes of the enemy, and that meant observers, but he never hesitated to tangle with fighters, even those superior to his own, when he found them. He went to bed on the night of the 20th having officially killed seventy-seven men in the air, wounded nineteen, and made prisoners of ten. All the figures could be higher, because some of his victims were never accounted for

---

* Billy Bishop, the Canadian ace, was one of them. In a biography, his son quotes him as saying: "Richthofen's fighting methods were typically German. That is not said to belittle the Baron's qualifications [as the ace of aces], but it is certainly not said in admiration of his qualities either. . . . He flew with a cold calculating skill and his great trick was to withhold from battle himself until his flying mates had set up a target for him. Then Richthofen would come whisking down out of the sun for the kill, pop off the lame duck, and fly away home with another great victory under his belt!"

and some of those who were wounded were also made prisoner. A mist spilled off the Somme and across Jasta 11's base on Sunday morning, April 21, allowing Richthofen to sleep until almost eight o'clock, which he always liked to do when possible. After a light breakfast, he stepped out of his quarters and confronted a military band. It had been sent to Cappy by a local division commander who thought Richthofen should be serenaded for his eightieth kill. Richthofen thought otherwise. He scowled, complained that the music was too loud, and walked to his triplane. The military music did not spoil his best mood in a week. He enjoyed the air, which was crisp, and which would become pleasantly warm if the sun came out at midday, as was expected. He was also looking forward to another peaceful hunting trip. Werner Voss's father had invited him and Lieutenant Hans Joachim Wolff (no relation to Kurt Wolff) to go woodcock-hunting at his lodge in the Black Forest, and they were scheduled to leave in two days. The train tickets had already been bought. The Rittmeister looked over his fourth triplane, which was entirely maroon, as it was being serviced. One of his mechanics asked him to autograph a postcard for his son. "What's the matter?" asked Richthofen. "Don't you think I'll come back?" He signed the card, finished inspecting his scout, and walked back to the ready area, where his pilots were lounging on deck chairs and cots, waiting for a take-off order.

Richthofen noticed that Lieutenant Richard Wenzl, who had only come to Jasta 11 a month before, was sleeping on one of the cots. In a playful mood, he kicked the cot out from under him, and Wenzl, showing mock anger, walked away. Another pilot took Wenzl's place and was soon dozing. Again Richthofen kicked out the cot's supports, and again one of his pilots picked himself off the ground, wiped dirt and grass from his flying suit, and left. The second pilot joined the first, out of their commander's sight, and planned revenge. It came a few minutes later, when Moritz walked slowly up to his master, dragging a heavy wooden wheel chock tied to his tail. Richthofen laughed, removed the wooden bar, and embraced his grateful dog. Someone snapped a picture, which again changed Richthofen's mood. He did not like having his picture taken before a flight. Boelcke's photograph had been taken before *his* last flight, and his most famous and longest-lived pupil never forgot it.

Bodenschatz announced that the weather had cleared enough for the first patrol to start. Soon, Richthofen's triplane was leading five others into a westward climb. They were helped along, he noted apprehensively, by a rare wind blowing toward the Allied lines. It could take them farther than they wanted to go. One of the six triplanes was being flown by another Richthofen. It was Wolfram's first combat patrol, and he was under orders from his cousin to avoid fighting at all costs, and to race home if attacked.

Twenty-five miles from Cappy, in the direction the wind was blowing, stood the Royal Air Force base at Bertangles. It was the same airfield where, less than a year and a half before, Lanoe Hawker had been stationed. One of the new groups at Bertangles, No. 209 Squadron, had been posted for an 8:15 A.M. patrol, but the same mist that delayed Jasta 11 also grounded No. 209 Squadron for more than an hour. Its first flight, led by Captain Arthur R. Brown, of Toronto, Canada, got off at 9:35 A.M. and climbed to 12,000 feet for what its five members thought would be a routine patrol. One of the Camel pilots, Second Lieutenant Wilfred R. ("Wop") May, was on his first combat flight. May was an old friend and schoolmate of Brown's, so the flight leader advised him to avoid fighting with the Hun and get out of a battle at all costs. May resolved to do as he was told and, since his friend had changed from a happy-go-lucky boy to a man in no mood to be crossed, to stay out of trouble altogether until he had permission to look for it.

Brown had started piloting at the Wright Flying School in Dayton, Ohio. He joined the Royal Naval Air Service in 1915, but crashed and snapped his spine during a training flight in England and spent most of 1916 in the hospital. He was sent to No. 9 Naval Squadron in October, 1917. When the Royal

Air Force came into being, naval squadrons added the number
200 to their existing numbers so that there would be no duplication of the numbers of Royal Flying Corps groups. No. 9
Naval Squadron therefore became No. 209 Royal Air Force
Squadron on April 1, and Brown, who was by that time a flight
lieutenant, was given the army rank of captain. He had joined
the navy, was now in the air force, and did not like either.
Many of his comrades' nerves had been shattered in combat,
and they had been removed from the front, which Brown considered lucky. He hated the war, was admittedly frightened,
but instead of losing his mind, had developed an ulcer. He fed
it with brandy and eggnog and refused to have it treated in a
hospital. Roy Brown was therefore in no mood to be crossed.

His flight was followed into the air five minutes after it left
Bertangles by a second flight of five Camels, and five minutes
after that by a third flight of five. When all fifteen reached the
southernmost point on their patrol line, the last five spotted two
Albatros observation planes, and peeled off to attack them.
One of the Albatroses went down on fire and the other disappeared in a cloud. The British flight decided to stay in the area
and look for it. Brown, who was also in charge of the entire
squadron while it was in the air, led his remaining two flights
back over the patrol line in a northeasterly direction about
halfway between Bertangles and Cappy. Less than five minutes
later, two Camels in the second flight developed engine trouble,
so their pilots dropped out for home, leaving Brown with eight
of his original fifteen fighters. He continued to lead them
northeast toward the Somme, which was exactly where Richthofen was headed on his westward patrol, but at a different
altitude. The Jasta 11 group had, in the meantime, been joined
by scouts of Jasta 5 and, together with Wolff, who had taken
off after the rest of Jasta 11 was in the air, numbered thirteen.

The British and German formations might not have seen one
another through the lingering clouds, except for two R.E. 8's.
They were on a photo-reconnaissance mission 7,000 feet over

Le Hamel when they were seen by the Germans. Four triplanes left the formation and dove on the R.E. 8's. They were beaten off, with one Fokker shot down, and the other three breaking off to rejoin Richthofen. The wind had blown them farther west than they thought, however, and when puffs of antiaircraft fire began exploding around them, they realized they were over British positions. Brown, attracted by the explosions, rocked his wings and turned toward the triplanes as they sped to get under Richthofen's protection. The Rittmeister saw the eight Camels chasing his three triplanes and, in turn, signaled his group to intercept the British. They did not get there in time. The Camels caught the three Fokkers, sending one of them down, before Richthofen and his eight companions plunged into the fight. As the controlled attack degenerated into a typical free-for-all, a Camel pilot, shot in the back, fell out of the fight. He managed to machine-gun a triplane on the way down, and it, too, fell.

May tried hard to obey Brown's warning. He circled at 12,000 feet while the battle went on under him, and even let a triplane pass close by without chasing it. Everyone was singling out an opponent except him, he thought. When a second triplane flew by, he could restrain himself no longer. He pushed his stick forward and followed the German right into the middle of the fight, shooting all the while, and finally hitting him. May was credited with destroying the triplane, which did not crash, but made it back to Cappy. Its pilot was probably his opposite number, Wolfram von Richthofen, who had no more restraint than the Canadian, and who paid for it with a badly punctured tail. May did not chase him. Instead, he looked around, and seeing that triplanes were passing close by on all sides, decided to pull the trigger for a long burst in the hope of hitting any German who flew in front of him. Predictably, both guns jammed, and that was when May decided to get home as fast as he could. He dropped out of the swarm, straightened out, and followed the sun westward toward Bertangles. The novice felt "pretty good" when he looked behind and did not see anyone. Brown was fighting two triplanes on the edge of the main battle. He saw May streak for their airfield, and was about to turn his attention back to the Germans when he saw another scout leave the melee. It was a maroon triplane, and, judging by its speed and direction, was obviously trying to overtake May. Brown broke off and went into a long dive after the Fokker that was going after the Camel.

May stopped feeling pretty good when he heard machine-gun fire behind him, looked back, and saw a Fokker gaining on him. He put his Camel into a shallow dive, kicking the rudder pedals and jerking the stick in a frantic effort to dodge the bullets that were going by at a rate of 600 a minute. No matter what the Canadian did, though, he could not shake the Fokker, which drew closer every time he maneuvered. Brown was by that time above the German and close enough for a burst. All three airplanes were now within 200 feet of the ground and following the Somme above a low ridge a half-mile east of Vaux-sur-Somme. Brown fired a short burst close behind the triplane, saw its pilot turn as if to look at him, and then slump as bullets went into maroon linen. Brown's diving attack brought him behind and below the triplane after he got off the burst, and when he pulled up, May and the German were gone.

May was terrified. He skimmed over trees that lined the river parallel to Morlancourt Ridge, which rises abruptly from the Somme to about 200 feet, and then climbed up and over the ridge past Vaux-sur-Somme. The German anticipated May's maneuver and cut over the ridge inside of him, still firing, and getting closer. May thought the German had him, and seriously considered deliberately crashing into the water. "Had I known it was Richthofen," he said later, "I should probably have passed out on the spot." The ridge was covered with Australian riflemen and machine gunners, and many of them started shooting at the Fokker as it passed, now a hundred yards behind May and still closing. Sergeant C. B. Popkin and Gunner R. F. Weston, of the Australian 24th Machine Gun Company, fired a burst at the triplane after it passed over Vaux-sur-Somme, and both said they saw pieces breaking off as their bullets hit. The Fokker also came under fire from an antiaircraft battery controlled by Sergeant Alfred G. Franklyn (who subsequently claimed to have been at the gun that killed Richthofen), and probably dozens of riflemen. As it flew over the Bray-Corbie road, antiaircraft guns of the Australian Field Artillery's 53rd Battery opened up, with Gunners W. J. Evans and R. Buie at the trigger. The unit's commanding officer reported later that after Evans and Buie fired, the triplane turned unsteadily and went down. As it turned, however, Sergeant Popkin fired again, and he said his target then swerved and crashed.

There is no telling how many Australians did actually fire at the Fokker, but Richthofen *was* caught in a hail of bullets. At some point between when Brown fired and the last Australian did, Richthofen died. His triplane staggered, slipped, glided a couple of hundred yards, then slipped again and crashed just north of the Bray-Corbie road, a mile and a half inside contested territory held precariously by the Australians.

The Fokker's landing gear was smashed and its gas tank collapsed, but everything else was intact when the first soldiers reached it. Looking inside, they saw that the pilot's nose and jaw had been smashed by impact with the machine-gun butts in front of him, and they realized he was dead even before they unstrapped him and laid his body beside his airplane. The body was searched. When it was discovered that the corpse at their feet was Manfred von Richthofen's, a wild rush started for souvenirs. Men shouted over the ridge that the "Red Devil" was dead. "They got the bloody Red Baron!" Half an hour later, the triplane had almost been picked clean, and patches of maroon linen were being distributed throughout the area and its propeller was being cut to splinters. Germans with telescopes had followed it all, and while a telephone message describing the scene went back to a command post, their artillery started a box barrage around the skeletonized airplane, sending Australian souvenir-collectors running for cover. Personal items taken from the body—at least some of them, like a wristwatch that stopped at 11:30 A.M.—were collected by officers and officially registered. Other items—a silk scarf, monogrammed handkerchief, and boots—disappeared. Some of the triplane's instruments were pulled out and never recovered. That evening, Richthofen's body was tied with rope to a sheet of corrugated steel and dragged, as if on a sled, down the far side of the Morlancourt Ridge and away from the anxious Germans who had continued to watch and send progressive reports to their rear positions which were, in turn, relayed to Cappy. The remains of the triplane were then lashed with a rope, and it was dragged along the same sunken road as its pilot and down into the Ancre Valley. Richthofen's body was taken to Poulainville, five miles from the crash site, and laid in a hangar belonging to the Australian Flying Corps. While the Fokker's machine guns were being removed and the airplane hacked to pieces away from German guns, Richthofen was given an autopsy. It became evident before the sun went down that both the Royal Air Force and the Australian gunners were claiming to have killed him, with as much relish as the Rittmeister himself had shown on his victorious days. And it was somehow fitting that souvenirs of the souvenir-hunter should be so highly prized, perhaps underlining a common denominator of men who strike down others in war. The only part of the triplane put to official use was an oil specimen, which was siphoned into a small bottle and taken to an R.A.F. laboratory for analysis of its quality. Intelligence would want to know that.

The autopsy showed that a single bullet entered the right side of Richthofen's chest, ricocheted off his spine, and came out two inches higher on the left side of his chest. The bullet was never found, and since the Fokker was by that time being carried in the pockets and bags of perhaps a hundred men, any holes in the fabric that might have given a clue as to whose bullet killed Richthofen were gone forever.

When Roy Brown landed at Bertangles, he thought he had killed the German pilot, but had no idea it was Richthofen. His report said:

"(1) At 10:35 a.m. I observed two Albatross burst into flames and crash.

"(2) Dived on large formation of 15-20 Albatross Scouts, D 5's and Fokker triplanes, two of which got on my tail and I came out.

Went back again and dived on pure red triplane which was firing on Lieut. May. I got a long burst into him and he went down vertical and was observed to crash by Lieut. Mellersh and Lieut. May.

I fired on two more but did not get them."

So far as the Royal Air Force was concerned, there was no question but that Brown killed Richthofen, and he was officially credited with the victory. The motto of No. 209 Squadron was even made: "A Red Eagle—Falling." Brown was convinced he had shot down Richthofen.

The Australians were just as convinced that their gunners had brought down the war's ace of aces, and a handwritten report by the Australian 5th Division said: "Airman shot down by 53rd Battery AFA this morning was famous Baron von Richtofen [sic]." The Australians accepted their generals' congratulations for the kill.

Richthofen's last battle has been called the "fight that will live forever" because the question of who actually killed him has never been completely resolved. Most evidence points to the Australians. Richthofen flew about two miles after Brown shot at him, which, medical officers have agreed, would have been impossible, given the nature of his wound, had Brown's shot been responsible. Second, the bullet hit him on the right side and came out two inches higher on the left, indicating that it was fired upward, and not from above. Finally, since he was strapped in his seat, he could have turned his head toward Brown, but not enough of his body so that Brown, flying behind, could have hit him in the right side of his chest and have the bullet come out on the left. If it was an Australian who killed Richthofen, no one will ever be able to prove which Australian, so it is a moot point. It was his life and legacy that were important, not his death; and certainly not the man responsible for it.

The Jasta 5 and Jasta 11 scouts that returned to Cappy came in at relatively long intervals, since their formation had been scattered in the fight. The first pilots on the ground reported that the Rittmeister's triplane had definitely been seen to go down inside British lines. Calls were put out to forward observation posts half a mile east of Vaux-sur-Somme, and the infantrymen who had watched Richthofen's fall confirmed the worst. Second Army headquarters was told before sunset that the Red Battle Flier was officially missing, although his death could not be confirmed. The message was passed to supreme headquarters, and hundreds of senior officers spent the night of the 21st–22nd waiting for word from the British. Albrecht von Richthofen was told that his son was missing. He showed no emotion, and two days later, when he received a condolence telegram from J.G. 1, answered this way: "My son still lives in your model."

Richthofen was buried by the British and Australians, with full military honors, late on the afternoon of April 22. His coffin was carried from the hangar by six captains—soldiers of rank equivalent to his—and laid on the back of a small army truck. The procession, led by twelve rifle-carrying soldiers, included official mourners, an infantry platoon, and other soldiers and local residents who wanted to see the burial. The line of people in front of and behind the sputtering truck walked slowly down the main street of Bertangles under a bright spring sun and into the small cemetery a half-mile west of the town. A grave had been dug just to the left of two brick columns and a high wrought-iron gate that formed, as they still do, the entrance to the town's small burial area. Man-high hedges enclose the two-acre plot. The wooden casket was lowered into the grave, which was almost under the branches of a hemlock tree, while the twelve soldiers fired three volleys in solemn tribute. Then a line of officers filed past the grave to pay their respects, and a cross, cut from a four-bladed propeller, was banged into the soil above Richthofen's head. A round plate at the center of the propeller was inscribed: "CAVALRY CAPTAIN MANFRED BARON VON RICHTHOFEN—Age 22 years [sic], killed in action, aerial combat, near SAILLY-LE-SEC, SOMME, FRANCE. 21st APRIL, 1918." The plate was eventually stolen.

The British announced Richthofen's death shortly before 10:00 A.M. on the morning he was buried. The communiqué was picked up by Reuters and released to neutral newspapers, from which the German press got it on the 23rd. The last sentence of the drily phrased communiqué was the one that ended any German hope that the Red Battle Flier had been captured: "The pilot of one of the hostile machines which was brought down in combat was the well-known German airman and fighter Rittmeister Freiherr von Richthofen, who claimed to have brought down eighty Allied machines. His body has today been buried with full military honours." The story made the New York *Times* edition of April 24. General von Hoeppner worded the official German communiqué thus: "Rittmeister Freiherr von Richthofen has not returned from a pursuit of the enemy. He has fallen. The German Army has lost its greatly admired pilot and the fighting airmen their beloved leader. He remains the hero of the German peoples for whom he fought and died. His death is a deep wound for his *Geschwader* and for the entire Air Service. The will by which he conquered and led, that he handed down, will heal that wound."

The prestigious British aviation weekly *The Aeroplane* praised Richthofen as "a brave man, a clean fighter and an aristocrat." All Allied pilots, the article said, "will be pleased to hear that he has been put out of action, but there will be no one amongst them who will not regret the death of such a courageous nobleman. Several days ago, a banquet was held in honour of one of our aces [Rhys-Davids, who killed Voss]. In answering the speech made in his honour, he toasted Richthofen, and there was no one who refused to join." Many letters were sent to London newspapers, however, which protested what their writers considered too elaborate burial for a Hun, even a noble Hun. Some German newspapers attacked the burial for the opposite reason, charging that it had been an act of hypocrisy. "This homage is nothing but the latest manifestation of the British self-advertisement of sportsmanlike knightliness," wrote Count Reventlow in *Deutsche Tageszeitung*. "For our part, we cannot look upon the ceremony shown as sincere. The Allied press is full of this cant and is beating the big drum of absurd British magnanimity in the accustomed fashion. But they say nothing about how many and how large money prizes were for the one who succeeded in killing von Richthofen. In truth, the monies must have amounted to an enormous sum. This explains why such a bitter controversy raged around the body of the fallen pilot, for there was money waiting for the one who inflicted the fatal wound. The very flying officers who bore our hero were all fortunate money-makers."

The R.A.F. pilot who flew over Cappy on the evening of the 22nd would have been unhappy had he read Reventlow's acid comments. He risked being shot down to drop a photograph of Richthofen's grave and this note: "To, The German Flying Corps, Rittmeister Baron Manfried [*sic*] von RICHTHOFEN was killed in aerial combat on April 21st, 1918. He was buried with full military honours."

The men of J.G. 1 had been stunned on the evening of the 21st. Lothar said he blamed himself for his brother's death, since he had not been flying with him, and he swore revenge. The next day, Hans Wolff shot down two Camels, and another Jasta 11 pilot, one. The Richthofen Wing felt grief, but it did not affect the group's flying, as the Allied airmen who fought against it could attest. When the letter Richthofen had given to Bodenschatz weeks before was opened, it turned out to be, as expected, his aeronautical last will and testament. "Should I not return from a flight," the handwritten note said, "Lieut. Reinhard, Jasta 6, is to command the *Geschwader*. —Frhr. v. Richthofen, Rittmeister."

Reinhard was a good commander, and under his leadership men like Erich Lowenhardt, Lothar von Richthofen, and Ernst Udet continued to build their scores. Lowenhardt was killed on August 10 after his fifty-third victory. Lothar survived the war with a score of forty. Udet, with sixty-two, also lived through it to become Germany's surviving ace of aces. But Reinhard was killed at Adlershof on July 3 while testing a new scout, which broke apart at 3,000 feet. The pilot who had taken the airplane up minutes before Reinhard, and had flown it successfully, became the last leader of the Richthofen Wing. He had been the commander of Jasta 27 the day Reinhard was killed, and he was notified on July 6 that he was to head the Circus.

Eight days later, Karl Bodenschatz handed Lieutenant Hermann Goering the ceremonial walking stick, or *Geschwaderstock*, of J.G. 1. It had been used by Richthofen and Reinhard, and the pilots who listened to Goering's first remarks kept looking at it and then at its new owner. From now on, Goering said, he would personally control every aspect of air fighting. He would not only tell his pilots where and when to attack, but also would see to it that there were no more free-for-alls after the ambush was sprung. The pilots of J.G. 1 shifted weight uneasily as Goering, who was a gifted orator, expounded on iron discipline and absolute control. At least one of them might have thought that Goering would make a better politician than a pilot.

ELEVEN · PHOENIX RISES

"Is war propaganda a means or an end? It is a means, and therefore it has to be judged from the point of view of the end."

—ADOLF HITLER

Ernst Udet, hands in his pockets, stood on the rear platform of a crowded Munich streetcar one cold afternoon toward the end of November, 1918, and watched raindrops spattering against the asphalt of a beaten city within a beaten nation. There was no longer work for men who shot down airplanes. Udet had destroyed sixty-two of them for the Fatherland, to become its highest living ace, but not one could be exchanged for a loaf of bread, so he looked at the glistening streets and wondered what he would do without the war. A man was staring at him. The man wore a gray-green army coat, but no regimental insigne, and had a red band tied around one sleeve. He also wore an untrimmed reddish beard, which covered most of a flabby face. Udet knew by the red band that the man was a member of a Soldiers' Council. He was a Communist, and he looked contemptuously at Udet's face and then at the Pour le Mérite under it. He reached out and touched the medal.

"So much old iron," he said, in a voice that wanted to be

heard by everyone on the platform. People looked and squirmed. Udet, still watching the raindrops, wondered what he would do if the Communist, who was much taller than he, hit him. A thick hand, covered with red hair, reached for the medal again, and pulled at it.

"Aren't you going to take off this bit of tin?" asked the loud sneering voice. Udet carefully measured the distance to the soldier's face, grabbed his beard, and pulled as hard as he could. "Aren't you going to take off your beard?" he shouted back.

The soldier screamed and struck out in all directions, hitting the conductor and several passengers, but missing Udet. The small platform turned into an arena, with the conductor finally punching the soldier in the head, stopping the streetcar, and throwing him off. Picking himself up from the wet pavement, he shook his fist at the aviator, the conductor, and the audience rolling away from him. Two fat men, whom Udet described as the "profiteer type," laughed. Germany's greatest living ace was too worried about his future to laugh at anything. He continued watching raindrops.

Hermann Goering had known he was through as an infantry officer one day in 1914 when, lying crippled in a Freiburg hospital, he was told he had arthritis. The twenty-one-year-old lieutenant was heartbroken until his inseparable friend, Lieutenant Bruno Loerzer, explained how he could transfer to the Air Service, where physical qualifications were less rigid and life was more exciting. Goering overcame his illness with remarkable courage and eventually flew, as observer, with Loerzer. Like so many others, his pursuit of fame led him to pilot training, and from there to Jasta 26, which, in 1916, was commanded by Loerzer. Within a year, he got his own squadron, Jasta 27, which, as luck would have it, shared an airdrome with Jasta 26. Goering and Loerzer often led their combined groups into battle, and they saw as much as possible of one another on the ground.

Goering's selection to be commander of the Richthofen Wing had surprised its members, many of whom thought that Lothar or Udet would become their leader after Reinhard was killed. Both pilots had more kills than Goering, and, like him, had the Pour le Mérite. But Goering had been in the service longer, had shown great organizational and leadership ability, and was anything but reckless in the air. In fact, he devoted much more time to administrative work than to flying after accepting J.G. 1's ceremonial walking stick on July 14, when he had twenty-one kills. When the war ended, four months later, he had twenty-two.

During those four months, J.G. 1 continued to move around the front, and it took such severe losses that its strength was finally reduced to that of a squadron. It was therefore sent into combat with the newly formed J.G. 3, commanded by Bruno Loerzer, and other groups. By the end of September, the Imperial Air Service had been bled and pounded to exhaustion, and not even Anthony Fokker's new D VII's * could hold back the Allied air armadas.

The Richthofen Wing fought its last battle on November 5, shooting down three SPAD's without loss. Then the rains came, and J.G. 1's young pilots, most of whom knew Richthofen only by legend—as the patron saint of their unit—settled down in their chairs and waited for orders. They came three days before the

---

* The Fokker D VII, a standard-looking biplane, has been called Germany's best World War I scout, and possibly the finest in the world. It was first tested by leading aces (including Richthofen) at Adlershof in January, 1918, and went into quantity service that May. It could fly at 125 miles an hour, climb to above 20,000 feet, and was superbly maneuverable. Armament consisted of the usual twin Spandaus. The D VII was so well respected by the Allies that it was the only airplane named in the Versailles Treaty. Many were used by German police after the war, and Anthony Fokker smuggled scores of D VII's into Holland, whose government bought them. Switzerland also used them. Goering's D VII was all white, and Udet painted "LO" on the side of his, in honor of his girl friend.

Armistice. Goering called his men for assembly at 11:00 P.M. on the night of November 8 and ordered them to demobilize, according to instructions he had received from Air Service headquarters. They would fly their scouts to Darmstadt, a major air center just south of Frankfurt, rather than be captured by the advancing Allied armies in France. Meanwhile, the whirlpool was inundating the rock. The Kaiser had abdicated and fled to neutral Holland, Ludendorff had resigned, army units were in open rebellion and already walking back to Germany, the Imperial High Seas Fleet had mutinied in Kiel, Berlin streets echoed with rifle fire, and Kurt Eisner, President of the Bavarian Workers', Peasants' and Soldiers' councils, had taken power in Munich after the King of Bavaria abandoned his throne. Germany was coming apart.

When Goering landed his D VII at Darmstadt on November 12, he found that the airdrome had been taken over by Soldiers' Councils, which began impounding each of J.G. 1's Fokkers as they set down. Enraged, Goering told the red-banded soldiers that if they did not release the captured Fokkers, he would instruct those still in the air to attack. He meant it, and the Communists backed down. Goering's last order instructed him to take his D VII's to Aschaffenburg and surrender them to the French. The order was carried out, but, as Goering later explained to angry French officers, it was not his fault if every one of the D VII's crash-landed so badly that they were almost total wrecks. That evening, Bodenschatz handed Goering a paper filled with statistics taken from J.G. 1's record book, and the Flying Circus's last leader read from it to his pilots. Since July 5 of the previous year, when Lieutenant Dostler shot down a balloon for J.G. 1's first victory, the group had officially accounted for 644 enemy airplanes and balloons. It paid for them with fifty-six pilots and six ground crewmen killed and fifty-two pilots and seven ground crewmen wounded. A pilot had, the day before, chalked his thoughts on a blackboard that had been used for flying orders: *"Im Krieg geboren, im Krieg gestorben."* The words summed up the rise and fall of the Imperial German Air Service and its Flying Circus even better than a gifted speaker like Goering could. "Born in war, died in war." The officers and men of J.G. 1, the Richthofen Wing, were dismissed and sent back to where they came from.

Goering returned to Germany filled with contempt for the floundering Weimar Republic and disillusionment at the seeming ease with which the Communists gained ground throughout the country. He took a job as a Fokker salesman in Denmark and then became the chief pilot for the Swedish national airline in Stockholm. In that capacity, he one day flew Count Eric von Rosen to his estate near Stockholm and, while stopping over, fell in love with Countess von Rosen's sister, Carin von Kantzow. Although she was married and had an eight-year-old son, and, to further complicate matters, was an epileptic, she had her marriage dissolved to wed the young war hero. They moved to Munich with her personal fortune, and Goering, trying to achieve respectability equal to his wife's, dabbled in studies at the university. It was in Munich, in 1921, that Goering met Hitler. He was attracted by the Austrian corporal's personal magnetism and his promises of revenge against those who had betrayed the Fatherland, who had stabbed it in the back. Since the General Staff had seen to it that civilians signed the Armistice, there was never any doubt as to whom Hitler meant, and it was not the army. The new leader of the National Socialist German Workers' Party realized that Goering was a valuable commodity. He was wealthy, had a Pour le Mérite that would show well in newspaper photos, and was the last leader of Baron von Richthofen's famous air group. Goering was a genuine war hero, and could therefore add priceless respectability to a party composed almost entirely of a malcontent rabble.

After being discharged from the hospital, where he had healed from the March 13 crash, Lothar von Richthofen went home to Schweidnitz, where he finished recuperating and helped his mother answer condolences for his brother. Doctors pronounced Lothar unfit for further duty, at least in the air, so General von Hoeppner offered him a staff job, which was refused. Weeks later, he called Hoeppner and reported that he had been medically cleared for combat. He was therefore ordered to Air Service headquarters, and from there back to Jasta 11. Hoeppner had taken him at his word, which was a mistake. Lothar, insisting that he felt fine, went back into combat and scored his fortieth kill on August 12. He had twice before been wounded on the thirteenth day of the month, but laughed when reminded of it, and took off on a patrol that day. He went into a fight that afternoon and came out with a bullet in his right thigh. Leaving the battle, he pulled his useless leg off its pedal and tried to parachute out.* No matter how hard he struggled, he could not climb far enough out of his seat to bail out, so, bleeding heavily again, he brought his scout far behind German lines and, fighting off a fainting spell, landed. For the third time he was taken to a hospital unconscious, and he finished the war as a convalescent.

He returned to Schweidnitz despondent and in poor health. Like most of his surviving comrades, he found it almost impossible to adapt to life in a country that had been beaten in eastern France and raped at Versailles. His father died in 1920. Most of his friends wandered around Europe bored and with empty pockets. Some, like Udet, performed stunt flying and mock air battles for beer money, but no one in Germany really wanted to see mock air battles in the early 1920's—not so soon after the real ones. Other friends, who months before had fought in the skies over France and Belgium, yawned over the textbooks that promised eventual employment. Lothar married the year his father died, had a son, named Wolf, and then sep-

---

* Parachutes were introduced to J.G. 1 around Christmas, 1917, but at first were distrusted and hardly ever worn.

arated from his wife. His infectious smile was gone, his hair
was turning prematurely gray, and he still could not find work
he liked. He took a job as a transport pilot the year his son
was born, and on July 4 of the following year crashed into a
tree while approaching Fuhlsbüttel Airdrome near Hamburg.
He died on the way to the hospital, and was buried in the
Schweidnitz garrison churchyard.

One day in mid-November, 1925, Karl Bolko Freiherr von
Richthofen, accompanied by an official of the War Graves Commission, entered the cemetery for German war dead at Fricourt.
Manfred's body had been removed from the plot at Bertangles
and reburied at Fricourt, with 18,000 other German soldiers,
soon after the war. Six thousand bodies were in separate graves
and 12,000 had been put in a mass grave. Baroness von Richthofen and Karl Bolko, who was then twenty-two, had decided
to bring Manfred back to Schweidnitz for reburial beside
Lothar and their father. By that time, however, many former
members of J.G. 1 had worked their way into responsible positions in airlines, airplane companies, lower and middle rungs of
government, and General Hans von Seeckt's quietly resurrected
army. When they learned of plans to lay their former leader at
Schweidnitz, they begged his mother to bury her son in Invaliden Cemetery, in central Berlin, as befit the Fatherland's
greatest combat hero. The Baroness had not wanted a spectacle,
but when newspaper editorials and letters backed the idea, she
agreed. After months of negotiations with the French, Karl
Bolko went to Fricourt with the papers necessary to have his
brother's body exhumed.

The caretakers at Fricourt had not been told that Bolko was
coming, and, as far as they were concerned, Manfred von
Richthofen's body was no more important than any of the other
18,000 Boche they had to look after. Bolko spent hours walking
past rows of crosses, many of them unmarked, until he found
one with the small zinc plate that had been nailed to his

brother's coffin at Bertangles. After another search, this time
for gravediggers, Manfred's body was dug up, transferred to a
new coffin Bolko had brought with him, and taken to Albert in
an automobile. There, it was put into a boxcar and, with Bolko
sitting alongside, was pulled through Strasbourg and on toward
the German border. The trip through France was uneventful.
At midnight on Monday, November 16, the steam engine rolled
slowly over the bridge that spans the Rhine near Kehl and
stopped in that German town. The few railroad men on duty
at that hour stopped working and took off their hats. After
helping to remove the coffin from the French boxcar, they lifted
it onto a German one and carefully laid it on fir branches.
Flowers, which had been sent for the occasion, were piled
around the metal coffin, which remained in Kehl all the next
day. Church bells tolled in the town on the night of the 17th,
and a torchlight procession came out of the little gingerbread
community and stopped in front of the boxcar. A handful of
former Air Service pilots had arrived earlier. They, with Bolko,
accompanied the Rittmeister to Berlin. Crowds gathered at every
stop to hand flowers to the men in the boxcar, while airplanes
flew escort and flags were brought to half mast. Another torchlight procession was waiting at the Berlin station to accompany
Richthofen's body to the Gnadenkirche, where it lay in state
for two days. An honor guard, made up equally of Richthofen
Wing pilots and 1st Uhlan cavalry officers, stood watch while
thousands filed past the closed casket and looked at the medals,
flowers, sword, and the wooden cross from Fricourt, which had
been laid on top.

On November 20, 1925—seven years after the Armistice—Manfred von Richthofen's body was taken to Invaliden Cemetery in
the largest and most glittering military parade Germany had had
since the war. Eight Pour le Mérite holders, including Ernst Udet,
placed the coffin on a shiny black horse-drawn gun carriage. An
army band played slow, solemn *Trauer* music with drums and
fifes as the carriage moved along crowded, silent streets. Baroness

von Richthofen, Ilse,* and Karl Bolko walked behind the caisson. Field Marshal von Hindenburg, the president of the convulsive republic, trudged wearily behind the family and was followed by a phalanx of dignitaries, most of whom wore uniforms. Hindenburg had been told to scatter the first handful of earth on Richthofen's coffin, and he did what he was told. It was a clear, crisp autumn day. The officers who had watched Richthofen's final burial left Invaliden slowly and in small groups. The Rittmeister was hardly mentioned. They talked instead about a lonely airfield 200 miles from Moscow, which the Russians had agreed to let them use as a testing and training center in exchange for technical aviation information. And there was plenty of that.

The ban on construction of civilian airplanes had been lifted by the Allies in May, 1922, and they were being built again. Ernst Heinkel was building small reconnaissance planes that looked like sport biplanes. Willy Messerschmitt was perfecting another sport plane, the M-17, which was the predecessor of the Bf-109 high-performance fighters. Claude Dornier and Hugo Junkers were designing twin-engine airliners that could be fitted with plastic noses for bombardiers and, when fully converted, would be the most advanced military aircraft of their time. In 1925, these were being smuggled into Russia in parts and put back together at the airfield southeast of Moscow. Two hundred German army officers, all aviation specialists, were sent there in civilian clothes. Their job was to test and perfect the new planes and invent techniques for their most effective use. The operation was well under way the day Richthofen was reburied.

The large tombstone placed over the grave the following year was a simple one, being completely unornamented and saying

---

* Ilse married Baron Karl von Reibnitz and had three children: Manfred, in 1921, Anna-Ursula, in 1922, and Nicol, in 1924. Manfred was killed in action in 1945. Ilse died on January 2, 1963, at the age of seventy-two.

only RICHTHOFEN in large block letters. It was not taken to represent the folly of a senseless war, but the promise of glory in another one, and Goering later had his photograph taken as he stood beside it. The tombstone is still standing, five feet in on the Communist side of the Berlin Wall. Two wire fences have been erected behind it. Dogs patrol between them, and beyond the second stands the brick part of the wall. The upper left face of the tombstone has been pockmarked by bullets, and, since photographs taken after World War II show no holes, they were presumably made after the wall went up. The Richthofen family paid the Communists in the 1950's to take care of the grave, and not only has that not been done, but also no member of the family is allowed to visit it. Signs in Russian, German, and English warn others not to approach within fifty feet because of its proximity to the wall.

Berlin was gray and rainy on April 10, 1935, but the weather did not dampen Hermann Goering's second wedding, and thousands of Berliners turned out to watch the procession move from the Reich Chancellory to the Town Hall. Goering had built a huge marble-and-stone home between two lakes in the Schorfhide Forest near Berlin. After his first wife died, he had her body brought from Sweden and placed in a mausoleum on this new property. His second bride, actress Emmy Sonnemann, was beautiful. The groom had more than doubled his weight since the first marriage, and if he was not handsome, he was at least resplendent in the uniform of a general of airmen. Goering was the head of the Luftwaffe, whose existence had been formally announced the month before, making him in fact, if not in title, the second most powerful man in Germany. The most powerful man had glorious plans for the new air force, and since Goering told his master that every task put to it could be achieved, he had found great favor and several titles. Among others, he was also Reichjägermeister, or the Fatherland's

Master Hunter, which pleased him because he loved animals and loved to shoot them. As General and Mrs. Goering stood in front of the Town Hall after their wedding ceremony, the people who had come to see them cheered and chanted, "*Hoch* Hermann," and "*Heil* Hitler," above the roar of airplane engines. The seventeen biplanes that Goering saw as they passed over him in a perfect swastika formation belonged to his Luftwaffe's first fighter wing, which had been ordered into existence less than a month before by order of Hitler. It was named Jagdgeschwader 2 "Richthofen."

The young pilots who came to J.G. 2 in 1935 were trained by the innocuous-sounding League for Air Sports. Their "sporting" planes were painted with civilian registration markings, but were similar to, or better than, other nations' fighters. During the next decade, increasing numbers of Luftwaffe pilots were graduates of the Nazi school system, the Hitler Youth, and a vast complex of glider and aviation clubs. As was the case with their parents and friends, Germany's young pilots and future pilots were trained ideologically as well as technically. The writers who had gone up in smoke in Berlin on the night of May 10, 1933—Einstein, Mann, Freud, Gide, Wells, Sinclair, London, Proust, Zola, and others—were replaced by new ones who volunteered or were persuaded to write for the Fatherland. To write for the state was to glorify the state. Heroes of the past would point the way to the future, and Dr. Joseph Goebbels' Proganda Ministry had many heroes to work with, not the least of whom was Manfred von Richthofen. Schoolchildren and members of the Hitler Youth were told about Der röte Kampfflieger as only one of a galaxy of national heroes, but those in glider and aviation clubs were treated to lectures that recounted his achievements in dazzling, if distorted, detail. And while writers outside Germany were writing about Richthofen to entertain, or to bicker over who killed him, his biographers in the Third Reich did so with a far more serious purpose. The Nazis officially credited gunners on the ground with killing Richthofen, incidentally, on the theory that no one could have bested him in the air.

The first Richthofen book published in Nazi Germany was a reprint of the original *Red Battle Flier,* and it appeared in 1933. It was enlarged, however, to include a sixteen-page introduction entitled "My Brother Manfred" and an eight-page epilogue, by Karl Bolko, who had been asked to lend his name and memory to the volume. Bolko did not argue with the Propaganda Ministry, but he wrote without touching on politics and without using sentimental adjectives. He ambled over his brother's experiences as a combat leader and mentioned the luminaries who fought at his side. Goering wrote the foreword, which said, in part, "Countless are the heroes brought forth by the World War, and gigantic were the efforts accomplished all over the world during the four years of conflict, wherever men fought against men with all the weaponry designed for victory. But no other weapon in that admired and shattered age was so impressive as the knightly fights that existed among the battling aviators who rose from their camps to pit man against man— he or I—and who well knew that they could only return as victors, or not at all. . . . For Germany's grandeur, Manfred von Richthofen fought, educated, and readied for battle and led hundreds and hundreds of German men and youth, and finally gave his own life. He knew how decisive the air force was, even at that time, for the struggle of the people. And he surely foresaw its part in defending the holiest belongings of the people in the future. . . . We want to adhere to the great example set by Manfred von Richthofen. We want to remember him in order to bring into play all of our might to reach our national goals—to give Germany once again an air force physically equal to the other nations', but superior in spirit, courage, sacrifice, and equal to the Richthofen Wing in the World War." *The Red Battle Flier* was reprinted several times and updated as outstanding fighter pilots achieved mention in its epilogue.

More than 877,000 copies were printed by 1937, and well over a million by the end of the war.

A 112-page book called *Richthofen: King of the Air* was written by Hermann Kohl, a German aviation historian, and appeared in September, 1937. Kohl, who also wrote a book on Immelmann, recounted Richthofen's war experiences with boundless enthusiasm, and ended with a list of Pour le Mérite winners, which, of course, included Goering's name as well as a full-page picture taken of him in 1918.

The twentieth anniversary of Richthofen's death came the following year and occasioned a small pile of books, including an eighty-two-page volume about Lothar, entitled *The War Flier.*

Richthofen was an "example of a military leader who will remain unforgettable in the glorious war annals of the German Army," said a red-covered, gold-lettered thirty-two-page commemorative book entitled *Captain Manfred Baron von Richthofen: His Military Legacy.* When Boelcke was killed, said the anonymous writer in the Luftwaffe's Military Science Section, Richthofen stepped into command "with tireless will, and inspired the young men in his wing to the highest combat readiness and sacrifice. . . . He lived and fought for his Fatherland. He found the hero's death that he never feared. Fear and death were unknown to him. He had willed his life only to the service he had wanted to live it in. So, therefore, his soul will live on in undying glory forever. His courage and deeds give the newly-formed Air Force imperishable lessons. The first wing of the new Air Force carried the name Captain Manfred Baron von Richthofen to honor the greatest hero of the old airmen."

"In grateful devotion, the German nation bows to the mothers— the women of the Great War—who gave their husbands and sons selflessly for Germany's greatness, freedom, and strength," wrote Goering in the foreword to Baroness von Richthofen's contribution, *My War Diary.* "The spirit of that attitude," he continued, "must remain alive for coming generations and must remain an example. May this book be part of a lasting monument for German mothers and women." He ended his unusually brief foreword with a favorite quotation from Kant: "Those whose lives are of greatest value, fear death the least." Baroness von Richthofen, like her surviving son, had been enlisted to write for the Fatherland. The product, which apparently did not have to be tampered with, was a sentimental collection of Manfred's and Lothar's letters, those of their comrades, and notes from the Baroness's wartime diary. The book was not smoothly written, but since the loving reminiscences came from a mother, it could not be challenged by the other mothers who were supposed to read it before giving *their* sons.

The Baroness also turned the entire first floor of her home at Schweidnitz into a museum devoted to souvenirs and relics belonging to her dead sons. Richthofen Street in Schweidnitz led to the home, a placard in front of which advertised the five-room museum, and an attendant at the door sold tickets and postcards. Baroness von Richthofen wrote the leaflet, describing how her oldest son had been killed, that was sold at the door. The museum was opened on April 21, 1933—the fifteenth anniversary of Richthofen's death—to help offset the effects of the depression that had ruined the family's finances.

Even the heroism of ancient times pales against the "symphony of heroism, leadership, bravery and disdain for death of the Richthofen Wing," wrote Goering in the foreword to *Hunting in Flanders' Skies*, by Karl Bodenschatz, Richthofen's last adjutant and a general in the World War II Luftwaffe. The German military sacrificed for four years "in a morass of smoke, fire and steel," added Goering, and was then betrayed. "But in the middle of the bloodiest of nights," he continued, referring to Germany's low ebb in the 1920's, "arose the first spark of a new faith—a faith based on the blind trust of the German people that had performed miracles before. And from that spark, a flame arose, and from the flame, a fire, and from the fire, a whole sea of light in which the whole German people were forged to new greatness. . . . We have again found the destiny of our cause. The blood we shed has again found a cause and now, from the ashes of that unique Richthofen Wing, rises new as a phoenix, the German Air Force. We must be worthy of the Richthofen Wing, and in the German sky, brave pilots must again show their [black] cross." German pilots are "filled with the spirit that Richthofen has instilled in them. Out of that spirit," Goering finally concluded, comes "a holy responsibility to be prepared every hour to give their lives for the freedom and honor of our country."

There were other books about the Rittmeister, including Rolf Italiaander's *Manfred von Richthofen: The Best Combat Flier of the Great War*, whose title sums up the thrust of its 155 pages. The volume, which also appeared in 1938, included the usual photograph of Goering, this time posing with a hand on Richthofen's tombstone. There were also magazine and news-paper articles, similar to those of the time of World War I, and documentaries for the movies that tried to blend Richthofen, Boelcke, Immelmann, and the others into the emerging Luft-waffe, into the future.

But Richthofen's presence was more than spiritual. It was flesh and blood. His cousin Wolfram, who was on his first patrol the day the Rittmeister died, and who finished the war with eight kills, studied engineering until he heard about the new Luftwaffe, and then re-enlisted. There is no evidence to indicate that Wolfram especially liked the Nazis, at least ideologically, but, like most World War I officers who went back, he liked military aviation, and he owed his job in it to them. He was sent to Spain in civilian clothes in 1936 to help perfect German airplanes and techniques in the civil war there. He was pro-moted to general, at least partly because of his name, and be-came a specialist in dive-bombing and ground support. Close support of the army would be important in the next war, so the lessons Wolfram learned in Spain with JU-87 "Stuka" dive bomb-ers and Messerschmitt Bf-109 fighters made him important, too.

Memories of the moribund life in the trenches in World War I, and of being gassed there, made Hitler decide that the only way to win campaigns was to move quickly. Moving quickly meant using airplanes to "soften" enemy ground defenses before German soldiers attacked in lightning strikes. That, in fact, was what Hitler called his innovation: blitzkrieg, or lightning war. Wolfram was given command of the Luftwaffe's Eighth Flying Corps when the war started. His dive bombers and fighters pounded Poland so hard that it collapsed within a month of the invasion. The Eighth Flying Corps was then pointed westward and, with the German army, accomplished in four weeks in France what the Kaiser's armies had not been able to do in four years. Wolfram was then sent to the Balkans and the Soviet Union, and from there to the Mediterranean. He developed a brain tumor in 1943, was retired, and died a year later at the age of forty-nine.

Ernst Udet was poor, but carefree, until Goering persuaded him to accept a generalship in the Luftwaffe. He had married his wartime sweetheart, Lo Zink, in 1920, but the marriage ended in 1922, and Udet became a playboy. He also designed and built a racing plane, which he used to win a 200-mile race in Italy, started an aircraft manufacturing company that produced "Flamingo" sport planes, and went into full-time air racing when the depression forced him to liquidate his small firm. He toured the Western Hemisphere in search of air races. While in the United States, he saw a Curtiss dive bomber, and returned to Germany convinced that such airplanes could win wars almost entirely by themselves. After flying for movie-makers in Africa and entering more races, Udet was talked into joining the Technical Department of the Luftwaffe by Goering, who was much better at talking than understanding the limitations of his air force. It did not take Udet long to find himself in the middle of several palace intrigues, which he never really understood, but which genuinely upset him. Furthermore, he was a nationalist, but openly disliked Nazis. He came to treat

Goering with contempt or indifference, and publicly called him
the "fat man." Goering repaid Udet by blaming him for the
Luftwaffe's beating in the Battle of Britain and nearly every
other reverse the air force suffered through 1941. If dive bombers were not doing what they were supposed to, Goering told
Hitler, it was Udet's fault, since he had been their chief pro-
ponent and was in charge of the dive-bomber program. Udet
was blamed for the planes' technical shortcomings, for inadequate matériel, and for everything else his "ink-spilling"
enemies could think of. By November, 1941, Udet was sinking
in paper work, which he hated, and besieged by men he loathed,
which made him sick. His few supporters in the Technical Department were quietly transferred, and when Germany attacked the Soviet Union, which he thought was a ghastly mistake, it became too much. On the morning of November 17,
1941, Udet climbed out of bed, put on a red dressing gown,
poured himself a brandy, and blew his brains out with a Colt
revolver. Dr. Goebbels told the press that Udet had died testing
a new weapon. Goering, who delivered the funeral oration while
movie cameras hummed, said all the right things with suitable
sadness. The Fuehrer ordered Udet's name to be perpetuated
forever, so the Luftwaffe's Third Fighter Wing became Jagdgeschwader 3 "Udet."

The surviving members of the original Richthofen Wing
whom Udet had nicknamed the "Gray Eagles," met every April 21
to commemorate the Red Battle Flier's death. The meetings were
usually held in the Berlin Aero Club, and, far from being sad,
they occasioned nostalgic toasting and the retelling of scores of
battles over France and Belgium. Goering, Bodenschatz,
Loerzer, Udet, von der Osten, and many of the others attended
the meetings, including Willi Gabriel, who was referred to in
whispers as the man who had defied Goering.

Sergeant Major Gabriel came to the Flying Circus six days
before Richthofen was killed and was present when Goering
took command and delivered his dictum on tight control and

against free-for-alls. Gabriel did not agree with Goering. Four days later, he attacked a flight of SPAD's and shot one out of the air. Seconds later, he was attacked by several more, but they got in each other's way, and Gabriel was able to shoot down another. On his way back to the airdrome, he was attacked by still another of the fighters, and, after a four-minute battle, sent it down. Goering, in a rage, met Gabriel when he landed, and while the Sergeant Major stood at rigid attention, Goering screamed about insubordination and threatened everything he could think of. Gabriel, finally dismissed, sat on the grass with other pilots and grumbled about being condemned for scoring three kills within an hour. At that moment, three French airplanes flew over the Germans, and, impulsively, Gabriel jumped into his Fokker and took off. The engine noise brought Goering out of his tent. A dozen Jasta 11 pilots watched Goering as he watched Gabriel shoot down a fourth victim, for a Wing record. When Gabriel landed, he had again to face his commander, who was then quivering and red-faced. Gabriel obviously could not be court-martialed for destroying four enemy airplanes. Outraged commanding officers can always find a way to even things, however, so Gabriel was sent to an air park, where the overexuberant Sergeant finished the war in complete boredom but with the memory of his greatest day.

The red-nosed biplanes of the 1935–37 Richthofen Wing gave way in 1938 to the first production models of Messerschmitt's Bf-109. The new fighters, which became the Luftwaffe's standard throughout the war, carried white shields with a red R under their cockpits to symbolize their heritage. They were sent to Czechoslovakia in 1938 as part of the military provocations that brought on the Munich crisis. J.G. 2 "Richthofen" was moved to France in time for the Battle of Britain in the summer of 1940, and suffered its first serious losses to R.A.F. Spitfires and Hurricanes while escorting bombers over London and other cities in the south of England. The group was led by a succession of outstanding fighter pilots during World War II, all of whom died in the air. Major Helmuth Wick, who was killed on November 28, 1940, had fifty-six victories. Colonel Walter Oesau went down on June 30, 1943 with close to a hundred kills. Two other pilots, who started their combat careers in J.G. 2 "Richthofen," were Lieutenant Colonel Gerhard Barkhorn and Major Erich Rudorffer, who scored 301 and 222 kills respectively. Two more leaders followed, and went to their deaths leading the Richthofen Wing, the last of whom was shot down on April 27, 1944. By that time, the already understrength wing had been pulled apart, almost an airplane at a time, to fill holes on every side of the collapsing Third Reich. Goering's promises of an invincible air force came to nothing. "If an enemy bomber reaches the Ruhr," he had once told the German people, "my name is not Hermann Goering; you can call me Meier." By 1945, the bomb-shocked inhabitants of a nation that was supposed to last a thousand years were too debilitated to call him anything.

The first Richthofen Wing had surrendered in 1918. Twenty-six years later, the second disintegrated. Goering's exhortations in the front of the books about Richthofen, like the propaganda of the war before, were futile.

TWELVE · THE PAPER PHOENIX

"The tendency to compensate for one's deficiencies by sinking them into the glorious achievements of more fortunate mortals may be an ever-present feature of social life."

—SIDNEY HOOK,
The Hero in History

Many of the young Americans who had flown in Eddie Rickenbacker's 94th "Hat in the Ring" Pursuit Squadron and other air groups faced the same problems when they returned to civilian life as their German counterparts did. Unlike Germany, the United States prospered after World War I; prosperity, however brief, was what happened to winners in those days. But aviators were still considered a little mad, and since no one wanted to hire madmen, they had to stop flying or go into business for themselves. The only business open to pilots was one that capitalized on their madness—barnstorming. Later, some would approach respectability by starting airlines or flying the mail, and others would die trying. The barnstormers bought war-surplus airplanes and squeezed out livings by stunt flying at fairs and giving lessons to the generation of teen-agers that followed theirs. By the mid-1920's, most Americans still thought aviators were mad, but they were by then familiar enough with flying so that the madness intrigued them. They knew enough to want a closer look, and the closer they looked, the more romantic it became. The majority were not yet brave enough to fly, but they could read and look at pictures. Thousands of vicarious pilots began planting themselves in overstuffed parlor chairs on Sunday afternoons and tensing over sentences like "It's murder to send a kid up in a crate like that" and "Should she let him sleep peacefully on or awaken him and perhaps send him to his death?" The armchair pilots and the youngsters who saved their pennies so they could be real ones bought a lot of books and magazines and went to a lot of movies.

Of all the writings between the wars about air heroes, none sold better than those on Manfred von Richthofen, who was a natural. He had been a baron, which to European immigrants and their sons was still exotic. He had flown a red airplane, which to conservative Americans was brazen. He had shot down more victims than anyone else—at least officially—which to the scorekeepers was heroic. No one could prove beyond doubt who killed him, which for the detectives was mysterious. He had been German, which for people who fought the "Kaiser's war" to make the world safe for democracy was villainous; and there *is* something wonderful about a villain.

Floyd Gibbons, a journalist, wrote the first book about Manfred von Richthofen. It was serialized in twenty-three consecutive installments in *Liberty* before being published in 1927 with the title *The Red Knight of Germany: The Story of Baron von Richthofen, Germany's Great War Bird*. Gibbons did extensive research, which included a pilgrimage to Schweidnitz to interview Baroness von Richthofen and read her son's letters, and to Berlin to go over official records and combat reports. He also went to England to talk with some who had survived attacks by Richthofen, and carefully studied the airplanes Richthofen flew and fought against. Since Richthofen's letters were among the items that disappeared from Schweidnitz when the Russians took it in 1944,* and since most official records were destroyed by bombings at about the same time, Gibbons's book remains the best source for such documents. His writing style gave the American public the kind of color it wanted in the heady, victorious days after the war and before the Depression. *The Red Knight of Germany* begins like this:

"To kill and kill and kill was the cry. To burn, to destroy, to devastate, to lay waste. Men heard the madness and knew it for madness and embraced it, some with fear and some with joy. Kill or be killed. Survive or perish.

"Pink, yellow, and green patches on maps personified themselves. The personifications glared at one another, then snarled, then cursed. Millions of hearts heard and beat faster. Males strutted; females loved them for it.

"It was the march beat of tramping feet. It was the sharp staccato of steel-shod hoofs. It was the whir and growl of speeding motors. It was the shriek and roar of troop trains forward bound.

"His mother had not raised him to be a soldier. . . ."

Gibbons's aviators were "war birds," "knights of the blue," and "cavaliers." A war bird shot down was a "fallen falcon." Richthofen, besides being the Red Knight, was the "Flying Uhlan." His victims' deaths were described in multiple adjectives calculated to juxtapose the glory of winning an air battle with the horror of losing. Readers loved it and bought twenty-one reprints between January, 1928 and April, 1940.

Roy Brown also told about Richthofen in print, but out of necessity, not desire. His stomach trouble became so bad after the fight with Richthofen that he had to be hospitalized. After release from the hospital, he crashed in a fighter, fracturing his

---

* The Soviet government has refused to comment on the whereabouts of the relics and documents that were in the Schweidnitz museum, so it is not known whether they were officially confiscated or looted by the first soldiers in the house. The latter is most probably the case.

skull, breaking his neck in three places, cracking seven vertebrae, and puncturing both lungs. He was pronounced dead and sent to the morgue. If a fellow pilot who came to pay his respects had not noticed that Brown was still bleeding on his slab, he probably would have been buried alive, instead of finishing the war in another hospital. He returned to Canada after the Armistice, married, had a son and two daughters, and tried to become an accountant. When the Prince of Wales, on his tour of Canada in 1920, presented Brown with a bar to his Distinguished Service Cross, newspaper reporters made the shy aviator recount his battle with Richthofen. Letters soon began arriving at the newspapers and at Brown's home. Some praised him, but others attacked him for being a murderer and a liar. He was warned by friends in Toronto that German-Americans in Detroit were planning to kill him, and was advised to keep a revolver at home and in his office. His ulcer became worse. He left the accounting firm to join a paint-and-varnish company, and, in order to bolster a depleted bank account, agreed in 1927 to have his encounter with Richthofen ghostwritten for *Liberty*, which bought "true aviation exploits" by the score. The first of Brown's four-part series started in November, the month that *The Red Knight of Germany* was published.

Part I of "My Fight with Richthofen" (*"Reading time: 17 minutes 30 seconds"*) left no doubt as to where Brown stood, or where the *Liberty* editors said he stood, in the controversy over who killed the Rittmeister.

"I never saw Richthofen until ten minutes before I shot him down.

"Even then he was—to me—merely a begoggled unknown, hunched in the cockpit of his red triplane; just another cipher in the succession of enemy fliers with whom I had tilted to a finish.

"Living, I never really looked into his eyes in this strange fighting of the skies that was quicker than the warfare of chance-met eagles.

"Dead, this dread Red Knight of Germany was simply a nude corpse on the shelf of a front-line morgue—stripped for the post-mortem which proved that my machine-gun bullet had killed him."

Liberty readers had to pay another nickel for Brown's climactic fight (Part III, "A Warm Sunday on the Somme." *"Reading time: 16 minutes"*).

"I was in perfect position, above and behind. It was a mere matter of straight shooting. Neither plane was aware of me. ["Wop"] May was wriggling like a hooked fish. The tripe [triplane] was pointing for a burst when the correct split second came.

"That was the moment May gave up. 'I'm through,' he thought. 'I can't do another thing.' He set himself for death in the back. Then he heard my guns. He flashed a look. 'Thank God, it's Brownie!'

"Richthofen's end was exactly like that of the majority of his own victims. He was caught cold. He was dead before he had time to recover from the full shock of the surprise.

"It was all so casual—so simple.

"I had dived until the red snout of my Camel pointed fair at his tail. My thumbs pressed the triggers. Bullets ripped into his elevator and tail planes. The flaming tracers showed me where they hit.

"A little short!

"Very gently I pulled on the stick. The nose of the Camel rose ever so slightly. Gunnery-school stuff!

"Easy now. Easy!

"The stream of bullets tore along the body of the all-red tripe. Its occupant turned and looked back. I had a flash of his eyes behind the goggles.

"Then he crumped—sagged in the cockpit. My bullets poured out beyond him. My thumbs eased on the triggers.

"Richthofen was dead.

"It was all an affair of seconds, faster than the fastest telling.

"The triplane staggered, wabbled, stalled, flung over on its nose, and went down."

Brown and his ghost writer devoted Part IV ("What Price Glory?," "*Reading time: 15 minutes 40 seconds*") to the controversy with the Australians over who actually killed Richthofen. Although not as exciting as the combat sequences, it is by far the most interesting part, because it typifies the vehemence peculiar to all of the partisans in the debate over who killed Richthofen.

"It looked as if credit for his death was not going to be won without a second battle.

"I felt suddenly sick of the whole business. What, in a way, did it matter whose hand had done the trick? The main thing was that his career of killing was at an end.

"In my mind's eye I could see the tracers strike his elevators, tear along the fuselage, pour into the cockpit. I could see him crumple. And yet Australian machine-gunners were emphatic in their contention that they had brought him low by bullets from the trenches.

"Indeed, the Australian command had lost no time in recommending that two infantrymen be awarded the Distinguished Conduct Medal for their allegedly successful effort in potting him. They meant to grab glory while the grabbing was good."

Bitterly, the article went on to charge that the Australians had demanded decorations for their gunners and recognition for killing Richthofen. "There had been friction, as it was," the story continued, and "it had become a kind of international complication within the British Empire.

"The British authorities, bowing before the ruckus raised by the Australian command, had thought it wise to make no recognition of my part in it, lest they—the Australians—be offended. It was apparently a question of army and imperial politics, the point of which I, in my dull way, could not quite grasp. But I was just a simple flight commander, merely a Canuck pilot in the Royal Air Force, without anyone particularly interested in pushing my claims. We Canadian fliers had no identification with the Canadian Expeditionary Force, else there might have been a proper rumpus: Canada *versus* Australia."

The Australians eventually answered in their own magazine articles. Robert Buie, the gunner in the Australian 53rd Anti-Aircraft Battery, had an article entitled "I Killed Richthofen!" in the December, 1959, issue of *Cavalier,* an American magazine of the barbershop variety. In what *Cavalier's* editors called the "most amazing war story we have ever printed," the then retired fisherman described his side of the controversy:

"I can still remember Richthofen clearly. His helmet and goggles covered most of his face and he was hunched in the cockpit aiming over his guns at the lead plane. It seems that with every burst he leaned forward in the cockpit as though concentrating very intently on his fire. Certainly he was not aware of the danger of his position or of the close range of our guns.

"At 200 yards, with my peep sight directly on Richthofen's body, I began firing with steady bursts. His plane was bearing frontal and just a little to the right of me and after 20 rounds I knew that the bullets were striking the right side and front of the machine, for I clearly saw fragments flying.

"Still Richthofen came on, firing at Lt. May with both guns blazing. Then, just before my last shots finished at a range of 40 yards, Richthofen's guns stopped abruptly. The thought flashed through my mind—*I've hit him!*—and immediately I noticed a sharp change in engine sound as the red triplane passed over our gun position at less than 50 feet and still a little to my right. It slackened speed considerably and the propeller slowed down, although the machine still appeared to be under control. Then it veered a bit to the right and then back to the left and lost height gradually, coming down near an abandoned brick kiln, 400 yards away on the Bray-Corbie Road." Buie added that Richthofen was hit in his left breast, abdomen, and right knee, which, except for the chest wound, was not the case, and that all of the wounds were "frontal," meaning that they were not made by bullets coming from Roy Brown's direction. The Canadian's plane "was definitely not in the action at all. No plane pursued Richthofen. There was only May pursued by Richthofen. *Two planes only!*" Buie concluded.

The parts of the cannibalized red triplane that ended up in museums also reflect the controversy. Aside from its engine, which rests in a corner on the first floor of the Imperial War Museum in London, all pieces that were not kept by souvenir-hunters were presented to museums in Canada and Australia by their respective soldiers. The Imperial War Museum, incidentally, has remained neutral on the question of Richthofen's killer. One of the triplane's six black crosses was autographed by the pilots of No. 209 Squadron and given to the Canadian Military Institute in Toronto, and the other, which bears a brief description of Richthofen's death, was donated to the Australian War Memorial in Canberra. The Canadian Military Institute has Richthofen's aluminum seat, which was given by Roy Brown, but the Australians have one of his fur boots, the sight from Buie's Lewis gun, and the triplane's compass, joy stick, and a piece of the propeller. Many other items, some of which are not authentic, are held by private collectors and relatives of men who were there when Richthofen crashed.

Roy Brown left his job with the paint-and-varnish company to start an airline in 1934. When it failed just before World War II, he tried unsuccessfully to get a staff job in the Royal Canadian Air Force, and then took up farming near Stouffville, Ontario, where he died of a heart attack on March 9, 1944, at the age of fifty.

During the late 1920's and up to World War II, there were dozens of articles about Richthofen in aviation magazines, and when the facts were exhausted, anecdotes like the following, which appeared in the March 4, 1939, issue of *Flying*, a British publication, were invented. The story claims to explain how

Richthofen won his Pour le Mérite, which, the article said, in late 1916 required fifteen downed airplanes and one balloon. When Richthofen had shot down his fifteenth airplane, but had not yet brought down a balloon, the unsigned piece explained, the General Staff asked him to rectify the situation so it could award him the medal. According to the article, "Richthofen did not reply, but carried on with his usual war against the R.F.C. The German General Staff were rather nonplussed by his silence, and a few days later, they sent him a telegram:

" 'Where's your balloon?'

" 'Still in the sky,' Richthofen wired back.

"The General Staff were furious, but the truth was that Richthofen was not interested in balloons. He had made a couple of unsuccessful attacks on them when learning his business as a fighting pilot, but soon decided that blimps were a mug's game. He therefore made no attempt to get one.

"The General Staff were worried. Richthofen was now Germany's leading ace and popular hero. The general public who read of his victories in the Press were beginning to ask why he had not yet received the distinction which Immelmann and Boelcke had obtained for only eight victories. At last, an adjutant who knew the Red Knight personally offered to ring him up and put the situation to him in plain language.

"He got through to Douai, where Jagdstaffel 11 was then stationed, and Richthofen came to the telephone.

" 'Look here, what about that balloon?' asked the adjutant.

" 'Balloon? What balloon?' inquired Richthofen suavely.

" 'The balloon you've got to shoot down before you get the Pour le Mérite.'

" 'I've no intention of shooting down any balloons. I'm far too busy with enemy machines,' Richthofen told him.

" 'But you can't have the Pour le Mérite without a balloon! The regulations distinctly say that you've got to shoot a balloon down to make yourself eligible.'

" 'Then keep your Pour le Mérite. I don't want it,' Richthofen informed him, and hung up the receiver.

"Matters were at a deadlock, but they did not remain so for long. For once, red tape was not allowed to prevail. Richthofen got his Pour le Mérite without the balloon, and there is nothing on record to say that he ever attacked one afterwards."

As Richthofen material began to run out by the mid-1930's, aviation writers, particularly in England, began concentrating on the Circus stars who had flown with him. Udet, Voss, Boelcke, and others appeared in profile pieces that were usually written by R.A.F. officers trying to supplement their income under pen names. The government had regulations against its officers writing for the popular press, so pseudonyms such as Vigilant, Spin, Contact, Wings, Theta, Wing Adjutant, A Pilot, Spinner, Observer, Mewgull, and Atlantis began to appear. Vigilant, which belonged to Captain Gerdon Jones, who received the Military Cross for his flying in World War I, was the best known. In addition to many magazine articles, Jones wrote three books— *Secrets of Modern Spying, German Warbirds,* and *Fighting the Red Shadow*—before writing one on Richthofen. It was published in 1934 and entitled *Richthofen, the Red Knight of the Air.* Jones openly admired Richthofen and called him a genius.

Hollywood, whose technology had not advanced enough to compete with newspapers, magazines, and books in the early 1920's, began to catch up by the end of the decade. Air epics such as "The Lone Eagle" and "Wings" (1927), "Lilac Time" (1928), and "The Dawn Patrol" (1930) put movie audiences into the swirling world of combat above the clouds for the first time. Authentic airplanes, some in pieces, were bought, reconditioned, and flown by pioneer stunt pilots, including Paul Mantz, and record breakers like Roscoe Turner. Directors' efforts to get absolute realism cost some pilots their lives, but audiences were never satiated, so almost anything was considered worth the price. "Hell's Angels," produced and directed by a twenty-two-year-old named Howard Hughes, was the most ambitious air saga of them all. Hughes assembled fifty airplanes, including a Gotha bomber, into the largest nongovernmental air force in the world, and based them on a complete period airdrome near Van Nuys, California. Several miles up the San Fernando Valley, another field was rented for the "Germans" to use as the "Jolly Baron's Nest." The filming of air scenes (in which the "Germans," characteristically, did most of the attacking and seemed the more ruthless fliers) took place over large portions of California. Ten camera planes were used to photograph what, by December, 1927, had become eighty-seven combat airplanes. The movie's climax, a spectacular free-for-all, was shot against giant clouds over San Francisco Bay, and pitted the good guys against the bad guys at a cost of $250,000 for that scene alone. The cost of the entire film, which was released in 1930, came to about $4,000,-000, and it could be seen on Broadway in New York for $2.50. The belligerents were backed up by Jean Harlow in a low-cut evening dress, so "Hell's Angels" had something for everyone.

"Here I am flying high over France in my Sopwith 'Camel,' searching for the infamous Red Baron!" says the dog in the cartoon. He sits on top of his doghouse, which he imagines is a World War I scout, and wears a leather flying cap and goggles. A silk scarf flutters behind him in an imaginary air stream. Suddenly, bullets coming from above and behind puncture the Sopwith doghouse, causing it to smoke, and narrowly missing him. He glares over his shoulder at the invisible attacker. "Curse you, Red Baron," he shouts as his doghouse spins out of control. Sometimes the dream ends there. Other times he crash-lands and crawls through a barbed-wire, shell-holed no man's land toward his own lines, and mumbles, "I should have stayed in Paris!" The Red Baron has even shot Snoopy, the beagle, down at Christmas. Snoopy was angry enough at the Baron's disregard of the holiday to vow never to send him another Christmas card.

The beagle was created by Charles Schulz for his comic strip,

"Peanuts," and is one of several characters—all of them children except Snoopy—who act out parables of adult life in witty, sophisticated ways. "Peanuts" had already become popular enough by the summer of 1965 to warrant syndication throughout the United States. It is one of the few comic strips to accumulate dedicated followers among the country's intellectuals, the better-educated, largely urban so-called "trend-setters." "Peanuts" characters are therefore quoted in East Side New York pubs, at San Francisco cocktail parties, in Chicago corporate offices, and on college campuses from coast to coast. They have become "camp," and have therefore spread off the newspaper pages and onto sweatshirts, note pads, calendars, greeting cards, buttons, pillows, and all of the other gimmicks that people who want to be "in" use to advertise themselves.

Schulz was inking in a strip one day in the summer of 1965 when his son, Monty, walked into the studio with a model of a red World War I airplane. When the cartoonist asked his son about the model, Monty answered that it was the Red Baron's plane, and both began thinking about introducing the Red Baron to "Peanuts." To this day, each claims to have had the idea first. The Red Baron initially appeared on Sunday, October 10, 1965, and was an immediate success. He was, in fact, second only to Linus's security blanket in terms of reader appeal, according to Schulz. Unlike the blanket, however, the Baron is never seen. But whenever Snoopy dreams that he is a dashing World War I pilot, he is shot down by the arch villain, who relentlessly stalks his delusions of grandeur. After all, there is still something wonderful about a villain, which is why another generation of Americans has been introduced to the Red Baron.

Schulz insists that there are no "deep, psychological" meanings behind his use of the "cursed Red Baron," but most of the strip's readers think otherwise. For some, the Red Baron shoots Snoopy down and destroys his dreams to bring him down to earth, to remind the pretentious dog that he is not a man, much less a heroic one, but only a dog. Others interpret the Red Baron as the embodiment of the evil that haunts all of us, ever ready to strike when it is tempted. Whatever the interpretation, the Red Baron has achieved a notoriety because of his dogfights with a dog that far surpasses what it was in the United States after his dogfights with men. A New York war-surplus goods distributor is advertising "Real Oldtime 'Red Baron' Flying Helmets" for "Snoopy fans and other high flyers (including sports car, hot rod, and motor cycle fanatics)" in "Buttersoft Black Leather" or "Brown Glove Leather" for $6.95. "Red Baron Goggles" with adjustable head straps cost $3.95. All are United States army surplus, and therefore not authentic, but they are selling anyway.

At least two movies have been made since the Red Baron began appearing in the "Peanuts" comic strip. The first, "Fanny Hill Meets the Red Baron," was a low-budget adults-only film whose advertising stated: "Dog-fights as hot-blooded Fanny meets the cold-hearted Ace!" The other movie, "Negatives," was a more serious study, "about the many bizarre faces of love," and dealt with an erotic relationship between a man and two women who dress in different costumes to broaden the "framework for physical communication." "What lover would you like to be tonight?" asked the advertising. "The notorious wife-murderer, Dr. Crippen? The famous war ace, Baron Von Richthofen? The possibilities are infinite. . . ."

Then there is television, whose possibilities are also infinite. Viewers of the "Get Smart" series, a weekly parody of spy films that centers on an extraordinarily inept agent named Maxwell Smart, were introduced to the Red Baron on September 28, 1968. Case #1173 had the Baron threatening to destroy the entire potato crop in the United States (to be followed by broccoli, rhubarb, squash, and kumquats) unless a large ransom was paid. The half-hour show ended with Smart, the good guy, taking off in a biplane to shoot down the Baron, while his boss looked on admiringly and whispered, "Darn fool kid." Smart was victorious in the dogfight that followed. World War I aviation buffs and Richthofen specialists who saw the program might have objected to the Baron's not only flying a Fokker D VII, which he did not live to use in combat, but also one with LO painted on its side, in reference to Udet's fiancée, whom he never even met. They might have objected, but did not, because they have come to accept such bastardization stoically. The Red Baron may be "high camp," but it is too high for his real devotees. They ignore the mistakes and rarely discuss him, except with each other.

Richthofen specialists constitute a subdivision of World War I aviation enthusiasts, and are probably better defined as cultists, rather than hobbyists. There are about a half a dozen of them in North America, including an officer in the Royal Canadian Air Force and a retired lieutenant colonel of the United States Air Force. They have taken their studies seriously.

Pasquale J. Carisella, a forty-seven-year-old, Wakefield, Massachusetts, television repairman, practically lives in his basement, which amounts to a Richthofen museum and library. One wall is filled with books about World War I aviation, and the desk at which he corresponds with other enthusiasts and people who have Richthofen relics he wants, is nearby. He has estimated that four hours a day are spent writing letters. There is a painting of Richthofen over the desk, an imitation Pour le Mérite, and plastic model airplanes of World War I. A display case stands on the other side of the room and, next to it, a life-size manikin of a World War I German pilot in a dress uniform. Another Pour le Mérite hangs at the manikin's throat. The glass display case is the central feature of the museum, because it contains items that, Carisella says, belonged to Richthofen. There are pieces of aluminum tubing cut from his last triplane, a few inches of his ammunition belt, goggles, and other small items. Carisella's proudest possessions, however, are a handkerchief with a maroon "MvR" monogram and a silk scarf whose faded gray spots are Richthofen's bloodstains. He bought both of them a few years ago from another collector for $350, and he is now trying to buy a boot owned by a woman in Germany. There are two large models of Fokker triplanes on the other side of the display case, one of which is maroon and represents the last one used by Richthofen. Beyond the triplanes, there are shelves full of non-Richthofen relics, including a full-size wooden propeller and a machine gun. There are also files of letters and photographs, but Carisella does not show them, because, he explains, they contain a picture of Richthofen's body which proves conclusively that he was killed by a shot from the ground. The photograph has never been published, he adds proudly. A visitor is struck by the basic similarity between Carisella's basement and his hero's room at Schweidnitz.

Collectors like Carisella are closely bound to each other by their specialized interest, but they tend to be so fanatically proud of their relics and material that they are openly contemptuous of those owned by the others, whom they consider rivals. Carisella related to me an incident that happened recently involving himself and Charles Donald, another Richthofen specialist, who lives in Union City, New Jersey, which underscores the seriousness of the competition. Although they have corresponded for years, they have yet to meet.

"Donald told me where I could get something that belonged to Richthofen [it was his flying helmet] and I spent about a year trying to track it down—writing letters just about all over the world—a whole year. Then I found out that it was bunk, that I couldn't get it, and that Donald tricked me. It was a wild-goose chase." He decided to get even by sending Donald a photograph supposedly of Richthofen's wrecked triplane before it was torn apart. No such picture is known to exist. "It served him right," said Carisella with obvious satisfaction.

Donald, who is fifty-seven years old and a security guard, received the photograph, which was accompanied by this anonymous typed note: "The only known picture of Richthofen's crashed tri-plane." The New Jersey collector took one look at the photograph and knew it was phony. "The triplane had Maltese crosses, and since the Germans used Latin crosses in 1918, I knew it was a fake. It was a drawing from a magazine, and since the envelope was postmarked from Massachusetts, I figured it was from Carisella. That's the thanks I get for trying to help him," said Donald.

Charles Donald became interested in World War I German aviation after reading Gibbons's book, which his father bought for him in 1927. "When I read about the fabric and pieces in his [Richthofen's] home, I got interested, too, and started saving all the relics I could. I never dreamed I'd have so many relics." His collection includes the fuselage side of a Lafayette Escadrille Nieuport, the rudder of another Nieuport, flying helmets, goggles, and original oil paintings and photographs of the aces on both sides of World War I. His Richthofen material features many relics but is primarily devoted to what he calls the "Richthofen Archives"—photographs, letters, articles, and books numbering in the thousands. He has corresponded with Australians, Germans, Canadians, and anyone else who could supply firsthand information about the first war in the air and particularly about incidents relating to Richthofen's life and death. For such correspondence, he uses stationery embossed with a scarlet triplane, and all answers are carefully indexed and filed to help future historians, he says. The accent is on information, he adds, not on relics. "Maybe I got interested in World War I aviation because I was over here, and Germany is over there. I suppose many German youths wanted to collect Allied things, although I was interested in the Allied aces, too. I always liked flying, loved planes, and saw all the big fliers like Earhart, Post, and Lindbergh. Air combat in World War I was something that happened for the first time. It was the legends of the old knights. I guess I got interested in Richthofen because he was the top-ranking ace. He saved relics, and I went right along with him, and fixed up *my* room like that."

Donald says that Richthofen was an ordinary man who has been treated "maliciously," when he was only "a soldier fighting for his country, the same as you and I would do if we were in Richthofen's place. I don't believe all that stuff about him being sadistic. It wasn't his fault that the Allies were behind [in the quality of their airplanes]. He was built up like Immelmann and Boelcke. A lot of it was propaganda. Germany was always a more militaristic nation, and was great for building up national heroes."

Manfred von Richthofen was, indeed, "built up." And in the building, man and myth were merged into an enigma of surprising durability, into the total hero (or antihero). Carisella and Donald, and their interest in Richthofen and penchant for collecting relics of him, are, in many ways, no more difficult to understand than the thousands of baseball fans who would probably pay $350 for a bat used by Babe Ruth or the movie fans who would give at least as much for one of Charlie Chaplin's bowlers. The obvious difference, of course, is that Richthofen was a war hero, and therefore achieved fame through violence. Unlike Babe Ruth, who could lose only a game by performing poorly, and Chaplin, who could lose only box-office receipts, Richthofen could lose his life by a poor "performance." He finally did, and in a world that places man's highest allegiance to his nation, dying for it—especially as a youth—brings martyrdom. Homage is a small price to pay a young man for giving up something those who adulate him would not give up, and it is so much the better if the hero is killed where they would not dare venture even in times of peace. The air was such a place in World War I, and if that is now difficult to comprehend, one has only to estimate how many otherwise patriotic people today would volunteer to make the trip to the moon.

Heroes—war heroes—may be invented by government and the press, but they are "built" by the ordinary men who live vicariously through them to gratify their own unfulfilled yearning for power and glory. Hero worship brings new meaning to dull and emotionally barren lives and even sets standards for a few to follow so they, too, may become heroes. But the cost of war heroes is very high.

EPILOGUE · THE JET-PROPELLED, SUPERSONIC, MISSILE-FIRING PHOENIX

"Inventiveness has not yet come to an end. Who can tell what machine we shall use a year from now to penetrate the atmosphere?"
—MANFRED VON RICHTHOFEN,
The Red Battle Flier

Colonel Horst D. Kallerhoff, who has never heard of "high camp," leaves his brick home in Wittmund, Germany, early on most mornings and drives down Manfred von Richthofen Street until he comes to a six-mile-long two-lane highway that is so straight it could be used as a runway. There he turns left and for ten minutes drives past the flat pastures and dairy cows that cover the northern part of his country. Another left turn brings him down a secondary road to a sentry post, where his identity is checked, and then to a low modern building marked with a sign that reads: STAFFEL 1. After pulling on a bright-orange flight suit and picking up his helmet, he checks the weather, files a flight plan in the squadron's operations room, and walks out of the building's rear door and onto a concrete apron. It is dark, but he can see that one of the pencil-shaped gray-and-green jet fighters lined up in front of some hangars is already being prepared for him by two ground crewmen. It is a Lockheed F-104G Starfighter belonging to Jagdgeschwader 71 "Richthofen." Kallerhoff is the commander of the third Richthofen Wing.

He lowers his six-and-a-quarter-foot height into the Starfighter's small cockpit, then straps himself into the seat and the parachute under it, which will open automatically if he has to shoot the seat and himself out of the fighter in an emergency. He goes over the instrument check list, watching white needles on more than a dozen black dials and checking circuits while a ground crewman waits for the signal to begin feeding air to an engine that is about half as long as the fifty-five-foot fighter. A hose connected to a mobile air compressor is plugged into the F-104, and when Kallerhoff makes a circular motion with his forefinger, the man watching him adjusts the compressor for increased air pressure. The flow of air makes the engine's turbine wheels spin, and the low whine that Kallerhoff heard when he strapped himself in becomes higher pitched. One of the needles in front of him indicates 1,000 turbine rotations a minute, which he tells the ground crewman by holding up a finger. Two fingers mean 2,000. Kallerhoff holds up three fingers and presses the engine's starter button almost simultaneously. The turbines are now sucking in air by themselves, compressing it, and pushing it back into the engine, where it is mixed with fuel and lighted. Flames come out of the Starfighter's exhaust, and there is a lot of noise. The engine has started. Kallerhoff signals to unplug the hose and checks the fighter's controls—elevator, rudder, and ailerons—by moving the stick and kicking both pedals. He makes sure that the speed brakes, which are large, hydraulically operated doors behind the wings, are working, since popping them out is the fastest way to slow the fighter at high speed. When the flaps have been lowered to take-off position, he motions for the wheel chocks to be pulled away and radios the control tower for taxing instructions. He releases the brakes, pushes the throttle knob on his left forward, and rolls slowly out of the hangar area and along a narrow taxiway parallel to J.G. 71's 8,000-foot-long runway—its only runway—and to the far end of the take-off strip.

Another Starfighter, piloted by Captain Guenter Gebbers, a twenty-eight-year-old native of nearby Wilhelmshaven, has pulled in behind Kallerhoff and follows him to the starting position. Gebbers's fighter stops half a plane-length behind Kallerhoff's and just to its right. Both pilots, now listening to take-off instructions from the tower and to their own breathing through oxygen masks, make final instrument checks. At a signal from Kallerhoff, throttles are pushed full forward and brakes are kicked to release. The fighters begin to move. They roll slowly at first, at least for interceptors, but as the hot gases and unburned kerosene reach the exhausts, they are lighted again by afterburners, causing four successive jolts, each of which pushes the fighters faster. Halfway down the runway, Gebbers is still just behind Kallerhoff's stubby right wing, and they are rolling at 175 miles an hour. The acceleration pushes both men into their seats. When Kallerhoff calls "rotate," the control sticks in both fighters are eased back, and the planes come smoothly off the runway together. They climb steeply, fire coming from each afterburner, as two sets of landing gear fold neatly up into the fuselages and disappear behind doors that snap shut. The ground behind the interceptors trembles slightly. Six minutes later, Kallerhoff and Gebbers, still flying within thirty feet of each other, pass 35,000 feet at nearly twice the speed of sound as they range over the North Sea on a practice intercept.

At 40,000 feet, Gebbers turns his Starfighter sharply to the right. The force of gravity pulls the flesh on his face to the left, and his body becomes heavier. He flies northeastward for ten minutes, with the dazzling sunlight of early morning filtering so strongly through the canopy that he must pull down a tinted visor in his helmet to stop squinting. Then he pushes the stick forward and drops into a dive. He watches the horizon recapture the sun as his fighter passes 20,000 feet. When it levels out, a mile above the sea, the sun is gone and he is flying through the gray mist of dawn at more than 600 miles an hour. He points his plane toward land. Gebbers and Kallerhoff are going to have a dogfight.

As the Captain begins his simulated attack against an imaginary land target at dawn, his Colonel makes wide, sweeping circles in the morning of 40,000 feet. Then a clipped metallic voice in Kallerhoff's helmet tells him that ground radar has picked up a low-flying "unknown," and gives him a vector. The large ground radar at the Sector Operations Center at Brockzetel, eight miles south of Wittmund, has been following Kallerhoff and Gebbers and sending continuous information about them to a computer. Based on the altitude, speed, and direction of each, the computer has calculated the point at which Kallerhoff, the defender, should be able to catch Gebbers, the attacker, and has also figured what the defender must do to reach that point. Kallerhoff is given the information—vectored to an intercept—and obediently turns his Starfighter toward where the computer says it should be to meet Gebbers in eight and a half minutes. The control officer in the Sector Operations Center tells Kallerhoff what the radar has just told the computer—that the attacker has changed direction slightly—and gives him the computer's new vector. Kallerhoff again responds to the computer's orders. When he is seventy miles from Gebbers, Kallerhoff is told to switch on his own radar, and a dish in the needle nose of his plane begins scanning the sky ahead of it. His radar sees nothing, so he continues to take directions from the ground until he is within forty miles of Gebbers.

Kallerhoff is sitting behind a search-and-ranging radar that feeds information into its own small computer, in roughly the same way as the larger models do on the ground. The air-borne equipment can give him information for bombing in any weather, mapping ground contours, avoiding obstacles such as mountains while flying in poor weather or at night, and firing his four rockets and 6,000-round-a-minute Vulcan rotating cannon at another airplane. The computer-radar is the heart of the Starfighter's automatic fire-control system, and if Kallerhoff can get the fighter close enough to its target, the system will make the kill. He also has a position and homing indicator, which continuously calculates his position in relation to preselected geographical checkpoints and records all changes of speed and direction to tell him where he is and how to get home. At this moment, his radar has picked up Gebbers, who appears as a blip moving toward the center of the small radar screen in front of him. He tells the Sector Operations Center that he has Gebbers on his radar. The radar antenna has been making wide sweeps, but he is now so close to his target that he puts the dish on a five-degree sweep and tells Brockzetel that he has a "lock-on"— that he is following Gebbers's vector the way a dog follows a strong scent. Gebbers turns again, and Kallerhoff's computer tells him to turn accordingly, while his fire-control system begins figuring where the nine-foot-long Sidewinder missiles have to go to hit the target. He has now gotten Gebbers's blip into a small circle on his radar screen, and when his fighter has drawn to within two miles of the plane represented by the blip, a whistling sound comes through his earphones. The Sidewinders are sniffing a heat source. If fired, they would follow the heat from Gebbers's exhaust at two and a half times the speed of sound until they went into his plane's tail pipe and exploded. Kallerhoff, of course, does not fire. The radar and computers have brought him to within two miles of Gebbers, whom he can now see ahead of him, and have told him that had the missiles been used, he—or, rather, his fire-control system—would have made a kill.

Horst Kallerhoff's office, like most of the others in J.G. 71's two-story administration building, has a picture of Manfred von Richthofen on its wall. There is a model of a Messerschmitt Bf-109G on his bookcase, an accurate representation of the one he flew in World War II as a member of Jagdgeschwader 3 "Udet." He joined the Luftwaffe as an eighteen-year-old in 1942 and saw his first combat against American and British fighters supporting the

D-day landings in June, 1944. He was shot down by a Spitfire on his fifth mission, by a P-47 on his thirty-first, and the next time up by a P-51. Moved to the Russian front, he shot down eight Soviet aircraft by January, 1945. At the end of the war he had completed 108 combat missions.

Kallerhoff's father had owned a construction company before and during the war, but by 1945 had lost everything. He tried to start it again near Hanover, but there was not enough money, and the company did badly. Horst decided to study engineering, but when he told a university admissions office that he had taken preparatory courses in the Luftwaffe, he was informed that such study did not count and would have to be repeated. When the preliminary engineering studies had been retaken, by the end of 1946, he was told that he would have to work at construction engineering for practical background before the university could enroll him. He worked for the required six months, reapplied, and was again turned down—this time because he had been an officer in the war, he recalls.

The former fighter pilot started driving a staff car for the Royal Air Force at a base it was using in Germany in 1950. The base, Kallerhoff says, was built by his father. A year later, he saw a Coca-Cola truck and decided that there was more money in driving soft drinks than British officers. "I went to the Coca-Cola office a little dirty," he remembers, "and after looking at me, they told me to write them a letter. The next day, I went back wearing my best coat and told them I was with the R.A.F. I got an interview and started work the next day. The job lasted two years and I became a supervisor. Then I got together with a friend and bought six slot machines. Coca-Cola fired me for that, so I wrote to breweries for a selling job, and got one with a Hanover brewery as a representative. I did that until 1954, when I changed to a Munich brewery and became their representative for northern Germany. It was a good job, and I would have stayed there if the air force hadn't started again."

The Luftwaffe had been reactivated in 1955 and integrated with other NATO air forces. Kallerhoff received a letter from the new Luftwaffe in September, 1955, asking whether he was interested in rejoining. He answered that he was and was told to report to Bonn the following March for tests, which he did not do because of the demands of his job. A second letter, that June, told him that his last chance for induction was scheduled for the following month. It was answered when he showed up for the tests. Refresher pilot training in August, 1956, was followed by a trip to the United States for a course in fighter-bombers. He eventually became a wing commander, and flew North American F-86 Sabers, but when given the option to switch to Starfighters, he took a course in the faster planes. He was put in command of the F-104-equipped Richthofen Wing in April, 1967. The Wing had been re-formed in 1959 with F-86's. It had been given the name "Richthofen," appropriately, on April 21, 1961, and had received its first Starfighters two years later. There are at present two other named wings in the Luftwaffe—JABO 31 "Boelcke," a fighter-bomber group, and A. G. 51 "Immelmann," a photo-reconnaissance wing. The new Luftwaffe has another interceptor wing, J.G. 74, but it is not named. "Someone wanted to name it after Werner Moelders, the World War II ace," says Kallerhoff, "but it is too soon."

His own recollections of first hearing Manfred van Richthofen's name go back to 1933, when he was a nine-year-old member of the Hitler Youth. "Wednesday and Saturday evenings," he recalls, "older boys, who were fourteen to eighteen, told us about German heroes, and there was often something about Boelcke, Immelmann, and Richthofen. They said Richthofen was one of the great German heroes, and was an example of leadership, clean character, and bravery. They said he was a typical German," he adds with a wry smile, "chivalrous and gallant." By the time he was an officer-cadet, he says, "I was expected to know about Richthofen, or I would not have been one."

Kallerhoff is not likely to forget what he was told. There are reminders all around him. He lives a block away from Manfred von Richthofen Street (there are also Richthofen streets in Bonn, Berlin, and Munich) and passes a large blue wooden sign on the way to his office that labels the airbase JAGDGESCHWADER 71 "RICHTHOFEN." Inside the entrance of the building that houses the officers' club and dining room, there is a large scale model of a scarlet Albatros with elevator and ailerons that move and a propeller that spins. A six-foot-high oil painting of Richthofen looks across the dining room, over the rows of linen-covered tables, to a piano and drums on the other side. Two bottles of champagne, whose gold labels show the Wing's insigne over the words "Jagdgeschwader 71 'Richthofen,' " stand behind the small bar where Kallerhoff often comes for a five o'clock glass of korn with his pilots before going home. If he wants to borrow a book from the base library, he must enter a room that looks more like a memorial to Richthofen than a book repository. There is a wall-sized mural of Richthofen and his airplanes, two table-top displays of typical World War I and II Richthofen Wing airfields, and display cases holding some of Richthofen's personal effects— a woolen scarf, goggles, gloves, a belt, a tortoise shell, pens—and books and magazine articles written about him. And every time Kallerhoff climbs into his Starfighter, he sees the Wing's insigne, which is painted on both air intakes of each of the group's approximately thirty-six fighters. It is the same white shield and red R used in World War II, but the R is now superimposed on a blue four-pointed NATO star. The star was added by J.G. 71's first commander, Colonel Erich Hartmann, who, with an astounding 352 kills, is the world's leading ace, and is still in the Luftwaffe.

Kallerhoff, a large, heavy-set man with thick hands and a booming voice, is in Hartmann's generation, and both are on the other side of an age gap that has come to the Luftwaffe, too. He has been in war, shooting down and being shot down, but his sixty-five pilots have not. There was no fire-control system in his World War II Messerschmitt, and although he has mastered the one in his Starfighter, he has not really mastered the interoffice telephone. He shouts to the outer office for his adjutant when he is angry. He is surrounded by administrative assistants—junior officers and lower ranks—who are "doing their stint," and who will leave the Luftwaffe as soon as they can to pursue studies in philosophy, history, agriculture, engineering, and other university disciplines. His pilots fly because they love it, but many are thinking about going to Lufthansa when their stints are over, to make what they love earn more money. To the last man, they chose fighters because they wanted to fly as high and as fast as they could, but none think about kills. As one put it, "today, we can let the computers think about kills, and we can think about other things."

"I went to a regular public school," says Gebbers, a short, slightly stocky blond, "and I read *The Red Battle Flier* when I was twelve. In fact, I read as many adventures as I could, including those about American Indians. I gradually became interested in flying, so I built gliders and prop models, but there was no air force, so I also played soccer, the accordion, the guitar, and bongos. I think about Richthofen, but those times are gone, and everything is now much too organized. Regulations are tight and you can't do what you like. The F-104 is driven, not flown, and the dogfights we have are in no way like they used to be. In Richthofen's time, there was a spirit of competition—you saw your opponent—and they were knights, all right. Now, you can shoot someone down and never see him. You're also working with too many others. There are too many people involved and it's all too complicated. Besides, you're shooting at a blip, and anyone can shoot missiles at blips. I suppose the feeling of flying will always be the same, but the area of initiative is smaller, because you must fly the way they tell you. I learned to fly because I love it, not because of Richthofen, and I don't want to kill anyone. In World War I, you had to be in high society to fly, but not any more." *

---

* There are three men with "von" in their names among J.G. 71's sixty-five pilots. "Most aristocrats are air attachés," said one pilot, scornfully.

Captain Wolfgang Lohmueller, a twenty-eight-year-old native
of Berlin, is soft-spoken and married to a vivacious, freckle-faced
redhead who met him in New York. She was on vacation and he
was on his way to Starfighter school in Nevada. They were married in the United States. In the old days, says Lohmueller, "it
was easier to fly and you could do more. I think they had more
fun, and certainly had more to do with making a kill than we
would. Richthofen was a great pilot—I don't know how he was
as an officer—but it's over. Today, we use autopilots and things
like that. Furthermore, pilots in those days belonged to a certain
social group. I suppose it was a good thing at the time, but they
had nothing to do with the lower classes, and you can't do that
today. There is less difference today between the upper and lower
classes, and I think that's good. Richthofen? It's a name and it's
more than that. It's hunting for the air force—something to be
proud of and to get inspiration from—but it's over."

Captain Jürgen Bollman, also twenty-eight, is the father of a
son named Jesse, who was born in the United States while the
Captain was at Starfighter school. The name comes from Jesse
James, which, Bollman says, was the most typically American
name he and his wife could think of. Bollman read *The Red
Battle Flier* when he was fifteen years old. "He had no influence
on my joining the air force, and I learned most about him after
I joined, although no one here forces you to know about him—
I mean, there are no formal talks about him, or anything like
that. It's just that, well, you see his picture everywhere around
here. He must have been a good pilot, and a lucky one—you need
a lot of luck. It's easier to be a commander who is liked than one
who is not. But if you do what you have to do, you'll probably
be disliked many times, and I suppose that happened to Richthofen. I also don't think he would have liked Hitler, because
as a soldier, he had to fight for his country, but would not have
cared for Nazi politics."

Major Ernst Glockseisen, a thirty-three-year-old Bavarian and
the leader of the second of J.G. 71's two squadrons, adds: "He

wouldn't have liked Hitler because he was a Prussian aristocrat and soldier, but he would have fought for Germany for the same reason, Hitler or not."

These men who have only heard about Richthofen and some of those who knew him met on April 19 to 21 in 1968, at Wittmund. It was the fiftieth commemoration of the Rittmeister's death, and most of the thirty-seven surviving Gray Eagles came to J.G. 71, as did Karl Bolko von Richthofen, who is now a gambling-casino operator in Baden-Baden. Had Baroness von Richthofen not died on April 24, 1962, at the age of ninety-four, she undoubtedly would have been there, too. Only a handful of those who made the pilgrimage had known Richthofen personally—Bodenschatz, von der Osten, Willi Gabriel, and a few others. The old men toured J.G. 71's hangars, flight line, operations center, and living quarters. They looked mildly impressed by the Starfighters, but were only being polite. Bodenschatz spoke in praise of his master, Colonel Kallerhoff called him a "great soldier, great comrade, and chivalrous flier," and the Gray Eagles reminisced about real flying while they shot skeet, ate steak, and drank. Gabriel, according to one J.G. 71 pilot, would begin drinking after dinner and continue through the night while one group of young pilots after another came into the little bar, toasted the Rittmeister, listened to Gabriel's stories about the "real war," and left. Gabriel told them that he had waited most of his life for the reunion, and was now content to face the future in peace. He returned to his home in Berlin on April 22, and died a week later.

When Colonel Kallerhoff and Captain Gebbers finished their dogfight, one fell in behind and slightly to the right of the other, the way they had when they took off, and they flew that way back over the flat German coast. Kallerhoff radioed Wittmund for landing instructions. When he heard that he was cleared to land, he lowered his fighter's wheels and set its flaps to the "land" position. Then he turned for his final approach, while Gebbers continued south for another mile before following his commander down. Kallerhoff's air-speed indicator showed 155 miles an hour as he neared J.G. 71's runway, which is laid out in a northwest-southeast direction, just as the first raindrops hit his windshield. He looked to his left and saw one of the North Sea's typical summer thunderstorms building almost over him. It was being pushed by a strong cross wind that struck the Starfighter's left side and swept over the runway ahead. He trimmed the fighter to compensate for it and switched on his landing lights. The wind does not matter much any more.

BIBLIOGRAPHY · INDEX

BIBLIOGRAPHY

Air Ministry of Great Britain, *Handbook of German Military and Naval Aviation* (*War*), London, 1918

Bodenschatz, Karl, *Jagd in Flanderns Himmel*, Munich, 1938

Bishop, William A., *The Courage of the Early Morning*, McKay, New York, 1965

Craig, Gordon A., *The Politics of the Prussian Army, 1640–1945*, Oxford University Press, London, 1955

Edmonds, Sir James E., *A Short History of World War I*, Oxford University Press, London, 1951

Ellul, Jacques, *Propaganda: The Formation of Men's Attitudes*, Knopf, New York, 1965

Fredette, Major Raymond H., *The Sky on Fire*, Holt, Rinehart & Winston, New York, 1966

Galland, Adolph, *The First and the Last*, Henry Holt, New York, 1954

Gibbons, Floyd, *The Red Knight of Germany*, Doubleday, Page, Garden City, N.Y., 1927

Goerlitz, Walter, *History of the German General Staff*, Praeger, New York, 1957

Gray, Peter, and Owen Thetford, *German Aircraft of the First World War*, Putnam, London, 1962

Hawker, Tyrrel M., *Hawker, V.C.*, Mitre Press, London, 1965

Hook, Sidney, *The Hero in History*, Beacon Press, Boston, 1955

Johnson, Captain J. E., *Full Circle*, Ballantine, New York, 1964

Jones, H. A., *The War in the Air* (six vols.), Oxford University Press, London, 1937

Killen, John, *The Luftwaffe: A History*, Frederick Muller, London, 1967

Lasswell, H. D., *Propaganda Technique in the World War*, Knopf, New York, 1927

Ludendorff, Erich von, *Ludendorff's Own Story* (two vols.), Harper, New York, 1919

Moore, Harry T., *The Intelligent Heart*, Farrar, Straus and Young, New York, 1962

Musciano, Walter A., *Eagles of the Black Cross,* Ivan Obolensky, New York, 1965

Nowarra, H. J., and K. S. Brown, *Von Richthofen and the Flying Circus,* Harleyford, London, 1964

Pitt, Barrie, *1918: The Last Act,* Norton, New York, 1963

Richthofen, Freifrau Kunigunde von, *Mein Kriegstagebuch,* Ullstein, Berlin, 1937

Richthofen, Freiherr Manfred von, *The Red Air Fighter,* "The Aeroplane" and General Publishing Co., London, 1918

Shirer, William L., *The Rise and Fall of the Third Reich,* Simon and Schuster, New York, 1960

Slessor, Sir John, *The Central Blue,* Praeger, New York, 1957

Toliver, Colonel Raymond F., and Trevor Constable, *Fighter Aces,* Macmillan, New York, 1965

Tuchman, Barbara W., *The Guns of August,* Macmillan, New York, 1962

Udet, Ernst, *Ace of the Black Cross,* Newnes, London, 1937

Vigilant, *Richthofen: The Red Knight of the Air,* John Hamilton, London, 1934

Wood, Derek, and Derek Dempster, *The Narrow Margin,* McGraw-Hill, New York, 1961

Sunday Supplement Fiftieth Anniversary Articles

Burrows, William E., "Here He Is In His Fokker Triplane—The Red Baron," the New York *Times Magazine,* April 7, 1968, p. 37. This article also appeared in Chicago's *American Magazine,* June 23, 1968, and the Fort Lauderdale *News,* August 18, 1968.

Cross, Colin, "The Most Magnificent Man in a Flying Machine: The Red Baron," the London *Observer Magazine,* April 21, 1968, p. 10. This article also appeared in the Chicago *Tribune Magazine,* November 10, 1968, and *West,* July 7, 1968.

Drake, Hal, "Red Baron—The All Time Ace of Aces," *Stars and Stripes,* April 21, 1968, p. A-3.

INDEX

Prisoners of war, aviators, 82
Propaganda, 110–12, 219–20,
244. *See also* German Air Service; Information departments;
Movies; Press coverage; MvR,
legacy of; MvR, propaganda,
used for; Sanke postcards
Propaganda Ministry, German,
219–20
Prussian Army: history of, 22–24;
tradition of, 24, 27, 53, 61, 156,
174

Rees, Lt. T., 92–93
Reibnitz, Baron Karl von, 217n
Reichstag, 21, 24–25
Reimann, Sgt. Maj. Leopold, 81,
90, 93, 95
Reinhard, Lt. Wilhelm, 164–65,
169, 206, 211
Reusing, Fritz, 182
Reventlow, Count, 205
Rhys-Davids, Lt. A. P. F., 173,
205
Richthofen, Maj. Albrecht von
(father), 24, 26–27, 30–31,
34–35, 41, 49, 95, 114–15, 137,
145, 155, 165, 171, 174, 180,
203, 214–15
Richthofen, Ferdinand von
(uncle), 25–26
Richthofen, Frieda von (Mrs.
D. H. Lawrence) (cousin),
34–35
Richthofen, Ilse von (sister), 27,
29, 217
Richthofen, Karl Bolko von
(brother), 29–30, 47, 154,
215–17, 220, 222, 255
Richthofen, Kunigunde von
(mother), 27, 29–30, 35, 41,
46, 49, 54, 77, 94–95, 97–98,

101, 105, 126, 128, 144, 154–
55, 171, 174, 175n, 188, 214–
17, 221–22, 229–30, 255
Richthofen, Lothar von (brother),
27, 29–30, 46–47, 114–18,
137–40, 143, 147, 152–55, 171,
175, 177–78, 180, 184–85,
187–88, 205–6, 211, 213–15,
221–22
Richthofen, Manfred von
—childhood of, 27–28
—death of, 200; autopsy, 201–3;
burial, 203–4; controversy over,
202–3; mourning, 204–6; reburial, 215–18
—education of, 28–34, *see also*
Wahlstatt school
—family lineage of, 24–27
—hunting and, 30–31, 48–49, 76,
152, 154, 156, 171, 185, 195
—legacy of, 209–56; comics, 238–
40; death controversy, 202–3,
231–35; literary post-mortem,
221–23, 229–37; movies, 223,
237–38, 240; propaganda, 204–
5, 215, 220–23, 227; souvenir
collection, 200–1, 222, 235,
241–43; specialists, 241–44;
television, 240–41
—memoirs of, 101–2, 154–55,
174–76, 182, 220–21, 253–54;
censorship of, 128, 133n, 138n,
149, 174–76
—military career of: air victories
of, 13–20, 67–68, 77, 90–93,
96–97, 99, 101–5, 113–14, 118–
20, 123–24, 128, 130–36, 143,
158, 165, 169, 171, 178, 180,
188, 191–5; becomes ace of
aces, 120; last will and testament of, 39, 41, 191, 206;